THE SECOND MOURNING

Murder Ink Press

Austin * New York * Boca Raton

ALSO BY STEPHEN G. YANOFF

The Graceland Gang
The Pirate Path
Devil's Cove
Ransom on the Rhone

For more information, you can visit www.stephengyanoff.com

THE SECOND MOURNING

The Untold Story of America's Most Bizarre Political Murder

Stephen G. Yanoff

AuthorHouse™ LLC
1663 Liberty Drive
Bloomington, IN 47403
www.authorhouse.com
Phone: 1-800-839-8640

Published by AuthorHouse 04/14/2014

ISBN: 978-1-4918-9990-8 (sc)
ISBN: 978-1-4918-9989-2 (hc)
ISBN: 978-1-4918-9991-5 (e)

For more information, you can visit www.stephengyanoff.com

Since this book will probably be the most important book I write, it's dedicated to the most important person in my life, my wife, Patricia Yanoff

ACKNOWLEDGEMENTS

First and foremost I'd like to thank Rachel Zell for designing the cover of this book and the covers of my mystery novels. As always, she did an outstanding job.

I'd also like to thank Hazel Yanoff, Rebecca Yanoff, Glenn and Grace Yanoff, and Adam Zell for their continued support.

Special thanks to Karl Monger, my editor, and Emily Garrison, my typist.

Last but not least, my gratitude to the core of my fan club: Barbara and Max Talbott, Helena and Lee Bomblatus, Jaime and Gary Rubenstein, Susan Marquess, Thomas Mannion, Christine Nickles, Janice Baum, Gladys Deatrick, and Thelma Wilson.

CONTENTS

Acknowledgements....vii

Chapter One 1
Chapter Two 11
Chapter Three 21
Chapter Four....33
Chapter Five....43
Chapter Six 57
Chapter Seven 69
Chapter Eight....81
Chapter Nine 93
Chapter Ten 105
Chapter Eleven....117
Chapter Twelve 127
Chapter Thirteen....139
Chapter Fourteen 151
Chapter Fifteen 159
Chapter Sixteen....169
Chapter Seventeen....177

Chapter Eighteen 185
Chapter Nineteen 193
Chapter Twenty 201
Chapter Twenty-One 211
Chapter Twenty-Two 231
Chapter Twenty-Three 241
Chapter Twenty-Four 251
Chapter Twenty-Five 257
Chapter Twenty-Six 265
Chapter Twenty-Seven 273
Chapter Twenty-Eight 281
Chapter Twenty-Nine 289
Chapter Thirty 299
Chapter Thirty-One 307
Chapter Thirty-Two 315
Chapter Thirty-Three 323
Chapter Thirty-Four 331
Chapter Thirty-Five 335
Chapter Thirty-Six 345
Chapter Thirty-Seven 353
Chapter Thirty-Eight 361
Chapter Thirty-Nine 373
Chapter Forty 379
Chapter Forty-One 387
Chapter Forty-Two 393

Endnotes 401
Bibliography 471

It is as much the duty of all good men to protect
and defend the reputation of worthy public servants
as to detect and punish public rascals.

James A. Garfield
"A Century in Congress"
The Atlantic Monthly, August, 1877

CHAPTER ONE

Long before he became President, James Garfield told friends he was certain that he would not live to be older than his father was when he died, and that like his father, he would die in a sudden and violent manner. When pressed to elaborate, he would say he believed that he would fall between railroad cars or be killed while traveling.

"It seems to me as foolish as it does to you," he told a correspondent of *The New York Times*. "I do not know why it haunts me." Indeed, it was wholly involuntary, and the harder he fought it, the more it pursued him. "It comes to me sometimes in the night, when all is quiet. I think of my father and how he died in the strength of his manhood and left my mother to care for a large family of children, and how I have always been without his assistance or advice, and then I feel it so strong upon me that the vision is in the form of a warning that I cannot treat lightly."

Whether it was fate or coincidence, President Garfield arose early on the morning of July 2, 1881, anxious to begin a long railroad trip with his family. He would be traveling far away from Washington, bound for a place where he hoped to find some peace and quiet.

A place where his haunting visions would not follow him.

The timing seemed good, as Congress had recently adjourned and the Capitol was more or less deserted. Garfield had taken the oath of office in March, but unlike previous administrations, his had no "honeymoon period." On the contrary, the last four months had been marked by intense political bickering, culminating in the resignation of both Senators from New York.

Simply put, the new President was weary and badly in need of a vacation.

In the quiet hours before dawn, he stood on the back porch of the White House, admiring the neatly trimmed lawn that surrounded the ornamental garden. Most likely, his thoughts were not on politics, but on personal matters. Lucretia Garfield, the First Lady, was still in Long Branch, New Jersey, recuperating from a severe bout of malaria. God willing, she would join her husband in New York City, and together with their children—and a few members of the Cabinet—they would enjoy a long, leisurely trip through New England.

Upstairs, Garfield's elder sons, Harry and James, began to tease each other, and before long, they were engaged in a wrestling match. Soon, the President joined the fray, and then, on a dare from Harry, he executed a hand-spring over the bed. Years later, both sons would describe the morning as one of the bet they ever spent with their father.

The rest of the day would be far less enjoyable.

Shortly before nine o'clock, James G. Blaine, the Secretary of State, arrived at the White House to accompany the President and his sons to the Baltimore & Potomac Depot. On the way to the station, Garfield and Blaine chatted amicably, seldom mentioning the political turmoil of the past four months. Instead, they discussed the President's itinerary, which had been published in the *Washington Evening Star*—and every other newspaper in the Capitol. After joining his wife and daughter, the President and his entourage would sail up the Hudson River, stopping overnight in the picturesque village of Irvington. On Monday morning they would proceed to Williamstown, Massachusetts, where the President would attend commencement exercises at Williams College, his alma mater. They would remain in Williamstown until Thursday noon, and then take a railway car to St. Albans, Vermont, where they would spend Friday. From there they would travel to the White Mountains, staying at Maplewood or Bethlehem, and remaining there until Sunday. On Monday they would climb to the top of Mount Washington, and then it was off to Portland, Maine, and then Augusta, where they would be the guests of Secretary Blaine.

The Secretary had arranged for a revenue cutter to take them down the coast of Maine, stopping along the way to visit Mount Desert and other places of interest. Later in the week, they would travel to Boston, Hartford, and New York City. If all went well, they would be back in Washington on July 17 or 18.

Not only did the White House provide the press with a detailed itinerary, but they also mentioned that the President would be traveling without any guards. At Garfield's insistence, there would be no police presence, no military escort, and no agents from the Secret Service. To understand the President's thinking, one would have to understand the prevailing sentiment of the day, best expressed by a White House biographer:

> They would have the President surrounded by a bodyguard, by men able to prevent the approach of lunatics, and dangerous persons.

> This proposition should be opposed with urgency, as unpatriotic and harmful in a land where republicanism has found its fullest, most notable growth.
>
> . . . His [the President's] person is safe in the fifty million hearts of his people, of those who gladly consented that he should rule over them, and who will fly to his rescue if there is a danger.

At about 9:15 the White House carriages pulled up to the B Street entrance of the depot, causing some commotion among the bystanders on the sidewalk. Someone had recognized the President, and soon, a friendly crowd began to gather. Garfield and Blaine sat for a while, engaged in lively conversation, and then, about three minutes later, they climbed out of the carriage and strolled arm and arm toward the entrance.

There was a single policeman on duty.

Just before they entered the depot, the President turned to the policeman and asked, "How much time have I got?"

The officer, a man named Patrick Kearney, replied, "About ten minutes, sir."

Garfield shook a few hands, then was nudged forward by Blaine. Once inside, they walked briskly through the ladies' waiting room, which at the time contained less than a dozen people. They were halfway through the room when the first shot rang out. The bullet, fired from six feet away, grazed the President's left arm. "My God! What is this?" Garfield exclaimed.

Blaine grabbed the President's arm, intending to pull him out of harm's way, but it was too late. There was another thunderous clap, and this time the bullet found its mark. The second bullet hit Garfield square in the back, entering his body four inches to the right of the spine, and as we now know, fracturing two ribs, chipping the first lumbar vertebra, penetrating a major artery, and finally coming to rest just behind the pancreas.

A moment later, the President fell senseless to the floor, bleeding, vomiting, and barely conscious. Ignoring his own safety, Blaine spun around and ran after the assassin. "I immediately followed after the man instinctively and went, I suppose, the distance of eight feet," he later testified. "I remember I stopped just outside the door which led from the ladies' waiting-room."

In an instant the depot was bedlam. Many of the passengers ran for cover, but a few brave souls dashed to the President's side. "There he goes!" somebody shouted. "Stop him. He shot the President!"

Officer Kearney heard the shots and began to run toward the entrance, but before he got inside, he ran into the assassin. "Hold up," he said sternly, grabbing him by the arm. "There were two shots fired, and you are coming from the direction in which they were fired."

The assassin, a nervous little man, had just put his revolver into his pocket and seemed unfazed by his terrible deed. He was about forty years of age and stood five feet five inches tall. He had a sandy complexion and was slender, weighing not more than 125 pounds. He wore a mustache and a thin beard, slightly tinged with gray. His sunken cheeks and droopy eyes gave him a sullen appearance.

Kearny was terribly excited and barely able to retrain himself. "You shot the President of the United States," he said angrily.

"Keep quiet, my friend," the assassin said. "I want to go to jail."

Blaine instantly recognized the man and identified him as Charles J. Guiteau, a disreputable character of the lowest order. Guiteau had spent the last four months pestering Blaine for a political appointment, and recently, he had been banned from both the State Department and the White House. Nobody, least of all Blaine, ever imagined that he would resort to such violence.

Inside the depot, a crowd had gathered around the fallen President. Sarah White, the ladies' room attendant, knelt beside him and cradled his head. By now, Harry and James were also at his side, and soon they were joined by other members of the entourage, including Postmaster-General James, Treasury Secretary Windom, Navy Secretary Hunt, and the Secretary of War, Robert Todd Lincoln. Nobody was more visibly shaken than Lincoln. "How many hours of sorrow I have passed in this town," he said bitterly, as his mind flashed back sixteen years to the awful night outside Ford's Theatre when he watched his own father taken down by an assassin's bullet.

Dr. Smith Townsend, the Public Health Officer, was the first physician to arrive on the scene, and as he would later recall, he found the President lying on his side, completely bewildered by the pool of blood that engulfed him. Accounts would differ about the President's level of awareness, but all would agree that he remained calm throughout the ordeal. Townsend, on the other hand, was a bundle of nerves, certain that the President was dying. He had reason to fear the worse. Garfield's skin was cold and clammy, and his pulse was beginning to fade. Still, he remained composed, smiling at his sons as if to assure them that all would be well.

Not knowing what else to do, Townsend gave the President some brandy and administered a dose of ammonia aromatic smelling salts. "Where do you feel the most pain?" the doctor asked.

"In my right leg and foot," the President whispered.

Two more doctors appeared, and one of them was D.W. Bliss, the President's long-time friend. With Garfield bleeding profusely, they decided to move him to a private room on the second floor. Acutely aware of the patient's pain, they carried him upstairs on a mattress—yanked from a Pullman railroad car. After making the President comfortable they examined him for the first time. Without wearing gloves, Townsend stuck his finger into the hole in Garfield's back where one of the bullets had struck and probed it with his fingertip.

Garfield, who was still conscious, clenched his teeth, but he did not howl or whimper.

"I found that the last bullet had entered his back about two and a half inches to the right of the vertebrae," Townsend later stated. "When I placed my finger in the wound some hemorrhage followed. I then administered another dose of the stimulant, which again revived him."

Outwardly, Garfield remained stoic, but he knew he was seriously wounded. "What do you make of my wound?" he asked in a weak voice.

Townsend now believed that the wound was less serious, and he assured the President that he would recover.

The other physician concurred.

"I thank you, doctor," Garfield said grimly, "but I am a dead man."

Downstairs, an angry mob had gathered, and they were out for blood. "Lynch!" "Lynch!" came the frenzied shouts. "Hang the coward!"

Somebody grabbed for Guiteau's wrist; another knocked his hat off. Kearney kept his composure and led the prisoner outside, away from the mob. "In God's name, man," he shouted. "What did you shoot the President for?"

"I did it," Guiteau said calmly. "I will go to jail for it. Arthur is President and I am a Stalwart."

Kearney tightened his grip and marched his prisoner down Pennsylvania Avenue. The mob had grown substantially, but Kearney and Guiteau managed to reach police headquarters without incident. Yanking Guiteau to the front desk, Kearney said, "This man shot the President."

The announcement was met with stunned silence.

Lieutenant Eckloff of the Metropolitan Police Force began to laugh. "You are giving us taffy."

"No," Kearney replied.

Eckloff studied the prisoner carefully for the first time. The man was disheveled, but he did not appear dangerous. Even so, Eckloff stopped laughing and waited for an explanation. Meanwhile, Guiteau reached into his pocket and calmly pulled out his revolver. He politely offered the weapon to Officer Kearney. Kearney turned red, then grabbed the gun out of Guiteau's hand and slammed it on the front desk. When he searched Guiteau, he found two silver coins and two letters. The letters, Guiteau explained, were to be given to Mr. Byron Andrews on Fourteenth Street.

Lieutenant Eckloff, who was no longer skeptical, asked the prisoner if he had anything to say.

"I have nothing to say," Guiteau replied. "The papers speak for themselves."

By now, word of the assassination had spread across the city, and hundreds of angry citizens were flooding the streets and avenues of the Capitol. It was only a matter of time before the mob descended upon police headquarters. Realizing this, Lieutenant Eckloff decided to transfer the prisoner to the district jail. Eckloff was joined by Detective

McElfresh, and on their way across town, the following conversation took place:

"Where are you from?" McElfresh asked.

"I am a native-born American," Guiteau answered. "Born in Chicago."

"Why did you do this?"

"I did it to save the Republican Party."

"What are your politics?"

Guiteau mumbled something about a Stalwart affiliation, then asked, "Who are you?"

"A detective of this department," McElfresh said.

Guiteau smiled at him. "You stick close to me and put me in the third story front cell. General Sherman is coming down to take charge. Vice President Arthur is my friend, and I'll have you made Chief of Police."

McElfresh frowned. "Is there anybody else with you in this matter?"

"Not a living soul; I contemplated this thing for the last six weeks and would have shot him when he went to church with Mrs. Garfield, but I looked at her, and she looked so bad that I changed my mind."

Detective McElfresh shook his head, at a loss for words.

When they reached the district jail, they were met by Deputy Warden Russ. Inside, the detective explained the situation and requested a cell for their prisoner. Russ was visibly shaken, and when he got a good look at Guiteau, his mouth fell open. "This man has been here before."

McElfresh glared at the prisoner. "Have you been here before?"

Guiteau hesitated for a moment, then said, "Yes, I was down here last Saturday morning and wanted them to let me look through, and they told me that I couldn't, but to come Monday."

"What was your purpose?" McElfresh asked.

"He wanted a tour," Russ said sarcastically. "I sent him away."

Guiteau smiled sheepishly. "I wanted to see what kind of quarter I would have to occupy."

Once again, McElfresh was speechless. Other than stating his full Christian name—Charles Julius Guiteau—the prisoner had little else to say. As he was led to his cell, Guiteau walked past a large wooden scaffold in the center of the rotunda, and though he averted his eyes, he would later learn that this was the very scaffold that had been used to hang the conspirators who plotted Lincoln's assassination.

CHAPTER TWO

Back at the depot, Sarah White, the first to reach the President, was already being questioned by the police. Her eyewitness account would later be repeated in a court of law, and it would send chills down the spine of every member of the jury. "I had noticed this man [Guiteau] lounging around the ladies' room for a half hour before the arrival of the President. I did not like his appearance from the first time I saw him. I thought seriously of having him pointed out to our watchman, Mr. Scott, so that he should be made to stay in the gentlemen's room."[19]

But Mrs. White did not point him out.

When asked what happened next, she replied, "When the President and Secretary Blaine entered he [Guiteau] was standing near the entrance door. He wheeled to the left and fired, evidently aiming for the heart. It was a quick shot and struck the President in the left arm."

Apparently Garfield did not realize that he had been shot. He turned slightly, but before he could turn all the way around, the second bullet hit him in the back. Dazed and bleeding, he took one step forward, then fell to the floor.

While the police were jotting down statements, the President's Cabinet sprang into action. Secretary Lincoln issued an order for troops stationed at the federal arsenal to prepare to move out quickly. The order was echoed by the Secretary of the Navy, who directed the marines to be ready to protect the Capitol on a moment's notice. These actions were taken as a precaution, because nobody knew if the President had been attacked by a lone assassin or whether they were dealing with a full-blown insurrection. In any case, it was clear that the President had to be moved to the White House, which meant a risk-filled ride through the heart of the city.

Dr. Bliss and Dr. Townsend gave their tacit approval.

Before they left the depot, Garfield awoke from a half-conscious state and called for his aide, Colonel A.F. Rockwell. "Rockwell," he whispered, "I want you to send a message to my wife. Tell her I am seriously hurt; how seriously I cannot yet say. I am myself, and hope she will come to me soon. I send my love to her."

A few minutes later, a wagon was procured and the president was taken to the White House. By now, the streets were jammed with angry citizens, demanding swift punishment for the assassin. Ironically, Clara Barton, the founder of the American Red Cross, was leaving her house on I Street when she saw a crowd of people streaming downtown. When she heard that Garfield had been shot, she ran to the Capitol, but she found the gates locked.

Almost immediately, the Executive Mansion was surrounded by armed sentinels. They had been given orders to stop any and all intruders—by any means necessary. Nobody, absolutely no one would be admitted without authority from Joe Stanley Brown, the President's private secretary. Those Cabinet members who were not at the depot when the shooting took place were immediately summoned, and each advised to remain at the White House for his own protection.

The President was carried to his chamber and made as comfortable as possible. Accounts differ on who conducted the second examination, but the doctors found that the first shot had passed through the arm just below the shoulder, without breaking any bones. The second ball had entered the back just above the hips, but they could not be certain of its direction, nor did they know where it had lodged. They agreed to search for the ball as soon as the President's condition improved.

While the doctors watched and waited, Garfield turned to Secretary Blaine, who was sitting beside him, and said, "What motive do you think that man could have had in trying to assassinate me?"

"I do not know," Blaine answered. "He says he had no motive. He must be insane."

"Perhaps," Garfield said, with a smile, "he thought it would be a glorious thing to be a pirate king."

Blaine simply frowned.

Turning to Dr. Bliss, the chief attending surgeon, Garfield said, "I want to know my true condition. Do not conceal anything from me; remember, I am not afraid to die."

Bliss told him that there were indications of internal bleeding. In all likelihood, he would only live a few hours.

"God's will be done," Garfield replied. "I am ready to go if my time has come."

At eleven o'clock, Dr. Joseph k. Barnes, the Surgeon-General, conducted a cursory examination and released a statement that the

President's wounds would probably prove fatal. Naturally, this sent shock waves through the city, but by three o'clock Garfield's pulse was up to 80 and his temperature was 96, just two and a half degrees below normal.

The sea air had done wonders for Mrs. Garfield, who had spent the last two weeks in Long Branch, New Jersey. Her bout with malaria had almost proved fatal, but now she was back to full strength, ready to join her husband and sons on a long-awaited vacation. She had just finished breakfast when her aide, General Swaim, received word of the shooting. He thought it best to break the news slowly, but the moment he entered the room, she sensed that something was wrong.

"What is the matter?" Mrs. Garfield asked.

"The President has met with an accident," Swaim answered.

"Is he dead?" she asked.

"No!" he replied.

"What was the accident?"

"I think he was shot," Swaim said. "I think he must have been fooling with a pistol, and doubtless he shot himself. I can't think it is anything very serious."

Mrs. Garfield was skeptical. "It is impossible that he could have shot himself. He has been shot. Tell me the truth."

Seeing that it was useless to evade her questions, General Swaim told her what he knew. A few minutes later, the following telegram arrived:

Mrs. Garfield, Elberon, Long Branch:

The President desires me to say to you, from him, that he has been seriously hurt, how seriously he cannot yet say. He is himself, and hopes you will come to him soon. He sends his love to you.

A.F. Rockwell

"Mrs. Garfield," Swaim said softly, "it may be necessary for us to go direct to Washington." There was an awkward silence between them. "So far as I am informed," he went on, "the accident is not so serious as was at first supposed."

"I need to pack," she reportedly said.

General Swaim told her that he would make arrangements for a special train to Washington. With any luck, they would be at the White House by seven o'clock that evening.

Five minutes later, a second telegram arrived. It read:

Executive Mansion,
Washington, D.C., July 2.

To General Swaim:

We have the President safely and comfortably settled in his room at the Executive Mansion, and his pulse is strong and nearly normal. So far as I can determine, and from what the surgeons say, and from his general condition, we feel very hopeful. Come on as soon as you can get a special train. Advise us of the movements of your train, and when you can be expected. As the President said on a similar occasion sixteen years ago, "God reigns, and the Government in Washington still lives."

A.F. Rockwell

The Pennsylvania Railroad furnished a special train to retrieve Mrs. Garfield and bring her to Washington. Mollie Garfield, the oldest daughter, accompanied her. Neither spoke much, their thoughts and prayers focused elsewhere. The train left at 12:30, traveling at a rate of forty to fifty miles an hour, and but for an accident twenty miles from Washington, they would have arrived an hour early.

During the day, the White House released several bulletins, but they were at best contradictory. The first official bulletin, released at 11:30 a.m., read as follows: "The President has returned to his normal condition. Will make another examination soon. His pulse is now 63."

An hour later, a second bulletin was issued: "The reaction from the shot injury has been very gradual. The patient is suffering some pain, but it is thought best not to disturb him by making an exploration for the ball until after the consultation at 3 p.m."

For a while it looked like the President's condition was improving, but then he took a turn for the worse, and the following dispatch was issued: "No official bulletin has been furnished by Dr. Bliss since 1 o'clock. The condition of the President has been growing more unfavorable since that time. Internal hemorrhage is taking place, and the gravest fears are felt as to the result."

Confusion would reign for the rest of the day and into the evening. Fortunately, Mrs. Garfield and her daughter were not subjected to the contradictory messages that continued to flow from the White House. Mrs. Garfield arrived in Washington at 6:30 p.m., and by seven o'clock, she was at her husband's bedside. To her great joy, he had clung stubbornly to life, confounding the ten or so physicians in attendance. If he could make it through the night, she was told, he had a decent chance of making a full recovery.

But making it through the night would not be easy.

Continuous doses of morphine did little to alleviate the pain, and even with nothing in his stomach, Garfield continued to vomit every half-hour.

Shortly after 7:00, Secretary Blaine telegraphed Vice-President Arthur, telling him that the President had recognized his wife and had conversed with her. Still, he continued, most of the physicians thought he was sinking rapidly. Arthur was advised to prepare himself for the worst possible news.

Later that evening, sensing that the end was near, the President began to tell his wife how to raise the children after he was gone. Mrs. Garfield cut him off. "Well, my dear," she told him, "you are not going to die as I am here to nurse you back to life; so please do not speak again of death."

Exhausted, but unable to sleep, Mrs. Garfield remained by her husband's side. Finally, when the President dozed off, she left the room. When he awoke, he discovered that his hand was being held by Mrs. James, the wife of the Postmaster-General. "Do you know where Mrs. Garfield is now?" he asked worriedly.

"Oh, yes," Mrs. James answered, "she is close by, watching and praying for her husband."

"I want her to go to bed," Garfield whispered. "Will you tell her that I say if she will undress and go to bed, I will turn right over, and I feel sure that when I know she is in bed, I can go to sleep and sleep all night? Tell her that I will sleep all night, if she will only do what I ask."

Mrs. James conveyed the message to Mrs. Garfield, who simply responded, "Go back and tell him that I am undressing."

She went back with the answer, and incredibly, the President turned over on his right side and fell into a peaceful sleep. Surprisingly, he slept through the night, and in the morning, his pulse and temperature were almost normal. The doctors continued to give him atropia and morphine, which if nothing else, reduced the nausea and vomiting.

At eleven o'clock, the sixth bulletin of the day was released to the public.

> The President's condition is greatly improved. He secures sufficient refreshing sleep; and, during his waking hours, is cheerful, and is inclined to discuss pleasant topics. Pulse, 106—with more full and safe expression; temperature and respiration, normal.
>
> D.W. Bliss, M.D.

During the afternoon the back wound was examined by Dr. Bliss and his colleagues, and just as they had done before, each physician stuck a finger deep into the hole, probing to find a channel. None of the doctors bothered to wash their hands, and none wore gloves. Not surprisingly, the poking and probing made the wound hemorrhage, and soon thereafter, the President began to complain about the pain in his feet and ankles. Even worse, his pulse began to gyrate between 100 and 120. Once again, the prognosis looked grim.

Years later, Lucretia Garfield would remember thinking that there were too many "experts" hovering around her husband—and too many expert opinions to consider. She would also remember thinking that if the doctors focused on easing her husband's pain and allowed the wound to heal, he would probably survive.

Sadly, she was right.

CHAPTER THREE

If it is true that a person's life flashes before his eyes when close to death, then James Garfield would have beheld a truly amazing sight. The "canal boy from Ohio" had excelled in many areas of public service prior to winning the presidential election of 1880 and becoming the twentieth president of the United States. During his fifty years, he had been a teacher, college president, lawyer, congressman, civil war hero, and U.S. Senator.

A biographer of the day would suggest that Garfield's accomplishments were due, in part, to his ancestry. "The law of heredity has long been suspected," John Clark Ridpath wrote. "And, in late years, has been, to a considerable extent, regarded as the demonstrated and universal order of nature. It is the law by which the offspring inherits the qualities and characteristics of its ancestors."

In Garfield's case, those qualities and characteristics were inherited from two prominent groups, the Puritans and the Hugenots. Both groups had come to North America to worship God according to the dictates of their own conscience, not for the sake of gold, adventure, or discovery.

The earliest known mention of the Garfield name occurred in 1587, when James Garfield (or Gearfeldt) was given a tract of land in Chester, England by the Earl of Leicester. The tract was located near the beautiful vale of Llangollen, and was probably given as a reward for military service on the continent.

Fifty years later, Edward Garfield, a Puritan, emigrated from England to America and joined the colony of John Winthrop at Watertown, Massachusetts. He appears to have been a farmer and a deeply religious man, highly respected in the community.

While the Garfields did not descend from English nobility, they did receive, or adopt, a coat of arms. The armorial bearings consisted of a golden shield crossed by three crimson bars. There was a cross in one corner, a heart in the other, and above the shield was an arm and hand grasping a sword. A Latin motto, *In CruceVinco* ("In the cross I conquer"), completed the emblem. Though never proven, the motto suggests that the family may have been soldiers, and it is possible that the coat of arms dated back to the Crusades.

The Garfields lived in the Watertown area for eight generations, and, by all accounts, they were devout Christians and well respected citizens. The spirit of their faith—Puritanism—dictated a peaceful coexistence with the outside world, but that all changed the morning of April 19, 1775. On that day, Solomon Garfield, the President's great-grandfather, and Abraham Garfield, his great granduncle, became embroiled in the first skirmish of the Revolutionary war—the fight on Concord Bridge. While it is not certain that Solomon took part in the actual battle, he did risk his life by encouraging his brother to sign the Garfield name to the following affidavit:

> Lexington, April 23, 1775.
>
> We, John Hoar, John Whitehead, Abraham Garfield, Benjamin Munroe, Isaac Parker, William Hosmer, John Adams, Gregory Stone, all of Lincoln, in the County of Middlesex, Massachusetts Bay, all of lawful age, do testify and say, that on Wednesday last, we were assembled at Concord, in the morning of said day, in consequence of information received that a brigade of regular troops were on their march to the said town of Concord, who had killed six men at the town of Lexington.

About an hour later, twelve hundred British troops marched into town, prepared to teach the colonists another lesson. Garfield and his companions rushed toward the North Bridge, and when they were fired upon, they fired back.

The Revolutionary War was now under way, and by signing the affidavit, Abraham Garfield identified himself as one of the leaders of the rebellion. Furthermore, he had admitted—even justified—the act of firing upon British troops. From that moment on, both brothers were branded as traitors to the crown, and if caught, they would surely have been hung.

Little is known of Solomon's military service, except that he served admirably and survived the conflict. After the war he moved to Otsego County, New York and returned to farming. Apparently, he was a muscular man, capable of performing great feats of strength. One day, while buying provisions, a country merchant offered him a five hundred pound grindstone if he would carry the stone home on his shoulder. Supposedly, Solomon hoisted the stone and carried it to his house a mile and a half away without stopping to rest.

Solomon's eldest son, Thomas, was born in 1775—the year of the Concord fight—and he too became a farmer and spent his entire life in Otsego County. Thomas married Asenath Hill, of Sharon, New York, and together they had four children. Abram, their third child, was the President's father. Named for his patriotic uncle, he was rumored to be his father's favorite. When Thomas Garfield died of smallpox, Abram became the man of the family and worked as a "bound boy," which was akin to being an indentured servant.

During this period, Abram became acquainted with a young girl named Eliza Ballou, whose widowed mother had recently moved to Otsego County from New Hampshire. Eliza was a lineal descendant of Maturin Ballou, a French Hugenot, who had emigrated to America in 1685. Maturin Ballou was a prominent member of Roger Williams' colony at Cumberland, Rhode Island. Upon arriving he had built a widely acclaimed church—constructed without a single nail. He was also the first in a long line of distinguished clergymen.

One of his descendants was Revered Hosea Ballou, the founder of the Universalist Church in America. Eliza was Hosea Ballou's grand-niece and a devout Christian in her own right.

In time Abram and Eliza would marry and produce four children, including a precocious son named James A. Garfield. For now, though, they had to content themselves with being friends, and even that did not last very long. In 1814, the Ballous sold the family farm and moved to Ohio which was still considered the "far west." The journey was dangerous and difficult, requiring a strong will and an even stronger back. As they soon discovered, the roads that led to Ohio were in pitiful condition, and when it rained they became impassable. As one might expect, the wagons were constantly getting stuck in mud, and that meant that they had to be unloaded, lifted out with lever, and reloaded. The process took hours and resulted in numerous injuries, some of which proved fatal.

Another problem was food, which was always in short supply and usually rationed. Beans and biscuits were the mainstays of the pioneer diet, and if fresh meat was desired, it meant a foray into the woods and a possible confrontation with hostile Indians.

Water, on the other hand, was plentiful—too plentiful. On the way west, the wagon train was forced to cross rivers, streams, creeks, and swamps. Each obstacle presented its own unique challenge, and some were downright deadly.

Incredibly, there was not a single bridge from New York to Ohio.

Despite the impediments, the Ballous preserved, and six weeks later they reached the "promise land," the eastern edge of the Great Ohio Wilderness. By the time they rolled into Muskingum County, they were on the verge of exhaustion, so they decided to remain in Zanesville, one of the oldest settlements in the west.

The "Ohio fever" struck Abram Garfield five years later, and he, too, packed up and moved west. Although just twenty, he was highly ambitious, and he found work in Newbury, a small town east of Cleveland. At the time, jobs were scarce, but he managed to land a position with a local construction firm that was about to start building the Ohio and Pennsylvania Canal—the very canal that would play such an important role in James Garfield's life.

Before long, Abram learned that Eliza Ballou, his childhood friend, was teaching at a school in Zanesville. He immediately sought her out, determined not to let her slip away again. The couple resumed their friendship, fell in love, and became engaged. They were married two years later, on February 3, 1821.

Abram and Eliza lived in Newbury for nine years, and during that time they had three children together: Mehetabel, Mary, and Thomas. In 1830, they sold their property and purchased fifty acres of land in Cuyahoga County near the town of Orange. Cuyahoga County had taken its name from the river that ran through it, and as one might expect, the name had an Indian origin. The first inhabitants of the region were the Miami Indians, and in their language Cuyahoga meant "crooked river." The tribe had come to the Ohio Valley in the seventeenth century and was soon joined by the Chippewa, Delaware, Ottawa, and Shawnee. The tribes used the river for food and transportation. They also used it as a gathering spot for the start of their autumn hunting season.

White settlers began to arrive during the 1700s, and before long, the Indians were relocated by treaty. The tribal lands lying east of the Cuyahoga River were appropriated by the Treaty of Fort McIntosh in 1785, and the lands west of the river were lost under the Treaty of Fort Industry in 1805.

In the beginning of the nineteenth century, Cuyahoga County was part of the "Western Reserve," a large trct of land claimed by the state of Connecticut. The Reserve had been created by the Kings of England who gave the colonies permission to extend westward. After the Revolutionary War, many states claimed the right of "soil and jurisdiction" over large portions of unappropriated land originally embraced in their charters. Eventually, Congress urged the states to cede these lands to the Federal Government, and all signed on except Connecticut, which retained a fourteen-county tract starting at the

Pennsylvania-Ohio border and extending 120 miles westward. In its entirety, the Reserve contained slightly over three million acres and covered about five thousand square miles.

In 1801, Connecticut ceded her jurisdictional claims over the territory, but thirty years later it was still referred to as the "Western Reserve of Connecticut." Like the Garfields, many of the settlers were originally from New England, mostly from the states of Connecticut, Massachusetts, and Vermont. Unlike the Europeans that had preceded them, the New Englanders came to farm, not to traffic in the fur trades.

The town of Orange was only seventeen miles south of Newbury, but to Abram Garfield, it sounded like the Garden of Eden. If the stories were true, fish and game were plentiful, and fertile fields and virgin forests were spread throughout the valley. All in all, it seemed to be the perfect place to raise their fourth and final child, James Abram Garfield, who was born on November 19, 1831. "Little Jimmy," as he was called, was named after his father, which was fitting, because he immediately became his father's favorite. Like his siblings, James entered the world under humble circumstances. His birthplace was a modest structure made of rough logs and mud, about twenty by thirty feet, with a small loft above. The single-room cabin had a puncheon floor and a large fireplace that was used for cooking meals and staying warm. To the dismay of Mrs. Garfield, the homestead was located in a remote and unpopulated section of the county and was a two-day ride to town. To make matters worse, the closest neighbor lived seven miles away.

The location of Cuyahoga County guaranteed an abundance of resources, but those resources were often threatened by natural disasters. Floods and tornadoes were not uncommon, but the biggest threat was fire. In the summer of 1833, a huge blaze swept into the Ohio Valley destroying everything in its path. In a desperate attempt to save his cabin and crops, Abram Garfield battled the blaze to a standstill, but he won a Pyrrhic victory. Sometime during the night he began to experience a violent congestion of the throat and lungs, and this led to prolonged vomiting and a high fever. Unfortunately, the nearest doctor was miles away, so Eliza turned to a neighbor who claimed to have some medical knowledge. The neighbor applied a blister—or poultice, as it came to be known—to the chest area that aggravated the problem and hastened Abram's demise.

Abram Garfield succumbed to his injuries the following day, and his last words, spoken to his wife and children, were these: "I have planted four saplings in these woods; I must now leave them to your care."

The young widow, thirty-two years old, had no time to grieve or console her children. She was now the sole provider and solely responsible for their survival. Even in her darkest hour, she had to keep the farm running and put food on the table. Meanwhile, the men of the community built a rough wooden box and laid Abram to rest in the corner of a nearby wheat field. There was no sermon, and nobody made any remarks or sang any hymns. Simply put, they had no time to spare. If the Garfield family wanted to survive, they had to get back to work and bring in a crop. Fall was just around the corner, and then came the long Midwestern winter. A severe winter could prove fatal, and unknown to them, they were about to encounter some of the harshest weather in history.

The first storm arrived in November and caught everyone by surprise, including some new arrivals from the east. Overnight the temperature dropped to freezing, and by mid-morning the fields were covered with a thick blanket of snow. Wagon trains were stranded, and passengers were forced to abandon their worldly possessions and seek shelter in the nearest town. Many remained in those towns, some taken in by strangers or relatives—others in unmarked graves.

By mid-December, the Garfield cabin was completely buried in snow. Two weeks later, Arctic air swept into the valley and killed every animal on the farm. For the next two months, the region was hit by storm after storm, and it looked like the winter from hell would never end. During these bleak days, Eliza and her children remained inside their cabin, venturing out only for firewood. The day was spent reading and reciting the Bible and praying for a break in the weather. When darkness fell, the valley became an eerie place filled with the howls of wolves and the cries of panthers. The children would often lie awake, listening to the chorus of wild animals, wondering just how close they were. From time to time, one of them would begin to cry, certain that all would be eaten alive.

Eliza did her best to comfort the children, but her main concerns were to keep them clothed and fed. The young widow had no money, no source of income, and a sizeable debt on the farm. They managed to survive the winter, but, as spring approached, it became clear that the food stock was dangerously low. Apparently, Eliza had miscalculated the daily allowance of corn, and now the crib was nearly depleted. Something had to be done to preserve the remainder of the crop. They were already down to two meals a day, and the portions could not get much smaller. Eliza could think of only one solution, and it was a risky one at that. She decided to forego dinner and take only the morning meal. The decision was difficult, and it clearly endangered her health. However, it got them through the spring and summer and probably saved the family from starvation. Fortunately, the autumn harvest was bountiful, and they soon had plenty of food.

Once they were back on their feet, Eliza sold off twenty acres of land and retired the debt on the farm. In the spring of 1835, a new family moved into the area, and then hired Eliza to do some sewing for them. Before long, she had enough money to buy Little Jimmy his first pair of shoes. The new family had children of their own, and they introduced the Garfield youngsters to some of the most popular books of the day, including *the* most popular book of the day, *Davy Crockett's Almanac.*

As it happened, Crockett had recently decided to head west himself, and, one year later almost to the day, he would make his grand entrance at a Spanish mission known as the Alamo.

That fall, the Garfield children enrolled in a new school in Chagrin Falls, a quaint little town whose unusual name according to local lore, was the work of a Yankee merchant who had been fooled by Mother Nature. He had supposedly arrived during the dead of winter. After finding a flowing stream, he decided to erect a saw mill and corner the lumber market. What he didn't realize was that the stream was seasonal, and when summer came, the water disappeared—and so did the merchant. But the town remained. Despite its remote location, it had a decent pioneer school. The schoolmaster emphasized the traditional subjects—reading, writing and arithmetic. He also taught geography and spelling.

Young James Garfield became one of the best students, often outshining the older children in class. His strongest subjects were spelling and reading, but he also excelled in math. It was at this school that Garfield was first exposed to the most widely used texts of the day, which included *Webster's Spelling-book, The English Reader, Morse's*

Geography, and *Pike's and Adams' Arithmetic*. When he read for pleasure, he read *Pirate's Own Book*, a collection of vivid tales. Although he did not know it at the time, the pirate book would have a profound affect on his adolescent life and propel him toward his own nautical adventure.

By the time James Garfield was eight, he was a full-fledged scholar, capable of reading and reciting long biblical passages. The schoolmaster, imported from New Hampshire, was astonished by his student's ability to read and retain information. He had never witnessed such youthful intelligence, not even in the finest private academies of New England. Clearly, the young lad was destined for greatness.

"Who knows," the schoolmaster said on more than one occasion, "Garfield may even grow up to be President."

CHAPTER FOUR

In the nineteenth century, the Ohio Wilderness was a vast and untamed territory, filled with adventure and opportunity, but even that was not enough to hold the attention of a teenage boy who dreamed of going to sea. In 1847, young James Garfield, now sixteen, informed his mother that he was going to Cleveland to become a sailor. Back then, Cleveland was the logical choice as it had one of the best—if not the best—harbors on Lake Erie. Nature had provided a nearly perfect port, one that was well defended from storms, easy to access, and deep enough to accommodate any large craft. After the city's incorporation in 1836, the harbor was extended several hundred feet into the lake. The result of this construction was an effective breakwater and a pier system that provided ample room for loading and unloading of vessels.

Eliza Garfield was dismayed by her son's decision, and she had good reason to worry. A seafaring life was dangerous, and sailors were often away from home for many months, or even years. She suggested that James sail on a Lake Erie schooner first. Her instincts told her, in all probability, he would quickly tire of the monotony and hardship of life aboard ship. He would then return home, anxious to resume farming. In addition, she prayed for her son's "enlightenment."

Like most pioneer women, Eliza was a devout Christian, and she truly believed in the power of prayer. Many of her ancestors had been clergymen, and she herself was a fervent supporter of the Temperance Reformation that was currently sweeping through New England and into Ohio. Typically, she did not tolerate "ungodly behavior" in the home, and visitors were never permitted to drink alcohol, to smoke, or to use foul language in her presence. Occasionally, she would allow a grown-up to chew tobacco, but they always had to spit outside.

On arriving in Orange, Eliza had joined the Disciples' Church, whose members were known as Campbellities in honor of their founder, Alexander Campbell. Reverend Campbell had emigrated from Ireland to the United States in 1809 and began his religious career as a Presbyterian minister. One year later, he left the Presbyterian Church and organized a new order called Disciples of Christ. Unlike Presbyterians, the disciples accepted baptism by immersion and declared that the Bible should be the sole creed of their new church.

The Disciples had no ordained ministry, and like the Quakers in Pennsylvania, members could preach when the Spirit moved them. They viewed both the Old and New Testaments as the inspired word of God. At mid-century, they had about half a million members and were one of the fastest growing denominations in Ohio.

Outwardly, Eliza remained supportive of her son's plan, but, in her heart, she knew that he was making a mistake. Her fear, of course, was that James might experience a different type of immersion. Then as now the Great Lakes laid claim to many lives, and even though Lake

Erie sounded like an exciting place to work, it was actually one of the shallowest, most treacherous, and least picturesque of the lakes.

Nonetheless, Eliza gave her blessing, and young James Garfield set out for Cleveland. The trip took a bit longer than expected, but that was because Garfield had to walk most of the fifteen miles. By one account, he spent the first two days wandering around the city getting the lay of the land. Cleveland had grown rapidly since 1836. Now, with the arrival of a railroad, business was booming.

For all its growth, though, Cleveland remained a "frontier city." Just outside of town, large herds of cattle grazed along the banks of the Cuyahoga River. Every so often, a calf would be taken by a wolf or panther, and there were even rumors of Indian raids down on the remote sections of the flatland.

By now, of course, there were also signs of "progress." If Garfield had walked beyond the cow pastures, he would have witnessed the birth of a new industry, the production of refined petroleum. Few were aware of it, but Cleveland was about to become the first city in the world to produce this new product and would become the headquarters of a giant monopoly, the Standard Oil Company. Even now, the view was startling. Just beyond the flatland, the terrain became dotted with large factory plants that housed the new business of the Industrial Revolution: copper smelting, iron manufacturing, and lumber production.

Ironically, Cleveland was considered the most beautiful city on the Great Lakes. More than likely, this was due to the large number of elms that lined its streets. The trees were a great source of public pride and the reason that Cleveland was known as the "Forest City."

If James Garfield had been an arborist, he might have found work, but finding a job on a schooner proved to be difficult. Nobody was anxious to hire a landlubber, especially a young one. After several rejections and a nasty confrontation with a drunken captain, he decided to take a long walk. Before long, he probably crossed the intersection of Superior and Ontario Streets. If so, he undoubtedly noticed a ten-acre site filled with lovely elms. The site would soon become known as Monument Park. Three years later, it would contain a colossal statue of Captain Oliver Hazard Perry, the hero of the Battle of Lake Erie. (Perry had achieved immortality in 1813 by penning the famous words, "We have met the enemy and they are ours . . .") The statue would be made of Italian marble and stand about twenty feet high, making it the tallest monument in the city. It would also be the most expensive sculpture, costing the taxpayers nearly eight thousand dollars.

One day, a monument would be erected to honor James Garfield, and it would stand in the same park. Amazingly, this was the very spot where, in 1881, President Garfield would be laid in state, covered by a large catafalque and patriotic bunting.

Hours later, back at the pier, Garfield ran into his cousin, Amos Letcher. Captain Letcher was the pilot of a canal boat called *The Evening Star*, a seventy-ton-capacity vessel that hauled copper ore from Cleveland to Pittsburgh. Letcher was something of a legend on the Ohio and Pennsylvania Canal, and fortunately for Garfield he was in need of a mule driver. A canal boat was manned with two steersmen, a bowman, a cook, and two mule drivers. Each person had a specific job, and each task contributed to the smooth operation of the vessel.

The steersmen, as the name implies, were responsible for steering the boat in the proper direction and avoiding collisions with oncoming traffic. The bowman had to open the locks and stop the boat by throwing the bowline around a snubbing post. The drivers, who were usually young, had two mules, and they took turns pulling the boat along the tow path.

Captain Letcher was fond of young James, but he would only offer the going rate, twelve dollars a month plus room and board. Garfield jumped at the chance to get his feet wet, and that is exactly what happened. By his own account, he fell into the polluted waters of the canal no less than fourteen times, and on several occasions, he nearly drowned. Spills were unavoidable and were usually caused by high winds or passing boat traffic. In most cases, the tow ropes would suddenly tighten, jerking the driver and his team into the water. The driver was responsible for extracting the mules, and the crew was expected to rescue the driver. If all went well, the driver and the mules would emerge unscathed, but injuries and illness were not uncommon.

Canal work was dangerous and difficult, and it attracted a rough class of people. In general, boatmen were deemed to be coarse and vulgar with a fondness for whiskey. Alcohol and tobacco were among the necessities of life, and it was rare to meet a boatman who abstained from either. In this environment, family connections meant nothing. To be accepted by the crew, a man had to prove that he was able to defend himself.

In Garfield's case, the moment of truth arrived unexpectedly. One day, outside of Pittsburgh, a steamer pulled along *The Evening Star* and threw some tow ropes to the crew. One of the ropes sailed over Garfield's head and hit an Irish tough named Murphy, knocking his hat into the water. The hat was retrieved, but Murphy began to curse up a storm and aimed his anger at the youngest member of the crew. Garfield apologized, but Murphy charged forward attempting to knock him overboard. As the crew watched in disbelief, Garfield stepped sideways and struck his attacker with a hard blow to the head, knocking him flat on his back. The boatmen cheered loudly, encouraging young Garfield to beat Murphy senseless. Instead of punching him again, Garfield lifted him up and offered his hand in friendship. Murphy was flabbergasted, but he was smart enough to calm down and shake hands. From that moment on, the two were inseparable.

Garfield worked as a mule driver for four months, and, during this period, he was thrown into the canal roughly once a week. The last dunking was the worst, and it nearly cost him his life. One night, while still half-asleep, he came on deck to take a turn at the bow. As he stumbled to his post, a rope got caught on the edge of the deck. When he yanked it loose, it flew back and knocked him overboard. He fell into the water headfirst, and when he came up, he saw *The Evening Star* drifting away. He yelled for help, but there was no one on deck. Nobody had seen him fall overboard. Luckily, he still held the rope. Somehow, he managed to pull himself back to the boat and climb up the stern. When he crawled to the bow, he discovered that the rope had caught in a crevice and held fast, saving his life.

Garfield, still in virtual shock, was not out of danger just yet. During his ordeal, he swallowed quite a bit of water, and within minutes, he began to experience severe stomach pain. The cramping continued throughout the night and led to a bad case of "ague," a malaria-like illness marked by chills, fever, and prolonged sweating. When his condition worsened, he returned to Orange barely able to stand on his own two feet. Fortunately, Eliza Garfield knew exactly what to do in order to prevent the disease from running its course. She immediately concocted an "ague cake," a disc-shaped poultice made of calomel, commonly known as mercurous chloride. The cake was used as a purgative and was usually applied to the patient's side.

By day's end, Garfield felt better, but, even after his fever broke, other symptoms remained. In the end, it took a full six months for him to regain his strength. As he improved, others began to experience a different type of fever.

Shortly after President James K. Polk mentioned the "extra-ordinary character" of the California gold strike in his annual message of 1848, a mad rush ensued. Gold-seekers from across the nation poured into California determined to find the Mother Lode. Almost overnight, San Francisco became a ghost town. In Oregon, two-thirds of the adult population rushed to the western slope of the sierras. Over the next twelve months, 25,000 Americans made their way to California by ship and another 55,000 by overland routes.

For a while, it looked like the entire nation would move west, but not everyone succumbed to the temptation of gold. Now that he was back on his feet, James Garfield was interested in seeking a different type of treasure. He was finished with boats, mules, and polluted water. It was time to get an education. The canal boy was going to college.

Throughout the nineteenth century, it was customary for college-bound students to begin their academic career at a preparatory school, which were designed to nurture students and introduce them to the advanced subjects of the day. Back east, admission was reserved for the sons and daughters of the rich; however, out west class distinctions were not as defined. In the spring of 1849, Garfield moved to Chester, a small town about fourteen miles away. Chester was the home of the Geauga Seminary, a college preparatory school associated with the Free-will

Baptist Church. At mid-century, the school had six faculty members and a student population of one hundred. Both sexes were represented, and students were schooled in a variety of subjects, including Latin, Greek, and Natural Philosophy.

Garfield arrived in Chester on the fifth of March, accompanied by his cousin, William Boynton, and a life-long friend named Orrin Judd. The three boys traveled to school on foot, which was no mean feat considering the condition of the roads and the fact that the campus was ten miles away. Unable to afford a wagon, they were forced to carry their own clothing, food, and cooking utensils.

When they arrived in Chester, they proceeded directly to the principal, and, after a short interview, they were given permission to attend class. Each boy had about seventeen dollars in his pocket, which meant that they were obliged to share a modest room in a local boardinghouse. Once school began, they took turns cooking. Since they were on a budget, their meals did not require a great deal of preparation. Most mornings began with milk and mush, and the evening meal usually consisted of "pioneer bacon" and a bowl of beans. If they exceeded their food allowance, which was one dollar per week, they switched to a diet of bread and milk.

After a few weeks of class, Garfield joined the Debating Society and became a prominent member of the debate team, rarely losing a match. The eighteen-year-old student was unusually wise for his age and especially glib when the topic was political in nature. In those days, the Geauga Seminary library contained 150 books, and the talented orator made good use of them, often studying the upcoming topic well into the night. Despite his age, he possessed a ready command of the English language and had little trouble expressing his thoughts. Many opponents admired his eloquence, and several of them urged him to pursue a career in law—or politics.

Presently, however, Garfield was more concerned about staying in school than in finding a career. During the summer recess he took odd jobs, barely saving enough money to support himself. If he wanted to return to Geauga, he had to find a good paying job and find one quickly. His mother advised him to pursue a teaching position, and as usual her advice was sound. Jobs were scarce in rural Ohio, but there was still a need for teachers, especially young ones who could stay awake in the classroom. Garfield was fortunate and found a job at a nearby school, but it was a position that he had to literally fight to keep.

The altercation took place on the first day of school, instigated by a vulgar bully who was out to get the new teacher. Apparently, Garfield had to scold the student for a misdeed, but, instead of apologizing, the student became quite angry. When Garfield turned his back, the student tried to hit him with a billet of wood, but he missed his target. As a result, the young man received a thorough thrashing. Afterwards, he became a model student. Not surprisingly, there were no more displays of insubordination. By the time Mr. Garfield left, he was widely acclaimed as the best schoolmaster in the district.

Garfield returned to the Geauga Seminary in the spring of 1850, and shortly thereafter, he joined the Disciples Church. Naturally, this pleased his mother a great deal. Before long, his ability as a public speaker began to show itself, and the "born preacher" began to attract a following. Many members attended meetings just to hear him speak. As a rule, his sermons were simple, earnest appeals, always to the point and eloquently expressed.

One of his not-so-secret admirers was a fellow student named Lucretia Rudolph. "Crete," as she liked to be called, was seventeen years old and a real charmer. She was the daughter of Zebulon Rudolph, a Maryland farmer, and Arabella Mason, a native of Hartford, Vermont. The Geauga yearbook described her as ". . . a friendly young lady of unusual worth and intellectual ability." These were, of course, admirable traits, but she also happened to be one of the prettiest girls in school, a fact that was not lost on young Mr. Garfield.

A biographer who knew Lucretia Rudolph at the time described her in the following words:

"She was of medium stature, with dark hazel eyes, wavy brown hair, a rounded form, and an expression about her mouth denoting a calm sweet temper, combined with a strong will."

Garfield was enchanted by Lucretia Rudolph, but he was a shy young man, unable, or perhaps unwilling, to express his feelings. They became close friends, but there was no courtship. They eventually went their separate ways. Lucretia Rudolph became a teacher and James Garfield took the bold step of enrolling in college. In time, their paths would cross again, and whenever they spoke of their happiest days, they would mention the Geauga Seminary. Indeed, the time spent in Chester marked the beginning of a productive decade and provided the last few years of calm they ever shared.

CHAPTER FIVE

There were many strange things about Charles Guiteau, but the strangest, perhaps, was how much he had in common with the man he shot. Both Garfield and Guiteau hailed from the heartland of the nation. Each was the youngest child in his family and both lost a parent at an early age. As adults, both studied theology, practiced law, and expressed a keen interest in politics. Like Garfield, Guiteau had been raised in a pious and respectable family, and oddly enough, his parents were from upstate New York. Finally, both men had parents of English and French Huguenot ancestry!

Luther and Jane Howe Guiteau came to the Midwest in 1833. After a brief stay in Ann Arbor, Michigan, they moved to Freeport, Illinois. In 1839, Luther and his bride of six years purchased a modest Greek-style house on the corner of High and Galena Avenue. Charles Guiteau was born here on September 8, 1841.

Freeport in 1841 still benefited from its early reputation as a haven for cash-strapped settlers traveling in northern Illinois. The town took its name from the renowned generosity of its founder, William "Tutty"

Baker. Baker operated a free ferry across the Pecatonica River and was well known as an honest trader and a gracious host. He often invited complete strangers into his home for meals and lodging. According to one source, Freeport earned its name after Mrs. Baker asked her husband if his river port was a "Free Port" as nobody paid for the ferry. Whatever the truth, Freeport was growing quickly and its future looked bright. In 1839, the town erected a new courthouse and its very first school. Now the state was financing an even bigger project, a new stagecoach line that would link Freeport and Chicago. The line was destined to have an enormous economic impact on the region, and soon after its completion it would become a magnet for thousands of German settlers from Pennsylvania.

Upon their arrival, the German immigrants would produce a number of novel items, such as the Pecatonica Long Rifle and a twisted dough concoction covered with salt. The latter invention would become a lasting source of pride; one day, Freeport would be known as the "Pretzel city."

But in September 1841, the town was still a rural outpost perched on the edge of the western frontier. In this setting, doctors were rare and hospitals even more so. Most babies were born at home, and delivery problems were not uncommon. Shortly after giving birth to Charles, Jane Guiteau suffered "brain fever" as it was called back then. Her illness, now known as a postpartum psychosis, was debilitating, and it caused her to engage in a bizarre act of self-mutilation.

Using a straightedge razor, Jane Guiteau shaved her head, locked herself in her room, and refused to see family or friends. She remained in this self-imposed isolation for several months, never once inquiring about her newborn baby. As fall turned into winter, her condition worsened and she became thin and frail. She managed to live for seven more years, but she never fully recovered from the initial trauma. Sadly, neither of her last two children lived to his second birthday, and she herself died in a mental asylum on September 25, 1848.

Luther Guiteau blamed Charles for his wife's illness and death. After she was gone, he became a cruel and abusive father who frequently beat his bewildered son. In truth, Jane Guiteau's illness was probably hereditary. According to family records, Charles had one uncle, two aunts, and two first cousins who were diagnosed as insane.

Nevertheless, young Charles remained the target of his father's anger, and, as the record shows, Luther Guiteau was often angry. He was also a religious zealot, intolerant of the "unsaved" and secretly repulsed by the wickedness of the world. Even worse, he was enthralled by the religious rantings of John Henry Noyes, the founder of the utopian Oneida Community in upstate New York. In contrast to other Christian sects, the Oneida Community practiced "free love," shared labor, and mutual criticism. It was under Luther's tutorage that Charles first learned about "Bible Communism" and its unique view of sex. In Luther's mind, the world was a battleground between the forces of good and evil, and salvation came only through faith and submission to the Almighty. Selfish and sinful acts were viewed as satanic in nature, and they were dealt with firmly and forcibly. Luther felt that only frequent beatings and verbal abuse would lead his "devious" son toward salvation. "Spare the rod and spoil the child," he always said.

The rod was seldom spared, but it had no effect on its young victim. Part of the problem was Luther himself. The man engendered little respect. At times, his own children questioned his sanity, and their misgivings were well-founded.

While reading Noyes, Luther had an epiphany and became convinced that sickness and disease could be conquered through faith.

It was this belief that led to the conclusion that he might live forever by forming a "vital union with Christ." The pursuit of this union was often comical, but it also had a more serious side. Doctors were not permitted to treat the Guiteau children. If they got sick, they had to depend on prayer. When Luther's six-year-old daughter became gravely ill, he announced that he would heal her by putting his faith in Jesus Christ. As the other children watched, he began to manipulate his daughter's arms and legs, commanding the disease to disappear in the name of Christ. Miraculously, the little girl survived, but she and her siblings were traumatized by the incident. Luther, on the other hand, was now certain that he had found the key to everlasting life. From that moment on, no doctors were allowed in the house again.

Charles was probably appalled at the thought of his father living forever, but, of course, he never said so. In fact, the two seldom spoke. When they did converse, it was usually unpleasant. Sometimes, it was more than unpleasant. On one occasion, Charles attacked his father and threw him to the ground. No blows were exchanged, but the incident rattled Luther. From that moment on, he was convinced that his son had a murderous spirit. Time would prove him right.

In the spring of 1853, Luther announced that he was going to marry a Freeport woman named Maria Blood. The announcement surprised the children, who had mixed emotions about getting a new mother. As it turned out, Maria Blood was exactly what the family needed, and she turned out to be a vital and optimistic stepmother. Under her influence, Charles became a better student and more a confident twelve year old.

But the second major event of that year changed everything. A few months after Charles gained a new mother, he lost an adored sister. Frances Guiteau, his favorite sibling, announced that she was going to marry a prominent attorney and move to Chicago. "Franky" was six years older than Charles, and she was the one who actually raised him after their mother's death. The two had been inseparable during childhood and shared a special bond. Without Franky, life was dull and without joy. Maria Blood was a godsend, but she did not have the time or the inclination to dote on any one child. Furthermore, she did not believe that the children had to be protected from their father. Only Franky could provide the love and support that Charles needed, and, when she left home, he was devastated. Almost overnight, he became sullen and withdrawn. Before long, his schoolwork began to suffer. Poor grades led to a prolonged period of self-loathing and set the stage for a miserable teenage life.

The misery began with Franky's departure and continued the following year. In 1854, Charles learned that his older brother was moving to Davenport, Iowa. John Wilson Guiteau was an avid reader of Horace Greeley's *New York Tribune*, the publication that urged young men to go west. After reading about cheap land, he decided to try his luck on the other side of the Mississippi. There were risks, of course, but he was anxious to open a law firm, and Davenport seemed to be the perfect spot. The *Tribune* had described Iowa as a land of opportunity, and now that the Sauk and Fox tribes were gone the region was relatively safe.

After his sister and brother left, Charles fell into the darkest period of his young life. From 1854 to 1857, between the ages of 13 and 17, he engaged in a series of self-destructive acts. First he became a petty thief, robbing money from various employers. He also began to steal from family members. Once his pockets were full he began to spend freely and often did so at brothels. Moreover, his sexual appetites were insatiable, and by the age of sixteen he had contracted a venereal disease.

He became addicted to "self-abuse," a polite, Gilded Age term for masturbation. The frequency of his abuse was rather startling, and it resulted in a serious genital injury. While the exact nature of the injury is unclear, current medical knowledge indicates that excessive masturbation can lead to both physiological and psychological imbalances. The physical side effects of these changes include lower back pain, groin and testicular discomfort, and pain in the pelvic cavity or tail bone. The psychological side effects include stress and anxiety. In the case of prolonged addiction, severe depression, shame, and self-hatred may ensue.

Guiteau felt spiritually bankrupt by his addiction. The prevailing opinions of "self-abuse" were extremely critical, and many physicians claimed that it caused headaches, epilepsy, memory loss, blindness, and even psychosis. A popular 19th century health manual described the act this way:

> Masturbation is a very degrading and destructive habit . . . There is probably no vice which is more injurious to both mind and body. It retards the growth, impairs the mental faculties and reduces the victim to a lamentable state. The person afflicted seeks solitude, and does not wish to enjoy the society of his friends; he is troubled with headache, wakefulness and restlessness at night, pain in various parts of the body, indolence, melancholy, loss of memory, weakness in the back and generative organs, variable appetite, cowardice, inability to look a person in the face, lack of confidence in his own abilities. Eventually there will be an irritable condition of

> the system; sudden flashes of heat over the face; the countenance becomes pale and clammy; the eyes have a dull, sheepish look; the hair becomes dry and split at the ends; sometimes there is pain over the region of the heart; shortness of breath; palpitation of the heart; symptoms of dyspepsia show themselves; the sleep is disturbed; there is constipation; cough; irritation of the throat; finally the whole man becomes a wreck, physically, morally, and mentally.

The fear of masturbation was so great that throughout the nation, prominent citizens dedicated their lives to battling what one writer called the "shameful vice which decimates youth." In the early 1800s, Sylvester Graham led a health food crusade based on the idea that sexual excess was caused by rich and spicy foods. His thoughts on the subject were summarized this way:

> All kinds of stimulating and heating substance; high-seasoned food; rich dishes; the free use of flesh; and even the excess of aliment; all, more or less—and some to a very great degree—increase the concupiscent excitability and sensibility of the genital organs.

During his illustrious career, Graham lashed out against white bread, pork, tobacco, salt, condiments, and hot mince pie. Prior to his death in 1851, he was America's foremost authority on "self-pollution," and his *Lecture To Young Men* (a popular pamphlet) launched a whole new genre of medical research. In an effort to stop the spread of undesirable behavior, he invented a bland morsel that became quite popular among teenagers and adults alike. The morsel, originally designed to moderate sexual desire, soon became known as the "Graham cracker."

One of Graham's disciples was a quirky young doctor named John Harvey Kellogg. Dr. Kellogg was also concerned about sexual excess, but he spent most of his time experimenting with whole-grain foods. One day, he mixed oatmeal and corn meal together, baked the mixture into biscuits, then ground the biscuits into bits. The finished product was rather tasty, and, by all accounts, the doctor's sanitarium patients loved the concoction. Eventually, the mixture was packaged as a breakfast cereal and called Granula, then Granola. The success of Granola enabled Kellogg to devote more time to the study of sexual excess and its effect on American youth. Like his mentor, he soon became obsessed with the subject. In time, he began to formulate some very strange ideas. When lecturing, he encouraged his audience members to abstain from all sexual relations regardless of their marital status. By abstaining, they would discover that sex was not necessary to promote good health. How the doctor came to this conclusion is unknown, but apparently he never consummated his own marriage. He and his wife lived in separate apartments throughout life.

Dr. Kellogg's view of self-stimulation was also unique: A remedy [for masturbation] which is almost always successful in small boys is circumcision . . . The operation should be performed by a surgeon without administering an anesthetic, as the brief pain attending the operation will have a salutary effect upon the mind.

Incredibly, the cereal magnate invented Corn Flakes to promote health and *decrease* sex drive. Whether or not he was successful is debatable, but he did have a profound influence on the subject, and his views were reflected in the business world. Between 1856 and 1932, the

U.S. Patent Office awarded 33 patents to inventors of anti-masturbation devices.

Clearly, society frowned upon anyone who engaged in this form of aberrant behavior. In Guiteau's case, the addiction produced a moral conflict between his ethical and religious values and his secret behavior. The result was predictable. It was, on the whole, a sad and lonely adolescence, made worse by uncontrollable urges and constant guilt.

Finally, at age eighteen, Guiteau had a spiritual awakening and realized that he was ruining his life. Seeking redemption, he returned to his religious roots and began to read the *Oneida Circular*, the theological newsletter published by John Henry Noyes. Shortly thereafter, he vowed to turn his life around and adhere to the principles espoused by Noyes. In order to convince his family that he was serious, he wrote a letter to his sister, Franky, promising to perfect and educate himself physically, intellectually, and morally.

"Dear Sister," he began:

> I think I should live according to the laws of health and physiology to arrive at the first part. [Physically] Secondly, to improve my mind by reading, writing, studying and thinking as much as possible without over taxing the brain. (sic). [Intellectually] Thirdly, to keep my moral character pure and spotless. (sic).

The letter raised a few eyebrows, but Charles kept his word and pursued a new course. He began to work long hours, taking on household chores and helping his father down at the Second National Bank of Freeport. Between jobs, he began to improve his health by taking up gymnastics and weight lifting. Finally, after weighing his future options, he decided to leave home and continue his education. "I want," he wrote his sister, "to go to school two or three years steady if I can, and I can if my will is large enough."

In a manner of speaking, a large will was exactly what saved the day. Luther Guiteau had no intention of subsidizing his son's education, and he made it very clear that Charles should forget about college and set his sights on the Oneida Community. As luck would have it, Charles was about to inherit a large sum of money from Major John Howe, his maternal grandfather. The major had always been partial to Charles, frequently reminding him that he had more brains than anyone else in the family. When the major died, he left his favorite grandson one thousand dollars, and that enabled Charles to enroll at the University of Michigan in Ann Arbor.

In the fall of 1859, Guiteau came to Michigan with high hopes and a renewed sense of purpose. The bad old days were behind him, and, from now on, it would be onward and upward.

But he soon discovered that he was ill-prepared for college and that university courses were beyond his grasp. Naturally, he was mortified, but the worst was yet to come. After reviewing his work, the registrar informed him that he would have to spend some time at Michigan's preparatory school. Even so, there was no guarantee that he would be readmitted to the university.

Unwilling or unable to blame himself, he blamed others, conjuring up wild theories to explain his failure. Once again, the wickedness of the world had crushed his dreams. The forces of darkness had won another victory, and for all Charles knew, Satan himself was celebrating. Tired of defeat, he began to ask some tough questions. How could he rid himself of these demons? Where would he find salvation? Who could show him the way?

Not surprisingly, he turned to John Henry Noyes, a "prophet" who had battled his own demons and rejoiced in triumph. Brother Noyes knew the way of salvation, and, more importantly, he and his followers had attained the kingdom of heaven on earth. Soon he began to correspond with several young men at the Oneida Community. Every letter was a revelation, and, as time went on, he became obsessed with utopian life.

The Oneida "Perfectionists," as they called themselves, had a truly radical vision of this life, even by today's standards. In essence, they believed that in order to attain the kingdom of heaven on earth, a follower would have to duplicate Heaven. To achieve this end, he would have to follow Christ's teaching on what the reign of God would be like. Some of their tenets were odd and several were downright bizarre. The most famous—or infamous—rule that Noyes imposed was based on Christ's teaching that there would be no marriage in Heaven. Perfectionists believed that on earth all men were married to all women and that men and women in the community should be sexually intimate with a variety of partners. Noyes called this practice "Complex Marriage," and it was regulated by another outlandish practice called "Male Continence," which was a type of birth control. In short, "a couple would engage in sexual congress without the man ever ejaculating, either during intercourse or after withdrawal."

"Ascending Fellowship" was a practice related to Male continence, and it was designed to properly introduce virgins into Complex Marriage. In this practice, an older male could choose any female virgin he wanted, and due to her lower status she was compelled to accept. If an older female was involved, she could choose a male virgin and he was obliged to honor the request.

The fourth major practice was called "Mutual Criticism." The way this worked was simple and cruel. If a member disobeyed the rules they had to subject themselves to either a committee or the whole community. The violator was forced to sit in the middle of a circle surrounded by a hostile group of his or her peers. The criticisms were usually directed toward a member's bad traits, and it was always a shameful and humiliating experience. Only Noyes was immune from Mutual Criticism, and that was because he felt that a group should not criticize its leader.

Outwardly, at least, Guiteau seemed unfazed by the rules and regulations of the community. On March 5, 1860, he bared his soul on paper, writing to his friends at Oneida that . . .

> I have been looking quite anxiously to hear from you for some time past . . . If the devil thought by preventing you from receiving my letter he would check my testimony for the truth, I would inform him that he is very much mistaken; that I am not (by the grace of God) thrown off the track as easily as that . . . . It would be very pleasant (and I trust profitable) for me to hear from Oneida often by letter in my present isolated circumstances. I feel that Christ is the only true friend I have in this world, except those that are united to him in the truth. I do not desire to have any others . . . . I desire to see glory of God in all things . . . . I feel united to you all by the body of Christ, that your sympathies are my sympathies; that my sympathies are your sympathies; that we are one in Christ.

One month later, he wrote: "My confidence in you is continuously increasing and especially in Mr. Noyes. I have perfect, entire and absolute confidence in him in all things. I believe him to be a man directly inspired by God."

Luther Guiteau believed the same thing. In early June, he wrote to Charles, urging him to devote his "faculties and powers" to the Oneida Community. Undoubtedly, it was this letter that convinced Charles to change his life and seek the truth:

> I cannot but in this connection confess my gratitude to God for His goodness in establishing on the earth a school where the young and inexperienced believer may find sympathizing friends and help such as his soul needs and hungers and thirsts for. Such a school I regard the Oneida Community; and in living and honoring Mr. Noyes and the generous and noble spirits associated with him, I feel that I am honoring God and the cause of Christ . . . . I am delighted with the idea of your going to Oneida, and have no doubt, with the spirit of faith and perseverance you now seem to have, you will very soon see, and feel, and realize that it is just the school you need, where there will be full opportunity for the highest and purest enjoyments of which you are capable of.

Later that month, Charles Guiteau left Ann Arbor for New York State. He had finally found his way. After years of strife and turmoil, he would now find peace and happiness. Nothing could stand in his way. Nothing except a civil war, and how likely was that?

CHAPTER SIX

The observant Frenchman, Alexis de Tocqueville, in an 1831 letter describing the American heartland, wrote: "[It is] . . . one vast forest, in the middle of which thy have carved out some clearings." There were some obvious exceptions to such a generalization: Chicago, for example, and Cleveland. These cities, built on the shores of Lake Michigan and Lake Erie, were quite cosmopolitan. By contrast, the rest of Illinois and Ohio was still untamed and would remain that way for another fifteen years. In 1845, a journalist named John L. O'Sullivan captured the new mood of the nation in a single sentence: "Nothing must interfere with the fulfillment of our *manifest destiny* to overspread the continent allotted by Providence for the free development of our yearly multiplying millions." In other words, Americans felt that the continent was theirs, not only to exploit, but to unite as one great nation. Consequently, the West was now seen as a "ripe apple, ready to be picked."

Not surprisingly, some Americans felt that there could never be enough apples. The intrepid pioneers loved to explore, but they seldom found contentment. For some reason, the grass always looked greener on the other side of the fence—and the other side of the continent. Tocqueville was amused by this uniquely American trait, which he described in his own inimitable fashion:

> In the United States a man builds a house in which to spend his old age, and he sells it before the roof is on; he plants a garden and lets it go just as the trees are coming into bearing; he brings a field into tillage and leaves other men to gather the crops; he embraces a profession and gives it up; he settles in a place, which he soon afterwards leaves to carry his changeable longings elsewhere. If his private affairs leave him any leisure, he instantly plunges into the vortex of politics; and if at the end of a year of unremitting labor he finds he has a few days vacation, his eager curiosity whirls him over the vast extent of the United States, and he will travel fifteen hundred miles in a few days to shake off his happiness. Death at the length overtakes him, but it is before he is weary of his bootless chase of that complete felicity which forever escapes him.

James Garfield was tempted to "carry his changeable longings elsewhere," but he had promised his mother that he would finish college. For himself, the best he could do was a short trip to Hiram, a small village in Portage County about thirty miles southeast of Cleveland. Hiram was the home of the Western Reserve Eclectic Institute, a newly chartered "college" known throughout the region as the Eclectic Institute. Technically speaking, it was not really a college as no degrees were conferred and nobody actually graduated. Nonetheless, eighty-four pupils enrolled on opening day, and, by the time Garfield arrived in August 1851, the school had 300 students. Most of the students were from Ohio, Pennsylvania, and New York, but the Institute also attracted young men and women from a number of southern and western states. The mix was quite unusual, and it produced a wide variation in age, ability, culture, and purpose. While some students received grammar school instruction, others were offered high school or college courses. The advanced courses, reserved for the older students, included language, mathematics, literature, science, philosophy, and history.

The Eclectic Institute was owned and operated by the Disciples Church, and, much to their credit, the Campbellites welcomed all comers. By and large, the students were young men and women, rough, crude, and untutored farm boys and girls, there to try themselves, and find out what manner of people they were. In 1851, the Institute was housed in a single brick building, erected on the top of a windy hill, and surrounded by corn fields. The founders referred to the spot as "the crown of Ohio," and, due to the elevation, a spectator could see for miles. Garfield captured the "feel" of the campus by providing the following description:

> In 1850 it was a green field, with a solid, plain brick building in the center of it, and almost all the rest has been done by the institution itself. Without a dollar of endowment, without a powerful friend anywhere, a corps of teachers were told to go on the ground and see what they could make of it, and to find their pay out of the tuitions that should be received; who invited students of their own spirit to come here on the ground and find out by trial what they could make of it.

Being devout Christians, the founders felt obliged to promote a "character building" philosophy. Therefore, students were told that they must work hard or leave. There would be no coddling, no excuses, and no second chances. The stated purpose of the Institute was "the instruction of youth of both sexes in the various branches of literature and science, especially of moral science as based on the facts and precepts of the Holy Scriptures." The goals were straightforward:

To provide a sound scientific and literary education.

To temper and sweeten such education with moral and scriptural knowledge.

To educate young men for the ministry.

Garfield had written the president of the Institute requesting an interview, but, for some reason, he had not received a reply. In a bold and audacious move that would one day mark his military career, he barged into an ongoing board meeting and asked to speak to the trustees.

Under normal circumstances, Garfield would have been ejected, but there was something about the brash young farm boy that the trustees admired. Maybe it was his tone or perhaps his forthright demeanor. Whatever it was, it won them over, and he was allowed to stay after the following exchange:

"Well, sir, what is your business with us?"

"Gentlemen," he answered in a firm, clear voice. "I am anxious to get an education, and have come here to see what I can do."

"Where are you from?" asked the chairman.

"From Orange. My name is James Abram Garfield. I have no father, he died when I was an infant. My mother is widow Eliza Garfield."

"And you want what education this institution can furnish?"

"Yes, but being the son of a widow, who is poor, I must work my way along; and I ask to me made your janitor." The request raised a few eyebrows, but Garfield went on: "Try me two weeks, and if you are not satisfied I will quit."

"I think we had better try this young man," said one of the trustees, addressing the Chairman.

"Yes," answered the chairman. "He has started out upon a noble work, and we must help him all wc can."

Plutarch, the Greek moralist, once said that the measure of a man's life is the well spending of it, and that was precisely what Garfield had in mind when he came to Hiram. He was determined to spend his time well and better himself. If that meant sweeping floors for a while, then so be it. Almost immediately he went to work, performing his janitorial duties between classes and late into the night. In addition to cleaning the building, he also became the school's bell-ringer, and he performed that task with equal enthusiasm.

One day a fellow student said to him, "Jim, I don't see but you sweep just as well as you recite."

"Why shouldn't I," replied Garfield. "Sweeping, in its place, is just as important as a lesson of Greek is in its place, and both should be done well. The sight of a half-swept floor would be an eyesore to me all the time."

Although he performed menial work, his kindness and earnestness made him a favorite with his classmates. A young woman at the Institute remembered him this way:

> When he first entered the institute, he paid for his schooling by doing janitor's work—sweeping the floor and ringing the bell. I can see him, even now, standing in the morning with his hand on the bell-rope, ready to give the signal calling teachers and scholars to engage in the duties of the day. As we passed by, entering the schoolroom, he had a cheerful word for all of us. He was always good-natured, fond of conversation, and very entertaining. He was witty and quick at repartee; but his jokes, through brilliant and striking, were always harmless, and he never would willingly hurt another's feelings."

The trustees were duly impressed. At the end of the two-week period, they promoted the energetic farm boy to assistant teacher of the Ancient Languages. Garfield, never shy in public, soon became the most popular teacher at the Institute. One of his students wrote:

> He was a most entertaining teacher,—ready with illustrations, and possessing, in a marked degree, the power of exciting the interest of the scholars, and afterward making clear to them the lessons.
>
> There were never any cases of unruly conduct, or a disposition to shirk. With scholars who were slow of comprehension, or to whom recitations were a burden, he was specially attentive, and by

encouraging words and gentle assistance would manage to put all at their ease, and awaken in them a confidence in themselves.

Every day brought a new challenge, but Garfield loved the classroom. In part, this was due to his interest in public matters, which was growing with the excitement of the times. In class, the main topic of conversation was The Compromise of 1850. Large numbers of Americans simply refused to embrace the six provisions of the bill, and it was no different on campus. In addition, there were lively debates about Stephen A. Douglas, the Illinois senator who had played a prominent role in steering the Great Compromise through Congress. Douglas was only 38 years old, but he had recently announced his intention to seek the Democratic Presidential nomination. Some felt that the "Little Giant" was too brash and too aggressive, especially on the subject of Manifest Destiny. He had recently begun to attack the European monarchs, and now he was demanding the annexation of Cuba. Even worse, he was convinced that Negroes were inferior beings, and he saw no moral issue in slavery.

The "slavery question" was evoking the most heated debate, and, even in an academic setting, there was little room for compromise. Generally speaking, northern Ohioans opposed slavery while those from the southern part of the state often had mixed feelings about the issue. The split was due to the geographic origins of the populace. The northern part of Ohio was dominated by New Englanders and the southern half by settlers from West Virginia, Virginia, and Kentucky.

The geographic mix on campus reflected the overall population and produced some loud arguments, especially when the topic touched upon the thorniest issue of the day—the Fugitive-Slave Law. The law was an integral part of the compromise of 1850, but many Ohioans rejected its premise, which called for the arrest and return of runaway slaves. Many students were uncompromising foes of slavery, and they were appalled by the outcome of the new statute. Throughout the country there was a sharp increase in the efforts of southerners to recover escaped slaves. Week after week the students were shocked by stories—real and imagined—of former slaves being abducted in the Negro communities of the north.

Shortly after the passage of the act, James Hamlet, a New York City Negro, was seized by bounty hunters and taken in chains to Maryland without even being allowed to communicate with family or friends. Northerners were outraged, but the abuses continued. In the months that followed, a woman who had lived for years as a free citizen in Pennsylvania was seized along with her six young children. A short time later, there was a widely publicized abduction in Boston, followed by another in Syracuse, New York. When word of these events reached Ohio, the northern part of the state was incensed, and the southern half was dismayed.

Even the mild-mannered Garfield spoke out, urging civil disobedience and condemning those who tolerated the new law. On this subject, there was no room for debate, and nobody was above criticism—not even the greatest orator of the day. Garfield had been a great admirer of Daniel Webster, but his advocacy of the Fugitive-Slave Bill turned admiration into contempt. While Webster saw compromise as a way to preserve the Union, Garfield saw it as something sinful. Never one to conceal his feelings, he described the bill as "a covenant with death, and an agreement with hell that will destroy the authors of it." Quoting from Isaiah, he added: "The cry of the oppressed and downtrodden will appeal to the Almighty for retribution, like that of the blood of Abel. The lightning of divine wrath will yet shiver the old, gnarled tree of slavery to pieces. Leaving neither root nor branch!"

As the year progressed, Garfield became increasingly troubled by the immorality of slavery, and he began to attack those who offered support from the pulpit. In his view, slavery was an absolute evil, a blight on the entire nation, and an abomination in the eyes of the Lord. Much to his dismay, there were many Clergymen who refused to condemn the practice, and, in some churches, slavery was actually supported with Scripture. The most frequently quoted passage was found in *Leviticus*: "Both thy bondmen, and thy bondmaids, which thou shalt have, shall be of the heathen that are around you . . . and they shall be your possession."

Garfield argued that the Biblical justification of slavery was intellectually dishonest, and he detested the southern view of the practice—a view that often painted a rosy picture of human bondage. Describing the lot of the Negroes in his poem "The Hireling and the Slave," William J. Grayson, a South Carolina planter, wrote:

Secure they toil, uncursed their peaceful life,
With labor's hungry broils and wasteful strife.
No want to goad, no faction to deplore,
The slave escapes the perils of the poor.

At about this time, Garfield began to teach Greek, which was one of the "Ancient Languages" offered at the Eclectic Institute. The class attracted some very bright students, including a former classmate named Lucretia Rudolph, whose father, Zebulon, was one of the original founders of the Institute. Garfield was impressed by Lucretia, and for good reason. She was articulate, compassionate, and smart.

She was also quite attractive. Taken together, Garfield thought she was as close to perfect as a woman could be—maybe too perfect. Would someone as refined as Lucretia Rudolph be attracted to a simple farm boy? There was only one way to find out.

The courtship began in 1852, which was quite appropriate since "The Romantic Age" was in full bloom. Like many students, James and Lucretia were involved in a mild revolt against the status quo and the "Age of Reason." The romantic view of life favored feeling and intuition over thought, and it was all the rage on campus. Though scorned by some, the movement had produced a literary renaissance sustained by some of the greatest writers in history. Between 1850 and 1855, Nathaniel Hawthorne published *The Scarlet Letter*, Herman Melville *Moby Dick*, Henry David Thoreau *Walden*, and Walt Whitman *Leaves of Grass*.

All across the country, "romantics" were turning away from the sterile confines of the Industrial Revolution, which Emerson described as "the mechanical powers and the mechanical philosophy of this time." Students were receptive to Emerson's emphasis on self-reliance and his assertion that "the less government we have the better." They were even more enamored by Thoreau, who took this view one step further, declaring, "That government is best which governs not at all."

Following tradition, Garfield courted Lucretia for several months, relying more on Longfellow's poems than New England philosophy. Maybe it was "*The Village Blacksmith*," or perhaps "*The Song of Hiawatha*," but in any case, the strategy worked. In 1835, Garfield proposed and Lucretia accepted, only to have their dreams put on hold. Lacking funds, they decided to postpone their wedding until Garfield completed his education. The hard part was deciding where to go. The logical choice seemed to be Bethany College, a Virginia-based institution established by Alexander Campbell. Eliza Garfield would have been pleased by this choice, but her son was reluctant to go to Bethany as he wanted to expose himself to other ways of thinking.

But this was not the only reason. In a letter to a friend, written one week before leaving Ohio, Garfield explained his decision:

> There are three reasons why I have deiced not to go to Bethany: 1st. The course of study is not so extensive or thorough as in Eastern colleges. 2d. Bethany leans too heavily toward slavery. 3d. I am the son of Disciple parents, am one myself, and have had but little acquaintance with people of other views; and having always lived in the West, I think it will make me more liberal, both in my religious and general views and sentiments, to go into a new circle, where I shall be under new influences. These considerations led me to conclude to go to some New England college. I therefore wrote to the Presidents of Brown University, Yale, and Williams, setting forth the amount of study I had done, and asking how long it would take me to finish their course. Their answers are now before me. All tell me I can graduate in two years. They are all brief, business notes, but President Hopkins concludes with this sentence, "If you come here we shall be glad to do what we can for you." Other things being so nearly equal, this sentence, which seems to be a kind of friendly grasp of the hand, has settled the question for me. I shall start for Williams next week.

Leaving for Williams College was one thing, but paying for room, board, and tuition was another matter. Garfield had only saved $300 during his years in Hiram, and that was hardly enough to cover his expenses. In desperation, he turned to his uncle for a loan. The structure of the loan was rather unusual, and it reflected Garfield's concern about repaying debts. Instead of simply borrowing the money, Garfield purchased a life insurance policy with a face value of $500 payable in the event of his death to his uncle. "If I live," he told his uncle, "I shall pay you; and if I die, you will suffer no loss."

Interestingly, this may have been one of the few times that Garfield thought about his own mortality. Unfortunately, it would not be the last. In the South, tempers were flaring, and the nation seemed to be inching toward the horrible vortex of war. Press reports warned that violence was inevitable, but for now, the world was still a sane place. Soon, however, neighbors would be fighting neighbors, and America would never be the same again.

CHAPTER SEVEN

Having never been out of Ohio, Garfield must have been astonished by the picturesque terrain of Williamstown, Massachusetts. The town was located in the northwest corner of the state bordered by the Green Mountains to the north and the Berkshire Hills to the south. In summer, the valley was a giant bouquet filled with all sorts of fragrant and colorful flowers. From his dormitory room on campus, Garfield's window looked directly out at "Old Greylock," the tallest peak in the region. Years later, he would remember its grandeur and how its shadow stretched across the horizon. Surprisingly, he had never seen a mountain before coming east. One day, he would make a point of climbing to the summit of Old Greylock, and then he would explore every glen and valley in the county.

Arriving at Williams College in June 1854, Garfield still marveled over the magnificent scenery. Initially, in fact, he was completely overwhelmed. The campus was beautiful, perhaps the most beautiful in the east. Most of it ran along the Hoosac River, and it was adorned by thick forests of maple, birch, poplar, and ash. In October, the trees began to show some color. By the end of the month, the colors were spectacularly vibrant. Even as he wrote to Lucretia, the lonely student had to admire the autumn splendor. Ohio was pretty, but there was nothing like this back home.

Williams College owed its existence to Colonel Ephraim Williams, who was killed in battle with the French and Indians near Lake George, New York in 1755. The Colonel's will, written shortly before his death, directed that the remainder of his lands should be sold at the discretion of his executors, within five years after an established peace, and that the interest of the money arising from the sale, and also the interests of his notes and bonds, should be applied to the support of a free school in a township west of Fort Massachusetts, and provided said township, when incorporated, be called Williamstown.

In 1785, a free school was established. Over the next seventy years, the college grew in size and usefulness. By the time Garfield arrived, Williams had a national reputation, and that reputation was about to grow more impressive. In a few short years, Williams and Amherst would clear some trees, draw some lines, and, on July 1, 1859, play the first intercollegiate baseball game in history. The game would create quite a stir, but it would not be remembered as a great "pitching duel." After some very long innings, Amherst would win by a lopsided score of 66 to 32.

At the beginning of the fall term, Garfield was required to take an entrance exam and present himself to Dr. Mark Hopkins, the President of the college. When they met, Garfield stuck out his hand and introduced himself. "My name is Garfield, from Ohio."

Dr. Hopkins was intrigued by the young Ohioan, whose clothing and speech were "thoroughly western." He would remember him as "a tall, awkward youth, with a great shock of light hair, rising nearly erect from a broad, high forehead, and an open, kindly, and thoughtful face, which showed no traces of his long study with poverty and privation."

Garfield too, would remember Hopkins, especially his warm greeting and kind words. He would also remember their first conversation, which turned into a lengthy debate on the President's lecture on the "Evidences of Christianity." Hopkins was a fine debater but, on this day, he met his match. When asked about Garfield's performance, he smiled. "He was not *sent* to college," remarked Hopkins, "but *came* . . . He not only came, but made sacrifices to come."

Once in class, Garfield became a voracious reader and made good use of the campus library, which contained over ten thousand volumes and was the envy of many larger institutions. During the fall semester he read the entire works of Shakespeare and Tennyson. He also completed a large portion of Goethe and Schiller. Naturally, his professors were impressed, and several of them recorded their thoughts for posterity. One wrote:

> Garfield, as a student, was one who would at any time impress himself upon the memory of his instructors by his manliness and excellence of character. He was one whom his teachers would never suspect as guilty of a dishonest or mean act, and one whom a dishonest or mean man would not approach. There was a manliness and honest about Garfield that gave him power to see and do what was for his own good and the honour of the college. His life as a student was pure and noble. His moral and religious character and marked intellectual ability gave great promise of success in the world.

Another professor said:

> The college life of Garfield was so rounded, so perfect, so pure, so in accordance with what it ought to be in all respects, that I can add nothing to it by eulogizing him. Everything about him was high, and noble, and manly.

For all his intellect, though, Garfield was not adverse to playing sports, and he actually gained a reputation as the best football player on campus. Apparently, he was rather agile for his size and incredibly strong. Some of his strength was probably heredity and some the result of hard labor. Whatever the mix, he became a formidable athlete. Opposing players would often marvel at his endurance, which was enhanced, no doubt, by clean living. Unlike some students, Garfield never drank alcohol or used tobacco, and as evidenced by his grades, he spent most of his time studying.

As Garfield progressed, he continued to write. During his senior year, he became one of the editors of the *Williams Quarterly*, a college magazine of "high moral character." Many of his contributions in verse conveyed his deepest thoughts and feelings. The following is an illustration of his poetic talent, copied from the pages of the *Quarterly*:

Autumn.

Old Autumn, thou art here! Upon the earth

And in the heavens the signs of death are hung;

For o'er the earth's brown breast stalks pale decay,

And 'mong the lowering clouds and wild winds wail,
And sighing sadly, shout the solemn dirge,
O'er Summer's fairest flowers, all faded now.
The Winter god, descending from the skies,
Has reached the mountain tops, and decked their brows
With glittering frosty crowns, and breathed his breath
Among the trumpet pines, that herald forth
His coming.

Garfield also had a sense of humor, which he displayed in his parodies. The following poem is modeled on Tennyson. It is entitled "The Charge of the Tight Brigade."

Bottles to right of them
Bottles to left of them,
Bottles in front of them,
Fizzled and sundered,
Ent'ring with shout and yell,
Boldly they drank and well,

They caught the Tartar then;

Oh, what a perfect sell!

Sold—the half hundred.

Grinned al the dentals bare,

Swung all their caps in air,

Uncorking bottles there,

Watching the Freshmen wile

Every one wondered;

Plunged in tobacco smoke,

With many a desperate stroke,

Dozens of bottles broke,

Then they came back, but not,

But not the half hundred.

Mostly, though, Garfield wrote prose: essays, literary reviews, and philosophical disquisitions. The latter were often religious in tone. Although he found himself in a liberal environment, his articles were generally well received. Writing on the subject of "The Province of History," he said:

> For every village, state and nation there is an aggregate of native talent which God has given, and by which, together with his Providence, He leads that nation on, and thus leads the world. In the light of these truths we affirm that no man can understand the history of any nation, or of the world, who does not recognize in it the power of God, and behold His stately goings forth as He walks among the nations. It is His hand that is moving the vast superstructure of human history, and, though but one of the windows were unfurnished, lie that of the Arabian palace, yet all the powers of earth could never complete it without the aid of the Divine Architect.

As his writing shows, Garfield had become a formidable thinker and philosopher, and he took great joy in discussing the exciting questions of the day: the Kansas-Nebraska question, the influx of foreigners, the domination of the Roman Catholic Church, and the desirability of an elective judiciary. Regardless of the subject, he displayed an intellectual capacity that was the envy of his peers. He also possessed a considerable amount of common sense, and, luckily, he was able to apply this gift freely. Before long, he became President of the Philogian Society, and during his final semester he made his first political speech. Up to this point, Garfield had not taken sides as a voter, mainly because both parties had exhibited pro-slavery tendencies, which, in his opinion, was inexcusable. When the Republicans denounced slavery, Garfield joined their ranks, and, shortly thereafter, he delivered a rousing endorsement of John C. Freemont, the Republican presidential candidate.

Freemont was well known and widely admired as an explorer and a soldier. In 1856, he was one of the most popular figures in the country.

"The Pathfinder" had led the conquest of California, and despite his political inexperience, he was favored to win the election. Unlike his Democratic opponent, he had a bold and articulate stance against slavery. He also had the best campaign slogan. [Free soil, free speech, Freemont.]

Anyone who thought the campaign would be dull was sorely mistaken. The candidates came out swinging, and the harsh rhetoric aroused political passions on both sides. Maybe it was the tone of the contest or simply a reaction to slavery, but things quickly turned ugly. In May 1856, two events took place, two days apart, that shook the nation and had a profound effect on the students at Williams College. The first incident involved Senator Charles Sumner of Massachusetts, one of the leaders of the anti-slavery forces in Washington. Sumner, a Harvard graduate, was quite articulate about his positions. He was also arrogant, combative, and totally prejudicial when espousing a cause. Once, when a colleague asked him whether he ever looked at the other side of the slavery question, he replied: "There is no other side."

In the debate over Kansas, which was exacerbated by the repeal of the Missouri Compromise, the Senate had come to the conclusion that the settlers of the new territory should be "perfectly free to form and regulate their domestic institutions in their own way"—even if those institutions included slavery. Sumner was outraged by this position. During the debate, he referred to his opponents as "liars" and "traitors." The tirade did not go unanswered. The oppositions called him a "filthy reptile" and a "leper," and they threatened to assassinate the meddling Yankee abolitionist.

Undeterred, Sumner delivered a two-day oration aimed at "The Crime Against Kansas," which he referred to as "the rape of a virgin territory, compelling it to the hateful embrace of slavery." During his speech, the senator attacked both Stephen A. Douglas, the author of the Kansas-Nebraska Act, and Andrew P. Butler of South Carolina, a leader of the pro-slavery forces. Butler was not present to defend himself, but Douglas heard every last epithet and was heard to whisper: "That damn fool will get himself killed by some other damn fool."

Two days later, on May 22, 1856, Sumner was attacked at his desk on the Senate floor. The attacker was Congressman Preston Brooks of South Carolina, a nephew of Senator Butler. Believing that Sumner had insulted his uncle, Brooks used his cane to beat Sumner unconscious. Brooks delivered about 30 "first rate stripes" to the head, permanently scarring Sumner *and* the nation. Overnight, the caning incident became a symbol in the North of Southern brutality, and it was only a matter of time before some hothead retaliated.

Forty-eight hours later, on the evening of May 24, a psychopathic free-soiler named John Brown stole into a pro-slavery settlement on Pottawatomie Creek in Kansas. Claiming to be an instrument of God, he and his followers brutally slaughtered five settlers, hacking them to death with sabers as they pleaded for their lives. Back east, the attack was viewed as an act of revenge, an inevitable consequence of the brutal assault on the free-state community of Lawrence. In the South, it was seen as cold-blooded murder.

Garfield and his fellow students were repulsed by the tactics of the anti-slavery forces, but their outrage was muted by the attack on Sumner. When the college held a "protest rally," Sumner was glorified. There was no mention of the massacre at Pottawatomie Creek. Ironically, Garfield and John Brown shared some common experiences. Both had been raised in northern Ohio, and each had been raised to revere the Bible and despise slavery. Additionally, both were "deep thinkers," and both spent a considerable amount of time brooding over the plight of the weak and oppressed. In a sense, they were both visionaries, but unlike Garfield, Brown was convinced that the Almighty had commissioned him to make his vision a reality. Such a man was unpredictable and, left to his own devices, was capable of horrendous acts.

One month later, as the nation continued to slide toward the abyss of secession and civil war, Garfield graduated with honors from Williams College. He had never wavered in his goal of obtaining a college education, but there had been moments of doubt and temptation. Earlier in the year, he was offered a teaching position in Troy, New York. The salary was generous, and there were several perks attached to the offer. If he had taken the job he would have been able to pay his debts, marry his fiancée, and live in a comfortable new home. Of course, leaving meant breaking a promise, and that was out of the question. Afterwards, he explained his reasoning to the gentleman who had tried to recruit him:

> You are not Satan, and I am not Jesus; but we are upon the mountain, and you have tempted me powerfully. I think I must say Get thee behind me. I am poor, and the salary would soon pay my debts, and place me in a position of independence. But there are two objections; I would not accomplish my resolution to complete a college course, and should be crippled intellectually for life. Then, my roots are all fixed in Ohio, where people know me and I know them, and this transplanting might not succeed as well in the long run as to go back home and work for smaller pay.

That June, forty-two students graduated from Williams College. Though small in number, the class of '56 produced many prominent citizens, including a President, a Treasurer of the United States, an Assistant Attorney-General, three renowned physicians, and many lawyers, ministers, and teachers.

A majority of the class would obtain fame or fortune, or, in some cases, both. Others would not fare as well. There were dark days ahead, and a few of the unlucky ones would not survive the gathering storm. By the end of the decade, the class of '56 would be embroiled in a deadly conflict. Along with the rest of the nation, they would learn about places called Shiloh, Antietam, and Gettysburg—idyllic settings where ordinary men would accomplish great things and become heroes, generals, and future presidents.

CHAPTER EIGHT

"Charles Guiteau?"

The new convert looked tired and a little confused by his surroundings. He was younger than most and seemed to be a man of few words. For a moment, his escort thought she had the wrong person, but then she remembered the young man's description: nineteen years old, five feet five inches tall, 125 pounds, sandy complexion, and neatly trimmed mustache and beard. Everything fit, down to the rumpled gray suit.

For once in his life, Guiteau was at a loss for words. He could scarcely believe his eyes. The woman was wearing what appeared to be a pair of baggy pants.

Actually, she was dressed in the everyday attire of the Oneida Community. Her long dress had been cut off at the knees, and the fabric sewn into pantalets or bloomers. The outfit was undeniably odd—and somewhat comical—but it was also comfortable and functional. The clothing had been designed in response to a complaint made by Brother Noyes, the founder of the group. Noyes had expressed his concerns about ladies' garments in a manuscript called "Bible Argument," writing that:

> The present dress of women, besides being peculiarly inappropriate to the sex, is immodest. Women's dress is a standing lie. It proclaims that she is not a two-legged animal, but something like a churn standing on castors. When the distinction of the sexes is reduced to the bounds of nature and decency . . . a dress will be adopted, that will be at the same time the most simple and the most beautiful, and it will be the same, or nearly the same, for both sexes.

The "distinction of the sexes" was further reduced by an innovation in hairstyle. As a matter of taste, it was decided that short dresses and long hair looked incongruous. Consequently, the ladies of Oneida wore their hair short, cut close to the scalp. By wearing their hair in this fashion, they saved hours of combing and arranging, and they reduced the risk of head lice.

If Guiteau was startled by the woman's appearance, there is no telling what he thought about Oneida itself. The community was located on a 386-acre tract in Leno, a small village in Madison County, New York. The site was roughly halfway between Syracuse and Utica and three miles south of the Oneida Depot. The Midland Railroad was the fastest way to get there; however, the trains were seldom on time, so most people came by carriage.

The carriage ride was quite difficult, however, usually taking forty-five minutes to an hour over rough terrain. At the time, there were only 200 members in the Oneida Community, equally divided among men, women, and children. Most of the members lived in the Mansion

House, a frame, three-story building that was about to be torn down and replaced with a brick structure.

By now the Oneida Community was twelve years old, and John Henry Noyes was one of the most controversial religious figures in America. Obviously, Noyes did not start out to become a target of scorn and ridicule; however, by August, 1860, he was widely viewed as a messianic madman. In the beginning, he was just a devout young man swept up in the religious excitement of 1831, "The Year of Revivals." After graduating from Dartmouth College, he continued his Biblical studies at Yale Theological Seminary, and it was there that he became convinced the millennium was at hand. So strong were his convictions that he began to preach a new doctrine called Perfectionism or Bible Communism. The notion that man could achieve perfection on earth was regarded as heresy. The New Haven clergy insisted that emancipation from sin could only be achieved in Heaven, not by presumptuous men on earth. Noyes rejected this theory, and, in turn, they rejected him. When he announced that he had actually achieved full salvation from sin, his preaching license was revoked, and he was expelled from the Theological Seminary.

Noyes made his announcement on February 20, 1834. Afterwards, he was branded a heretic and shunned by family and friends. Nonetheless, he remained defiant, telling anyone who would listen that "I have taken away their license to sin, and they keep on sinning. So, through they have taken away my license to preach, I shall keep on preaching."

If nothing else, Noyes was a man of his word. Over the next few months he crisscrossed the region, preaching the gospel and spreading the doctrine of Perfectionism. These were difficult days, and Noyes lived hand-to-mouth, dependent on "the kindness of strangers." Finding converts was never easy, especially when the messenger was viewed as an outcast. On one ill-fated trip to New York, Noyes found himself destitute and homeless, forced to wander the city in search of food and shelter. He wound up in a dangerous part of south Manhattan and later wrote about the experience: "When weariness overcame me in these excursions, so that sleep became inevitable, I would lie down on a door-stone, or on the steps of the City Hall, or on the benches of the Battery, and forget myself for a few minutes."

As one might expect, Noyes was often disheartened and depressed, and this led to a nervous breakdown followed by rumors of insanity. Noyes referred to his disorder as a "spiritual crucifixion," and adamantly denied that he was insane. Then as now, actions spoke louder than words, and the actions that followed were hardly normal.

Abigail Merwin was a longtime friend and supporter, and, according to Noyes, his very first convert. During his "crucifixion," he had a vision that she was "Satan transformed into an angel of light." Never one to question a vision, he ended all contact and never spoke to her again.

Shortly after this incident, he became convinced that *he* was Satan. In 1849, Noyes wrote: "A persuasion fell upon me that I was LUCIFER, the fallen son of the morning." He was smart enough to seek spiritual counseling, and with the help of friends, he began to pull himself together. In the end, he found comfort by returning to what he knew best—scriptural obedience. "By systematic temperance, fasting, exercise and prayer, I had satisfactorily overcome the bodily infirmities which troubled me at Andover. I was no longer tormented with inordinate alimentiveness, and other temptations to sensuality."

The ordeal would leave lasting scars and further damage his reputation, but, as Noyes often stated, he emerged with a clear mind and a renewed sense of purpose. In 1838, he returned to New England and organized a Perfectionist community in Putney, Vermont. The group was relatively small but not small enough to go unnoticed by the local authorities. On or about November 1, 1846, the group issued a "Statement of Principles," which proved to be a costly mistake. Instead of gaining acceptance, they were roundly condemned and criticized. Their enemies in the press trumpeted Item Number Three as proof of their misguided fervor: "John H. Noyes is the father and overseer whom the Holy Ghost has set over the family thus constituted. To John H. Noyes as such we submit ourselves in all things spiritual and temporal."

From this point on, Noyes was persona non grata, and the Putney Community was a blight on civilized society. Time ran out on October 26, 1847. After numerous complaints, Putney officials charged Noyes with adultery. He was released on bail but warned that other charges were pending. His trial was set for the following April; however, in November, a warrant was issued for his arrest. The warrant was devastating, but even more frightening were the rumors that a mob was about to attack his beloved commune. Noyes fled to New York City, abandoning Putney, but not his dream of building a utopian community.

Before long he was invited to visit an old friend in Upstate New York, and, shortly thereafter, he was offered some land on Oneida Creek. The tract had once been owned by the Oneida Indians and was quite scenic and completely unspoiled. As Noyes wrote in 1848, Oneida was a dream come true. "Everything conspires to bring about concentration here. There is one comfortable room with a buttery, a back kitchen for summer, a bedroom upstairs, a good barn, a small shoemaker's shop, and twenty-three acres of land. There is some romance in beginning our Community in the log huts of the Indians."

In these days before Guiteau's arrival, the community had 87 members, most of them from Putney, Vermont, and Upstate New York. Prior to joining, adults were required to abide by the "Terms of Admission" stated in the Register of the Association. In regard to personal property, the terms were as follows: "On the admission of any member, all property belonging to him or her, becomes the property of the Association." The surrender of worldly goods was justified by the "Theory of the Rights of Property," which held "that all the systems of property-getting in vogue in the world, are forms of what is vulgarly called the "grab-game," i.e. the game in which the prizes are not distributed by an rules of wisdom and justice, but are seized by the strongest and craftiest."

Accordingly, Guiteau was obliged to surrender his newly obtained inheritance, which he did freely and without hesitation. By luck, or perhaps by careful planning, he had arrived at Oneida shortly before the start of the Civil War. Luckily for him, Noyes was anti-war and fiercely opposed to the draft. Although opposed to slavery, Noyes remained neutral. His views were expressed in various issues of *The Circular*, the weekly newspaper of the Oneida Community. The following excerpts reveal his ambiguity and a fair amount of arrogance and disdain:

> May 2, 1861
>
> We have been stirred by the great pulse of patriotism that throbs throughout the North to such a degree that many have been willing to take an active part in the war. Two of our more impulsive youths

went so far as to give their names to a recruiting agent as volunteers, but on reconsideration concluded to abide the advice and direction of the Community. We desire to know exactly our duty, and do it . . . . We are called to the work of social and material construction, and our allegiance to Christ requires us to maintain the post where we are placed until other orders are issues.

August 7, 1862

Some discussion in our evening meetings relative to the true position of the Community in regard to war and public movements in society around us. The Community is devoted to The Establishment of the Kingdom of God; and wc cannot cooperate with any movement which is not directly tending to that end.

August 13, 1862

I submit myself to the Providence of God in regard to the draft; yet I shall advocate the policy of ransoming our young men, let it cost what it may. If not necessary, I will not give any of or bodies or souls to the work of destruction.

Little is known about Guiteau's view of slavery or the war, but it is known that he was something of a coward, preferring to assault his victims from behind. He also was afraid of the dark, and when left alone at home, he would often carry a loaded pistol. Young Guiteau may have brought a weapon to Oneida, but, if so, he would not have kept it long. All weapons, especially firearms, were forbidden. Indeed, many things were forbidden, and just to make sure that everyone knew the rules—residents and visitors alike—they were given a pamphlet of "suggestions." The main suggestions were as follows:

> *The Community does not furnish spirituous liquors or tobacco in any form*; and would prefer that they should not be used on the premises.
>
> *Card-playing* in the house or on the grounds, is offensive to the Community and to many visitors.
>
> *Purloining of fruit and flowers* in the gardens, is contrary to good morals.
>
> Careless driving of carriages on the borders of the lawn, and swift driving in the midst of crowds, are serious annoyances.
>
> *Boisterous talking*, and *heavy tramping* in the house, are needless disturbances of both inmates and visitors.
>
> *Scribbling* on window casements or the walls of rooms, is not in accordance with the tastes of the Community
>
> If visitors, in walking about the premises, leave the paths, and *trample cultivated grounds* among vines and fruit bushes, they make bad work for the gardeners.
>
> In rambling about the house, visitors should remember that all of the small rooms are occupied by the family as *private apartments*.
>
> The *trap works* in the factory south of the house, are not open to the public; and visits to them are regarded as intrusions, because they interfere with business.

The Community closes the labors of the day with a family *meeting* at eight p.m., and asks to be excused from waiting on visitors after that hour.

There is a story that Guiteau had taken great delight in torturing animals during his youth, and, on one occasion, he had dropped a puppy out of a second-story window, shattering the dog's leg. Supposedly, he wanted to find out if the puppy would land on its feet like a cat. Whether or not this was his motivation cannot be known, but apparently he disliked animals, which was somewhat ironic. Within days of his arrival, he was assigned to work at the animal trap factory—the only facility that did not permit visitors. It is clear from all the evidence that Guiteau was unhappy from the start, and he made no attempt to hide his disappointment. One of his co-workers at the factory described him as "a nervous quick-tempered man. If anything was said to disturb him he would get riled and gesticulate wildly and talk in a mysterious manner. He would sit for hours in a corner saying nothing to anybody. At other times he would be cheerful."

Guiteau, certainly, found the assignment demeaning, but a large part of the problem was Guiteau himself. He truly believed that he was a superior being, destined to achieve great things. The business manager of the Community thought differently, complaining that Guiteau was the most egotistical man he ever met. "Eccentric and different from other men," he told Noyes. "He was absorbed in himself and had such a high idea of himself as to think himself a superior being, qualified to be a leader and manager of men."

The interesting thing about Guiteau's resentment was that it was completely misplaced. Despite its bland name, the trap factory was the most important facility at Oneida. If Guiteau had not been blinded by egotism, he might have realized that his work was crucial to the Community. The factory was the brainchild of a woodsman named Sewell Newhouse, a Vermont transplant who became a Perfectionist in 1849. Prior to joining the Community, Newhouse operated a small blacksmith shop and sold his traps to the local Indians. In 1852, he expanded his operation, moving into a bigger shop that contained a forge and bellows, a swaging mould, and a common anvil. Newhouse turned out to be a gifted mechanic, and he produced a product that caught game and held it. The trap was affordable and lightweight, and it had one big advantage over the German models that dominated the market: tempered springs that did not break in the extreme cold. By 1855, the Newhouse trap was the most popular model in the United States and Canada, and shortly thereafter, it became the dominant trap in Russia, Australia, and South America. By the time Guiteau arrived, the trap factory was the most profitable business at Oneida, generating over $100,000 a year in sales.

Still, Guiteau was dissatisfied with is position. Building traps was beneath him, and no amount of spiritual counseling would change how he felt. What he did not know and would soon discover was that Noyes thought egotism was sinful, and he would not tolerate is existence at Oneida. Egotists were a threat to the status quo, and, once they were identified, they were subjected to "Mutual Criticism," a unique and degrading form of punishment. Noyes had devised the system of criticism to regulate social behavior, and, in most cases, it was highly effective. The process began with an investigation of the character of the individual to be criticized. After the investigation, the individual would be asked to sit in a room surrounded by a circle of spiritual "judges," who would proceed to offer sharp and unflattering critiques. In the words of one prominent member:

> The criticisms were administered in a purely clinical spirit. The subject sat in complete silence while each member of the committee in turn assessed his good points as well as his bad. In cases of unusual seriousness, perhaps involving the violation of a fundamental tenet of their common philosophy, the committee would be expanded to include the entire Community. This, however, was an ordeal that very few were ever obliged to submit to and the effect must have been drastic and frankly disciplinary.

Thanks to his father, Guiteau was used to drastic action and frank discipline. But he was not used to public humiliation, regardless of its "good intentions." Early on, he began to complain that Noyes was "harsh, cold, and cruel" and that he exacted the most degrading service. He despised criticism, describing it as something he could barely stand—the worst feature of the "terrible despotism" that Noyes exerted over the members. In retrospect, it seems natural that Guiteau would resent authority, but Mutual Criticism had served the Community well, and they were not about to cast it aside. Pierrepont Noyes, the founder's son, offered a different view of the process:

> The committees mixed praise with faultfinding. The essence of the system was frankness; its amelioration friendliness and affection. Yet it was always an ordeal. Without doubt, the human temptation to vent personal dislikes on a victim was not resisted by everyone, but I have heard old members say that the baring of secret faults by

> impartial criticizers called for more grace—as they used to say—than the occasional spiteful jab of an enemy. The same witnesses have testified that they were always happier and healthier after one of these spiritual baths; also that just because members had an opportunity to criticize each other openly, Community life was singularly free from backbiting and scandalmongering.

In light of these views, it was no surprise that Noyes often told his flock about the female member who, when a visitor from the outside commented on "the sweet clean smell" of the Community, answered gently, "It is the odor of crushed selfishness."

CHAPTER NINE

The two years that Garfield spent in Williamstown were among the happiest of his life, but now that he had a college degree, he was anxious to return to Ohio. He could scarcely contain his excitement as he contemplated a reunion with his fiancé, Lucretia Rudolph. Knowing that he had a job at the Eclectic Institute came as a great relief, and he was determined to do well. Garfield put it this way: "I have attained the height of my ambition. I have taken my diploma from an eastern college, and am appointed a teacher at Hiram Institute, and now I shall devote all my energies to my work there."

When Garfield arrived in Hiram, he discovered that little had changed during his absence. Still a lonesome country village, Hiram was built high upon a hill, overlooking twenty miles of cheese-making country to the south. By now, there were fifty or sixty houses clustered around the village green, but it was still a poor town. The teachers were poor, the students were poor, and the institution was poor.

After much debate, the Institute had changed its name to Hiram College, and, in the fall of 1856, the enrollment stood at three hundred.

Upon his arrival, Garfield was immediately appointed Professor of Ancient Languages and Literature. His salary was $800 a year, roughly half of what he was offered back east. Over the months that followed, he became one of the most beloved and respected teachers at the college. Henry James, the American philosopher, described his former instructor in the following way: "Then began to grow up in me an admiration and love for Garfield that has never abated, and the like of which I have never known. A bow of recognition, or a single word from him, was to me an inspiration."

Through all the acclaim and affection, Garfield remained humble, never losing his sense of humor or the desire to entertain. One of his favorite classroom tricks was writing Latin with one hand and Greek with the other at the same time. At the end of his first year on campus, he became the head of the school, "Chairman of the Board of Instructors." One year later, at the age of twenty-six, he was made principal or president of the institution. He may have been the youngest college president in history, but he was mature enough to get the job done. The trustees were amazed by his energy, vigor, and good sense. Under Garfield's supervision, the attendance at Hiram doubled, the standards of scholarship improved, and the faculty was increased and strengthened.

Although technically he was an administrator, he never lost touch with the students. A pleasant picture of his methods and manners can be drawn from the recollections of an old pupil, the Reverend J.F. Darsie:

> No matter how old the pupils were Garfield always called us by our first names, and kept himself on the most familiar terms with all.

> He played with us freely, scuffled with us sometimes, walked with us in walking to and fro, and we treated him out of the class-room just about as we did one another. Yet he was a most strict disciplinarian, and enforced the rules like a martinet. He combined an affectionate and confiding manner with respect for order in a most successful manner.

Garfield's "respect for order" was unceasing, and he insisted upon punctuality in all settings—at prayers, recitals, lectures, and social engagements. He demanded promptness as an essential duty, and his students were taught to honor this quality in themselves and others. Throughout his tenure, he lectured on "manners" and the "elements of success." One of his most interesting topics was the "turning point of life," in which he said:

> The comb of the roof at the court house at Ravenna [capital of Portage County, of which Hiram was a town] divides the drops of rain, sending those that fall on the south side to the Gulf of Mexico, and those on the opposite side into the Gulf of St. Lawrence, so that a mere breath of air, or the flutter of a bird's wing, may determine their destiny. It is so with your lives, my young friends. A passing event, perhaps of trifling importance in your view, the choice of a book or companion, a stirring thought, a right resolve, the associations of an hour, may prove the turning point of your lives.

For Garfield, the turning point was coming home. Northern Ohio was an unusual place. Because of its New England heritage, it was both pious and progressive, rigid and radical. Most of its citizens were

Protestant and quite devout, but there were also some skeptics who were known for their adherence to "spiritualism." The most prominent member of this group was Professor Denton, a critical scholar who attempted to prove by scientific discoveries that the Bible could not be true. Denton was a confident speaker, and he openly challenged any and all believers of the Bible to refute his statements. He had recently caused a stir by boasting that he had "closed up the churches and abolished the Bible from Chagrin Falls"—the town where Garfield had gone to school as a child.

The Church of the Disciples viewed the success of Professor Denton with dismay, and they were greatly alarmed by the loss of congregants in northern Ohio. Consequently, they turned to Garfield for help. The elders of the church had heard him preach in Chagrin Falls, and they knew that he could hold his own at the podium. At first, Garfield declined, believing that it would be unseemly for a Christian to debate such questions in a public setting. However, after repeated requests from family and friends, he relented and agreed to a public debate.

The following day, Garfield sent six of his most advanced students to the college library to look up a wide array of information. Then he procured a copy of Professor Denton's standard lecture, which he dissected line by line and point by point. He also obtained the learned opinions of some distinguished scholars. When the hour came for the discussion, he was thoroughly prepared.

The poor profession walked right into the trap, repeating almost verbatim, the lecture obtained by Garfield. As the audience watched in disbelief, Garfield systematically dismantled Denton's arguments, quoting from the Bible, the latest scientific books, and the professor's own sources. Everyone was spellbound, and Denton was forced to publically acknowledge defeat. Still reeling, he admitted that it was the first time he had met such a gifted and learned adversary. Afterwards, Denton faded into obscurity and the Churches of the Disciples grew in membership.

As a result of his performance—on and off campus—Garfield received many job offers, and almost all of them paid more than his present position. Some were in major cities. A few included room and board. So why did he remain in Hiram? When he was offered a position at the Cleveland Institute, at a salary of fifteen hundred dollars a year, he returned this reply:

> I am very much obliged to you for your kind offer, but you would not want to employ me for a short time, and I feel it my duty to say that some of my friends have got the insane notion in their heads that I ought to go to Congress. I know I'm not fit for the position, and I have fought against it all I could. I know nothing about political wire-pulling, and I have told my friends plainly that I would have nothing to do with that kind of business, but I am sure that I can be nominated and elected without my resorting to any unlawful means, and I have lately given authority to allow my name to be used. I don't know that anything will come of it; if there does not, I will gladly accept your offer.

Ultimately, Garfield did throw his hat in the ring, but it took an entire year to convince him to run for office. So happy was he during his first two years at Hiram that he did nothing but improve and promote the college, delaying his own wedding until he had accomplished certain goals. He had no intention, however, of remaining a bachelor. As always, it was just a matter of finishing one task before starting another. Accordingly, on November 11, 1858, James and Lucretia were finally married. Now that their four-year engagement was behind them, they had to find a place to live. Lacking funds, they were unable to build their dream house, but they could afford a neat little cottage fronting the college campus.

Shortly after his marriage, Garfield became a student of law, sponsored by the law office of Riddle and Williamson, attorneys in Cleveland. In those days, attaching your name to a firm was a formality meant to ensure admission to the bar. Surprisingly, Garfield had no intention of becoming a lawyer; he just wanted to learn the principles of law.

Apparently, he learned quite a lot. In later years, a colleague said of him: "Had Garfield gone to the bar for a living, his gift of oratory, his strong analytical powers, and his ability to do hard work, would soon have made him eminent. In the few law cases he took during vacation seasons he held his own with some of the best lawyers of the country."

Up to 1858, Garfield had taken little interest in public affairs. His focus had been on other matters. But now that Hiram College was on solid footing and he knew the law, his political pulse began to stir. Thus, he began to give speeches and lectures warning of the terrible conflict that was about to divide the country into two distinct camps: one advocating the separation of the Southern states from the Union and the retention of slavery, the other desiring one nation and the abolition of slavery.

Earlier that year, the subject had been debated by Abraham Lincoln and Stephen A. Douglas, the brilliant Republican orators who were vying for an Illinois seat in the United States Senate. Lincoln and

Douglas had agreed to seven debates, each to be held in a different town. The first debate took place in Ottawa, Illinois, and was seen as a draw. The second debate took place on August 27, 1858, and was widely thought to be the most significant of the debates. It was during this historic meeting that Lincoln posed the following question to his opponent: "Can the people of a United States territory, in any lawful way, against the wish of any citizen of the United States, exclude slavery from its limits prior to the formation of a state constitution?"

An estimated 20,000 people had braved the cold and rain to hear the second debate, and most of them were delighted to hear Douglas's reply. In essence, he said that the people did have a right to choose whether to exclude or include slavery within their territory. The answer helped Douglas win the senatorial race, but it cost him the support of the South and split the Democratic Party. Two years later, it would enable Lincoln to win the Presidency, which would lead to succession and then war.

Douglas's view of slavery became known as the "Freeport Doctrine," or as it was called in the South, the "Freeport Heresy." Both terms came from the town that had hosted the debate, Freeport, Illinois—the birthplace of a future assassin named Charles Guiteau.

In 1859, only three years after his graduation, Garfield was honored by the faculty of Williams College with an invitation to speak on commencement day. Garfield gladly accepted, but this time he brought Lucretia with him. Together they traveled the St. Lawrence River to Quebec and then crossed the New England states to Williamstown, Massachusetts. Fittingly, this was the first pleasure trip of his life.

Upon his return to Ohio, Garfield discovered that his name had been proposed for State Senator representing Summit and Portage

Counties. At first, he was reluctant to accept the nomination, but, after consulting with the trustees of Hiram College, he agreed to run for office. Naturally, his anti-slavery views were popular in northern Ohio. Those views combined with his speaking ability made him a formidable candidate. His campaign also got a boost from an unexpected source. On October 16, 1859, John Brown and 21 other men raided the federal arsenal at Harpers Ferry, Virginia. They had planned to arm the local slaves and establish a Negro republic in the mountains of Virginia, but the audacious attack ended in disaster. Federal troops, led by Colonel Robert E. Lee, trapped Brown and his followers in an engine house of the Baltimore and Ohio Railroad. A two-day battle ensued, and both sides suffered casualties. The fighting ended with ten of Brown's people killed and seven captured, Brown among them. "Old Brown of Osawatomie" was moved to Charlestown, Virginia, where in early November, he was tried and convicted of treason. Though initially repulsed by Brown's exploits, many Ohioans began to speak favorably of the militant abolitionist, and the entire state was shocked by the final outcome of the trial. Brown was sentenced to hang on December 2, 1859.

As a result of Brown's trial and the impending conflict with the South, Garfield was elected by a wide margin. He took his seat in January 1860, becoming the youngest member of the assembly and an integral part of the "Radical Triumvirate," a group of anti-slavery senators. Of course, slavery was not his only concern. During his first session, he promoted a State Geological Survey and authored a report authorizing measures to protect and instruct neglected, destitute, and pauper children. He also produced a controversial report on treason, stating that it was "high time for Ohio to enact a law to meet treachery when it shall take the form of an overt act; to provide that, when her soldiers go forth to maintain the Union, there shall be no treacherous fire in the rear." The strong start elicited the following opinion of the young senator: "He was a valuable man on committees and in party counsels. No senator was more frequently called to his counsels by the President of the Senate when knotty points of order were to be united or cut."

Far away in Washington, D.C., the government was sliding toward anarchy, and Garfield watched in dismay as the politicians tried to placate the rebellious South. Back in Ohio, he denounced Buchanan, the Democratic President, and characterized his cabinet as traitors to their country. According to at least one historian, Buchanan "never made a witty remark, never wrote a memorable sentence, and never showed a touch of distinction." One thing was certain, Buchanan was determined to follow a course of appeasement. In his last annual message, he displayed an unusual degree of weakness and indecision. After condemning the Northern legislatures for the passage of Personal Liberty Bills, he said:

> How easy it would be for the American people to settle the slavery question forever, and to restore peace and harmony for this distracted country. They, and they alone, can do it. All that is necessary to accomplish the object, and all for which the Slave States have ever contended, is, to be let alone, and permitted to manage their domestic institutions in their own way. As Sovereign States, they, and they alone, are responsible before God and the world for the slavery existing among them. For this the people of the North are not more responsible, and have no more right to interfere, than with

> similar institutions in Russia or Brazil. Upon their good sense and patriotic forbearance I confess I greatly rely.

During Garfield's second term in the Ohio Senate, the crisis escalated to the point of no return. Lincoln had been elected President, the Southern states were preparing to secede, and civil war was imminent. When Congress proposed a Constitutional Amendment prohibiting further restrictions on slavery in the South—a measure designed to prevent secession—Garfield denounced it in the Ohio Senate, calling it a "compromise with traitors, an unpatriotic and base surrender to the slave oligarchy." Furthermore, he declared that "his arm should wither in its socket before it should be lifted in favor of a measure that virtually abandoned liberty, and left slavery master of the situation."

Even Garfield must have been stunned by the swift Southern reaction to Lincoln's victory. Stimulated by indications of sympathy in Congress, the South Carolina legislature ordered its delegates to a special convention to decide the state's future. On December 20, 1860, the delegates passed the following ordinance:

> We, the people of the State of South Carolina, in Convention assembled, do declare and ordain, and it is hereby declared and ordained, that the Ordinance adopted by us in Convention, on the twenty-third day of May, in the year of our Lord one thousand seven hundred and eighty-eight, whereby the Constitution of the United States was ratified, and also all Acts and parts of Acts of the General Assembly of the State, ratifying Amendments of the said Constitution, are hereby repealed, and the Union now subsisting

> between South Carolina and other States, under the name of the United States of America, is hereby dissolved.

When the residents of Charleston learned about the ordinance, they began to celebrate, and the celebration lasted for several days. During the festivities, business was suspended, shops were closed, women displayed "secession bonnets," and the church bells rang out in joyous peals. A few brave souls gathered around the tomb of John C. Calhoun in St. Philip's churchyard and took a solemn oath to defend the honor of South Carolina.

By the 1st of February, all the other states of the Lower South had seceded. One week later, a provisional government was established in Montgomery, Alabama. The rebellious states had formed a confederacy, and now they were going to teach the meddling Yankee abolitionists a lesson.

CHAPTER TEN

When the Southern states began to secede, many Northerners were dismayed, but a few prominent citizens urged Washington to act with restraint. Horace Greely, the editor of the *New York Tribune*, argued that the Union would survive and advised the government to allow the wayward states to depart in peace. Throughout the North, Southern sympathizers began to question the government's authority to "coerce a state" to remain in the Union, and, before long, the topic of coercion was being flaunted at public meetings, in state legislatures, and occasionally from the pulpit. Garfield would have none of it. On January 24, 1861, he made a powerful speech in the Ohio Senate advocating a "Militia Bill" permitting the state to raise and equip six thousand troops. The bill was roundly attacked by his opponents, but, as usual, the criticism was muted by logic. To the charge of coercion, he replied:

> If by coercion it is meant that the Federal Government shall declare and wage war against a State, then I have yet to see any man, Democrat or Republican, who is a coercionist. But, if by the term

> it is meant that the General Government shall enforce the laws, by whomsoever violated, shall punish traitors to the Constitution, be they ten men or ten thousand, then I am a coercionist. Every member of the Senate, by his vote on the eighth resolution, is a coercionist. Nine-tenths of the people of Ohio are coercionists. Every man is a coercionist or a traitor.

As the tide of insurrection and rebellion rose higher, Garfield began to realize that war was inevitable. There was simply no way to justify or permit secession. "Would you give up the forts and other government property in those states, or would you fight to maintain your right to them?" he asked his colleagues. In Garfield's view, the Federal Government reigned supreme, but he was well aware of the consequences of this position. In January 1861, he wrote, "My heart and thoughts are full almost every moment with the terrible reality of our country's condition. I do not see any way, outside a miracle of God, which can avoid civil war with all its attendant horrors. Peaceable dissolution is utterly impossible."

Faced with the prospect of war, Garfield urged his fellow Ohioans to arm themselves and prepare for a long struggle. "The doom of slavery is drawing near," he wrote. "Let war come, and the slaves will get the vague notion that it is waged for them, and a magazine will be lighted whose explosion will shake the whole fabric of slavery."

In February, Lincoln reached Washington, D.C., barely escaping assassination by Secessionists in Baltimore. He was inaugurated on March 4, 1861, and in his speech on that day, he said:

> It follows, from these views, that no State, upon its own mere motion, can lawfully get out of the Union; that resolves and ordinances to that effect are legally void; and that acts of violence within any State or States, against the authority of the United States, are insurrectionary or revolutionary, according to circumstances.

Lincoln's position was clear, but his words fell on deaf ears. The South was in no mood to be lectured, especially by a Yankee politician who was threatening its very way of life. Soon, there were rumors of government forts and arsenals being seized across the South. In the North, militiamen began to arm themselves. The first shots were fired in April, and the news spread like wildfire across the nation. Confederate guns—nearly two hundred of them—had opened up on the Union garrison in Charleston Harbor. The garrison was ablaze. The Stars and Stripes had been downed at Fort Sumter. The Civil War had finally begun.

The attack on Fort Sumter shocked the nation and shattered all hopes of finding a peaceful solution to the Slavery Question. Once again, Garfield's words proved prophetic—civil war had become a sad necessity. Unfortunately, none of the Northern states were prepared to defend the Union. Still, Lincoln remained calm, certain that Union forces would overwhelm the enemy and produce a quick victory. The odds were certainly in Lincoln's favor. In 1860, there were almost twenty-one million people in the Northern states, excluding Kentucky and Missouri, where public opinion about slavery was evenly divided. By contrast, the eleven Confederate states had only nine million residents, and, of these, roughly one-third were slaves whom the Southerners were unwilling to trust with arms. The "loyal states" also had a huge economic advantage, primarily in the crucial area of manufacturing, which was seven times larger in the North than the South.

At the time, Ohio's population and wealth ranked third in the nation, but, despite its size and prosperity, the state was in danger of fighting its own civil war. Just like the nation, there were two distinct camps, Northern Ohio of Puritan stock and Southern Ohio of Virginia stock. To make matters more complicated, the state had a long border, and 426 miles of it ran along Slave States. Remarkably, most Ohioans remained loyal to the Federal government.

When Lincoln issued a call for 75,000 men, Garfield rose to his feet in the Senate and moved that "twenty thousand troops and three millions of money" should be Ohio's quota. The proposal was met with cheers and applause, but the public response was even greater. Before the smoke had cleared from Fort Sumter, twenty full companies were offered to the governor of Ohio for immediate service. All across the state, militias placed themselves at the disposal of the government. The list of names included the Cleveland Grays, the Columbus Videttes, the Dayton Light Guards, and the Guthrie Grays. Even a company of "colored men" offered to serve, but "in obedience to the temper of the times," they were refused.

Ignoring reality, the South continued its call to arms, believing that public opinion in the North would prevent Lincoln from using force. Many doubted the President's resolve, and few believed that Northern manufacturers would support a war against cotton, since "cotton was king." Senator Hammond of South Carolina had reminded his Northern colleagues of this fact by declaring that "you do not dare to make war on cotton. No power on earth dares to make war upon it. Cotton is king."

The South's intransigence forced Lincoln to abandon a measured approach, but, as he planned for war, he had to convince the populace that "the holy cause of freedom" was worth fighting for. In some states a war against slavery would not have been supported by a majority of the people. The cost was simply too high. So what could the President do or say to rally support? In the end, he took the very position that Garfield had advocated from the start—that secession was a rejection of democracy itself. If the South could arbitrarily decide not to abide by the results of an election, then anarchy would prevail and the nation would be destroyed. The logic of this position was inescapable and widely accepted, but, as Garfield knew, the Union army was in disarray and unprepared for war. Many of the Union's finest officers had left the military, unwilling to fight against their friends and neighbors in the South. Even worse, troops were scattered along the vast Western frontier, and bringing them together would take a great deal of time and energy.

Garfield decided to lead by example. Putting his life on the line, he resigned his college post and made a secret journey to Illinois to procure five thousand rifles for the Ohio militia. The mission was a complete success, and, on August 14, 1861, the Governor offered Garfield the lieutenant-colonelcy of the 42nd Ohio, a regiment formed with recruits from Portage and Summit Counties—many of them former students at Hiram College. Garfield was reluctant to accept the offer, not because he was afraid to fight, but because he was unsure if he was the right man for the job. After all, he was relatively young, and he had no military training or combat experience. Surely the Governor could find a more qualified person.

While contemplating the offer, Garfield began to worry about his family. He had a wife and child to support but only a few thousand dollars in the bank. What would happen to his family if he were killed in battle? Who would provide for them? How could they possibly survive a prolonged war? Of course, many men were asking the same questions, but there were no easy answers. Each man had to choose his own course of action. Knowing what he had to do, Garfield wrote: "I regard my life as given to the country. I am only anxious to make as much of it as possible before the mortgage on it is foreclosed."

The 42nd regiment was encamped at Camp Chase, just outside of Columbus. Each day at dawn the young recruits would be roused from sleep by the bugler's reveille and stumble into formation for roll call, tin cup in hand. After a cup of strong black coffee the troops would march to the commissary for breakfast. The morning meal was always the same: bacon, hardtack, and more black coffee. The coffee was supposed to clear the lungs of infection, but it was not much of an antidote. Even in Ohio, malaria was a serious problem, and each day there were fewer men at roll call.

Soon after his arrival, Garfield formed a school for his officers, and he required them to learn military tactics. The troops were required to drill six hours a day, seven days a week. At the end of the fifth week, the regiment was organized into various companies. By then, they had gained a reputation for being the best disciplined unit in Ohio. Though untested in battle, they had gained a newfound confidence and were now prepared to do the unthinkable—fire on their own countrymen.

In mid-December, Garfield was ordered to report to General Buell in Louisville, Kentucky. Don Carlos Buell was a graduate of West Point and a man accomplished in military science and experienced in war. He had been in the army for twenty years.

Besides other service to his country, he had distinguished himself in the war with Mexico. In some ways, he was the complete opposite of Garfield, who had spent the last five years on a college campus and learned about war by reading books. Oddly enough, the general wanted Garfield's advice about a military campaign. Taking a map of Kentucky, Buell showed Garfield the position of the Confederate forces and asked him to devise a plan of attack. Hopefully, the plan would make sense. In any case, it had to be ready by nine o'clock the next morning. Somehow, Garfield managed to submit a plan, and, later that evening, he received Order No. 35, which organized the 18th Brigade under his command. In addition, he was informed that he was to be sent against Humphrey Marshall, the Confederate general who was moving down the Sandy Valley and threatening to overrun Eastern Kentucky. Marshall was expected to advance toward Lexington, unite with another rebel force, and establish a provisional government in the state capital. So far, Kentucky had refused to secede, but if the rebel advance was successful, the state would undoubtedly leave the Union. Losing Kentucky would also have a devastating impact on morale. The army was still smarting from the debacle at Bull Run and another loss so early in the war might result in the dissolution of the Union itself.

The following morning, as the regiment moved out, Buell rode up to Garfield and made a simple statement. "Colonel, you will be at so great a distance from me, and communication will be so slow and difficult, that I must commit all matters of detail and much of the fate of the campaign to your discretion. I shall hope to hear a good account of you."

Following his own plan, Garfield led his troops to Catlettsburg and then proceeded to Louisa, twenty-eight miles up the Big Sandy. When he arrived in Louisa, he discovered that the 14th Kentucky, the only other Union troops in the region, had retreated to the mouth of the Big Sandy. The departure of the Kentucky brigade meant that Garfield now had two difficult tasks to accomplish. First, he had to locate the other half of his own brigade, which had been positioned to protect his flank. Second, he had to link up his forces and attack a much larger enemy—hopefully by surprise.

Garfield was able to contact his troops by sending out a messenger who knew the lay of the land, but linking up proved more difficult. The Ohioans were in rough and unfamiliar terrain, surrounded by a hostile populace. Winter travel was never easy along the Big Sandy. A recent downpour had made things worse, and now the roads were impassible to supply trains. There were, of course, other options. They could always commandeer a steamer and try to navigate the river. If they got lucky, they might survive the swift currents, overhanging tree limbs, and floating timber. They might even avoid a few of the Confederate sharpshooters positioned along the banks. Then again, they could march through the wilderness.

Outnumbered, but determined to fight, Garfield led eleven hundred men to the mouth of Abbott's Creek, three miles south of Marshall's main encampment. The Ohioans had marched eighteen miles, through sleet and rain, and were now within striking distance. Deeming it unsafe to proceed in the darkness, Garfield ordered his troops into bivouac, but nobody got much sleep. During the night a cold wind swept into camp, followed by a driving rain and dense fog. The men were roused from their beds at four in the morning, their icy uniforms clinging to their half-frozen limbs. The time had come to engage the enemy.

Marshall had split his forces into three groups, positioned on both sides of Middle Creek and directly in front of the Union army. The plan was to lure Garfield into the center and attack from all three sides, but a premature volley of cannon betrayed Marshall's intentions. Garfield reacted quickly and redeployed his troops to make a charge on one of the rebel positions. The maneuver forced Marshall to send reinforcements, but, more importantly, it bought Garfield some much needed time. As the sun began to set, the fighting intensified. For a while, it appeared as though the rebels would prevail. Suddenly the sound of bugles filled the valley.

When Garfield looked over his shoulder, he saw the remainder of his regiment rushing into battle.

Marshall ran to high ground and shouted for his men to retreat, but before he could turn he was hit by six bullets. When his troops saw him fall, they began to panic, and then they fled in all directions.

"God bless you, boys!" Garfield exclaimed. "You have saved Kentucky!"

Incredibly, a former college professor had given the Union its first decided victory—and he had done it without sacrificing his troops. Only one Union soldier was killed during the battle of Middle Creek. Eleven others were wounded.

When asked about the skirmish later in life, Garfield said: "I see now, that favorably as it terminated, the engagement was a very rash and imprudent affair on my part. A West Point officer would probably have had more caution, and would not have attempted so unequal a contest. I didn't know any better, then." Perhaps not, but the enemy had sustained a serious blow. After burning their supplies, baggage, and wagons, the remnants of Marshall's army fled through Pound Gap into

Virginia. Garfield was tempted to pursue the rebels, but his men had run short on food and ammunition. The weather was turning colder. The following day, he addressed his troops:

> Soldiers of the Eighteenth Brigade:
>
> I am proud of you all! In four weeks you have marched some eighty, and some a hundred miles, over almost impassable roads. One night in four you have slept, often in the storm, with only a winter sky above your heads. You have marched in the face of a foe of more than double your number—led on by chiefs who have won a national renown under the old flag—intrenched in hills of his own choosing, and strengthened by all the appliances of military art. With no experience but the consciousness of your own manhood, you have driven him from his strongholds, pursued his inglorious fight, and compelled him to meet you in battle. When forced to fight, he sought the shelter of rocks and hills; you drove him from his position, leaving scores of his bloody dead unburied. His artillery thundered against you, but you compelled him to flee by the light of his burning stores, and to leave even the banner of his rebellion behind him. I greet you as men. Our common country will not forget you. She will not forget the sacred dead who fell beside you, nor those of your comrades who won scars of honor on the field. I have called you from the pursuit that you may regain vigor for still greater exertions. Let no one tarnish his well-earned honor by any act unworthy an American soldier. Remember your duties as American citizens, and sacredly respect the rights and property of those with whom you may come in contact. Let it not be said that

good men dread the approach of an American army. Officers and soldiers, your duty has been nobly done. For this I thank you.

Garfield's victory did not go unnoticed by his superior officers or by the government in Washington, D.C. General Buell was so delighted that he sent a personal note thanking "General Garfield and his troops for their successful campaign against the rebel force under General Marshall, on the Big Sandy, and their gallant conduct in battle." President Lincoln, to whom the news of "Middle Creek" was a godsend, immediately promoted Colonel Garfield to Brigadier-General. In early spring, Buell and Garfield would reunite on the march toward Corinth, Mississippi, an important railroad junction. There they would meet at a country church called Shiloh.

CHAPTER ELEVEN

By the fall of 1863, Guiteau was becoming disenchanted with the menial labor that he was required to perform. Still, he was not about to confront Noyes and risk expulsion. For all his bravado, he was afraid of failure and deathly afraid of facing his father. The old man would be livid if things went wrong. In Luther's world, failure was never an option, especially when it came to matters of the soul. A year earlier, he had taken Charles to a prayer meeting, exposing him to a group of "true believers." During the meeting, an elderly gentleman began to expound on the doctrine of Perfectionism, indicating that he and his wife were anxious to join the Oneida Community. Unfortunately, their son was violently opposed to the idea. The couple had come to pray for guidance, but they were also seeking advice. As soon as the man finished speaking, Luther jumped out of his seat and said, "I will tell you what to do. Take a knife and slay him as Abraham did Isaac!"

The outburst raised a few eyebrows, but nobody said a word, possibly out of fear. Everyone knew that Luther's family was a bit odd. The oldest boy had recently died in a madhouse in New York City.

According to the police, he had fought a duel over a girl and killed his rival. Afterwards, he became despondent, melancholy, and eventually lost his mind. Then, to everyone's surprise, both of Luther's sisters went insane. Sometime later, Luther's niece was made feebleminded by her father. Some said the father had practiced "mesmerism" on the daughter, hypnotizing her almost daily for several years. Then, according to the authorities, a nephew went berserk because he failed to get a sales position with the Decker Piano Company. Clearly, it did not take much to push a Guiteau over the edge.

It is certain that Charles was afraid of his father but that was not the only reason he remained in the Oneida Community. People like Guiteau who had no intention of fighting for their country were welcomed by Noyes. "The community has been drawn into too much sympathy with the North," Noyes wrote. "The abolitionists refused to have anything to do with the war against sin, and now they are trying to draw us into a minor issue."

In other words, Guiteau had found a safe haven, a place to hide. The fact that he lived in the Oneida Community off and on for six years, from 1860 to 1866, speaks for itself. Whether or not he would have served if drafted cannot be known, but he clearly had no intention of volunteering.

In general, community life was pleasant but predictable. Each night, members were brought together by the ringing of a bell. After dinner, the adult members attended a general meeting, followed by a special program. The weekly schedule seldom varied, but there was something for everyone. A typical week might include the following:

Monday	—	Reading and report of newspaper
Tuesday	—	Lecture on social topics

Wednesday	—	Exercises in phonography
Thursday	—	Music, vocal and instrumental
Friday	—	Dancing
Saturday	—	Reading Perfectionist publications
Sunday	—	Bible class

To virtually everyone's surprise, Guiteau attended most of the programs. In truth, this was not because he wished to learn but because he wished to endear himself to the ladies. From the start, he displayed a keen interest in the opposite sex, and now that he was a productive member of the community, he wanted to experience "free love." Judging by what he had heard, the women at Oneida were not ashamed or embarrassed by the components of human sexuality. Noyes himself had written about the subject, and he too was quite liberal:

> Sexual shame was the consequence of the fall, and is fractious and irrational. To be ashamed of the sexual organs, is to be ashamed of God's workmanship. To be ashamed of the sexual organs, is to be ashamed of the most perfect instruments of love and unity . . . To be ashamed of sexual conjunction, is to be ashamed of the image of the glory of God.

What Guiteau did not know but would soon discover was that Free Love had two main components, and neither of them involved sexual promiscuity. The concepts of Complex Marriage and Male Continence were invented by Noyes in order to eliminate the pain and suffering of childbirth. By one account, Mrs. Noyes had given birth to five babies in six years, and four of them had been stillborn. Apparently the experience had scarred both husband and wife, and neither could find a religious justification for accepting such pain and disappointment.

In theory, Complex Marriage meant that all men were married to all women and that any man and woman could be intimate within the limits of the community. Noyes knew full well this would be seen as immoral, but he defended the practice by pointing to the absence of marriage in heaven. In addition, he claimed that:

> When the will of God is done on earth as it is in Heaven, there will be no marriage. Exclusiveness, jealousy, quarrelling have no place in the marriage supper of the lamb. I call a certain woman my wife. She is yours, she is Christ's, and in Him she is the bride of all saints. She is now in the hands of a stranger, and according to my promise to her, I rejoice.

In actuality, Complex Marriage was strictly regulated and members were required to follow the rules. Before a man and woman could cohabit, they were obliged to obtain each other's consent through a third party. Secondly, exclusive relationships were forbidden. If a couple became "selfish," they would be separated and not allowed to see each other for a certain length of time. Complaints were to be referred to the Book of Matthew: "In the Kingdom of Heaven, the institution of marriage which assigns the exclusive possession of one woman to one man, does not exist."

In order to prevent idolatrous attachments, members were encouraged to approach as many different partners as possible. Some men and women had intercourse seven times a week, but regardless of how often they mated, members were not permitted to sleep together overnight or to engage in long conversations. Both could lead to *exclusive love*, and that would be a very bad thing.

One of the strangest parts of Complex Marriage was something called "Ascending Fellowship." The purpose of this quaint practice was twofold. It was used to properly introduce the virgins into Complex Marriage, and it worked to prevent the young members from falling in love with each other and ignoring the older members. Perhaps because of his position, Noyes stipulated that the virgins be guided by a Central Member, a person who was older and closer to God. Central Members were allowed to pick any female virgin they wanted, and, due to her lower status, she was compelled to accept. Female Central Members were allowed the same privilege, and, when they chose a male virgin, he was obligated to honor the request.

One can only imagine how Guiteau felt when he learned that male members had to serve a term of two to three years before they could have sexual relations with a female member of the community. Of course, the second component of Complex Marriage was even more restrictive. Male continence, or *coitus reservatus*, was actually a form of birth control, and it was used to prevent haphazard procreation, which was said to result in the birth of deformed or mentally deficient children.

Basically, couples were allowed to engage in "sexual congress" as long as the man never ejaculated, either during intercourse or after withdrawal. "It is the glory of man to control himself," wrote Noyes. "And the Kingdom of God summons him to control all things." Perhaps inevitably, this belief led Noyes to conclude that every instance of self-denial was an interruption of some natural act. The man who contents himself with a look at a beautiful woman is conscious of such an interruption, as is the lover who stops at a kiss. Besides, he argued:

> The useless expenditure of seed certainly is not natural. God cannot have designed that men should sow seed by the way-side, where they do not expect it to grow, or in the same field where seed has already been sown, and is growing, and yet such is the practice of men in ordinary sexual intercourse. They sow seed habitually where they do not *wish* it to grow. This is wasteful of life, and cannot be natural.

If Guiteau had been able to control himself, he might have done well with the ladies, but he showed no aptitude for practicing self-restraint. Though it was not then widely known, an unsanctioned orgasm was called an "upset." Each upset had to be reported to a Central Member, and the guilty party was obliged to face Mutual Criticism. For a brief period—two or three months—Guiteau was subjected to intense scrutiny and constant criticism. Not surprisingly, he was embarrassed and humiliated by the experience. Finding himself miserable, he began to make others miserable. Before long, he became an object of scorn and ridicule, and some of the ladies began to refer to him as Charles "Gitout."

And the year would get even worse.

The criticism sessions were supposed to offer constructive criticism, not insults. Someone must have forgotten to inform the women of this fact, because their comments were often quite vicious. On one occasion, a young woman offered the following observation: "He is not as neat in his personal habits as good taste requires; he should pay more attention to outward adornment."

Shunned by the ladies, Guiteau sought happiness outside the community. In July 1864, he took a short trip to New York City. Whether or not he sought female companionship is unknown. From what he wrote, it seems that he remained celibate. In a letter written on the 12th, he describes his visit:

> Dear Friends:
>
> I have delayed writing until now, in order that I might give a better account of my visit . . . Sunday Mr. Bloom and myself heard Henry Ward Beecher. I was very much disappointed in him . . . . He failed entirely to comprehend the great spiritual object of Christ's mission, which was to destroy the works of the devil and to save his people from their sins. On the whole his discourse was a *bore* and he impressed me as being a very superficial man.

Obviously, Guiteau was not impressed by the most famous clergyman in America, but he did enjoy the city itself. He concludes his letter in some detail:

> Monday Mr. Bloom and myself visited Central Park, of course I was delighted. It is truly a grand magnificent, splendid place and especially at this season of the year when nature is adorned in her finest garb . . . Tuesday Mrs. Bloom and myself visited the ocean at *Long Branch*, in New Jersey.
>
> Wednesday I went over to Staten Island and enjoyed it much . . . Thursday I went to Barnum's and saw many things of interest.

The trip to New York City lifted Guiteau's spirits, but only for a while. When he got back to Oneida, he was treated poorly and began to sulk. By now, he had a reputation as a "careless man," unskilled in lovemaking. Needless to say, this curtailed his social contacts. Ultimately, he was forced to seek guidance from a prominent member of the community.

This was another blow to his fragile ego. Holding nothing back, he composed a touching letter, which reveals his frustration:

> Dear Mr. Hamilton:
>
> I have a delicate matter on my heart that I wish to mention to you. It pertains to my social experience. The case simply stated is this—For several months past I have found myself liking ________________, and have from time to time sought in a quiet modest spirit to manifest my feelings toward her, and on the whole have felt quite encouraged; but recently I have met an obstruction in her spirit that seems to prevent that free flow of fellowship that I desire.
>
> My object in writing to you is to express the hope that she may be advised to turn her heart toward me.
>
> I confess a good spirit in regard to love, and am willing to wait on God for it.
>
> Your Brother Chas. J. Guiteau

In hindsight, the letter can be seen as a cry for help, and it contains some interesting elements. The name of the young woman has been erased, ostensibly to guard her identity. Unwilling to accept the obvious, Guiteau wants her to be advised, or persuaded, to accept his affection. There is no mention of what, if anything, he might be willing to do in order to earn that affection. Finally, he states that he is "willing to wait on God," but that was simply not the case. By the time this letter was written, Guiteau had made up his mind to leave, and nothing was going to stop him. Considering the situation, who could blame him? Nobody, not even Noyes, could stop the subtle abuse. But in truth, nobody even tried. Day after day the insults continued—the sexual rejection, the harsh criticism, the whispering, the giggling, the dirty looks. In response, Guiteau fell into a deep depression, biding his time until he felt strong enough to leave.

How unhappy was he?

When his sister Frances finally went to see him, she was shocked to find him in a state of utter despair. What in the world had happened to her brother? He looked like he had the weight of the world on his shoulders. As she later testified, "She could hardly have any conversation with him as they were never left alone. She noticed that Charles acted like a person who had been bewildered, struck on the head, or had partly lost his mind."

Guiteau told her that he had a "dreadful feeling" about the community. In his words, "he had lost all of his free-agency." This so-called agency, or will, had been destroyed by his association and connection with the Oneida Community. Once a loyal member, he now characterized his experience as "the great misfortune of his life." Sooner or later, he told his sister, they would pay for their transgression.

In the meantime, he would satisfy himself by becoming a man of influence—the editor of a great newspaper. There were many who, like his sister, predicted failure, but Guiteau was determined to try his hand at publishing. "I am about to leave you," he wrote to the community. "The movement about to be made has been long pondered and well considered, and I make it in obedience to an irresistible conviction that if I do it not a woe will be upon me."

Naturally, Noyes tried to reason with him, patiently explaining the difficulties that lay ahead. A rational person might have learned something. Noyes was a prolific author and had a great deal of publishing experience, but none of this mattered to Charles Guiteau. In his arrogant reply, he wrote:

> Do you say that the establishment of a great daily paper is a stupendous work and only to be accomplished by extraordinary talents and energy? Of course it is . . . therefore, I say boldly, that I claim *inspiration.* I claim that I am in the employ of Jesus Christ & Co.; the very ablest and strongest firm in the universe.

Relations between Noyes and Guiteau were never great, but after this exchange, they deteriorated to such a degree that they seldom spoke to each other. Still, Guiteau was given a generous settlement. He left Oneida with $50 worth of books, $100 worth of new clothes, $100 in cash, and a note for $800. In return, he offered a final thought concerning his departure: "If a man have big ideas he is usually deemed insane; but I trust the Community will not thrust the charge of insanity at me; but will allow me to quietly follow my own inspiration."

CHAPTER TWELVE

In early January 1862, Garfield received orders from General Buell instructing him to leave a small force near Pound Gap and return with the rest of his troops to Louisville, Kentucky. From there, Garfield took command of the 18th Brigade and began to march south, engaging Confederate forces at Middle Creek on the afternoon of January 10. After a short, but intense battle, the Confederates retreated south, and were eventually ordered back to Virginia.

The Battle of Middle Creek was followed by another victory at the Battle of Mill Springs, and together, they served to cement Union control of Eastern Kentucky.

The most remarkable thing about the 42nd Ohio and many other regiments was that their soldiers were barely old enough to serve. In fact, over two-thirds of the Union forces were under twenty-two years of age. Out of a total enlistment of three million men almost half were under nineteen.

Unknown to General Garfield, the Army of the Ohio was on its way to join Grant at Pittsburgh Landing on the Tennessee River, and it had already moved beyond Nashville. Garfield left quickly and joined the army about thirty miles south of Columbia. Upon reporting to General Buell, he was given the command of the 20th Brigade. It was from Buell that he learned their destination—a small country church and meetinghouse called Shiloh.

The Battle of Shiloh began at dawn on April 6, and from all reports, it was not going well for the Union army, which was under the command of a shabby, cigar-smoking general named Ulysses S. Grant. Details were sketchy, but apparently Grant was caught by surprise and lost many men. It was odd that a seasoned warrior like Grant fell victim to a surprise attack, but as Garfield soon learned, the general had left the battlefield and was twelve miles down river.

Grant came south to invade Corinth, Mississippi, an important railroad junction twenty miles southwest of Shiloh. He planned to attack the Confederate stronghold and launch an invasion of the Lower South, but his Southern counterparts had their own plans. Albert Sidney Johnston and Pierre Gustave Toutant Beauregard had forty thousand men under their command, and on Saturday night, April 5, they moved into striking position, hoping that their attack could be a surprise. They were not disappointed. Some Union soldiers were caught half-dressed. Others were in the middle of breakfast or brewing their morning coffee. A few were killed in their blankets, shot at close range or pierced by the cold steel of a rebel bayonet. Unwilling to imagine such an audacious assault, Grant convinced himself that his was an army that was meant to attack, not to defend. Consequently, no protective fortifications had been erected and the Confederate cavalry charged directly into the Union camp.

The casualty reports were chilling, and like many other officers, Grant began to wonder about the Union picket lines. Had they sounded any warning? Had they fought a skirmish with the enemy? Had they been overrun and slaughtered? In time, the truth would come out, and it would almost ruin the careers of Grant *and* Sherman.

Ambrose Bierce, the famous American journalist, fought at Shiloh and later wrote about his experience in a book called *What I Saw of Shiloh*. Employing a healthy dose of sarcasm, he wrote:

> "On the morning of the memorable 6th of April, at Shiloh, many of Grant's men when spitted on Confederate bayonets were as naked as civilians; but it should be allowed that this was not because of any defect in their picket line. Their error was of another part: they had no pickets."

On April 7, the second day of the battle, General Garfield led his brigade against the weary, but tenacious Confederates. Garfield had whipped Marshall rather easily, but this time he faced General Pierre G.T. Beauregard, the "Napoleon of the South." Unlike Garfield, Beauregard had an impressive military background dating back to 1838, when he graduated second in his class at West Point. After graduation, he had served with Winfield Scott in Mexico and was then engaged to clear the Mississippi River of obstructions. In 1861, he became the superintendent of West Point, serving just five days before resigning his post to join the Confederacy. In February, he was placed in charge of the South Carolina troops in Charleston Harbor, where he won a nearly bloodless victory and became known as the "Hero of Fort Sumter." Five months later, he was at Manassas Junction, Virginia, defending the northern part of the state—and preventing an invasion of Richmond. On July 21, his forces came under attack on a branch of the Potomac

River called Bull Run. While he waited for reinforcements, he fought a defensive battle, stubbornly holding his position and checking the advance of 30,000 Union troops. Late in the day his left flank collapsed. For a while it looked grim, but then a Virginia brigade under Thomas J. Jackson rushed to the field and saved the day. During the counter attack, a South Carolina general pointed to the hill where Jackson was directing his troops. "Look," he shouted, "there is Jackson with his Virginians, standing like a stone wall against the enemy." Thus, Jackson received his famous nickname, and Beauregard became a fighting legend. Now the legend was commanding the Army of the Mississippi, and he had every intention of enhancing his formidable reputation.

Quite naturally, Garfield had other ideas. As Ambrose Bierce once wrote, "war is God's way of teaching Americans geography." True or not, Garfield was forced to make a quick study of the terrain and mount a counterattack. During his advance, Beauregard tried to turn his right flank and then his left, but the 17th Brigade held tight and the maneuver failed. Instinctively, Garfield called up his reserves and drove against Beauregard's right, causing him to retreat and regroup. The struggle continued for hours, but in late afternoon, the Union troops recaptured the ground they had lost the day before. The Confederates fell back toward Corinth, bloodied, exhausted, and demoralized. They had lost over ten thousand men, including General Johnston, one of their finest commanders. The cost was high for the North, too. Buell's army lost two thousand men, and the total number of Union dead exceeded thirteen thousand. Sadly, more Americans died at Shiloh than in all the battles of the Revolutionary War, the War of 1812, and the Mexican War combined. Grant was so shaken by his losses that he failed to apply the coup de grace that might have destroyed the Army of the Mississippi. Instead of pursuing the enemy, he allowed them to escape, which damaged his hard-earned reputation and prolonged the war in the West.

As it turned out, Grant's army did not reach Corinth until the end of May, and, by then, the town was nearly deserted. Beauregard had moved his troops farther south, leaving his adversary a few old guns and four hundred prisoners. Garfield wanted to march south, but his brigade was ordered to repair the railroad east of Corinth, an arduous task that proved to be of little or no value. Following orders, the 17th worked its way toward Huntsville, Alabama, hacking through marsh and swamp and exposing itself to malaria.

When Garfield finally reached Huntsville, he was given another thankless task, only this one required brains, not brawn. The Union army was about to court-martial one of its own, and the War Department needed a special kind of judge, an officer who had both legal and military experience and a sterling reputation. Garfield fit the bill and was conveniently stationed in Alabama, so he was made President of the panel. By strange coincidence, the courtroom battle involved not only the Army of the Ohio, but also its commander, General Don Carlos Buell.

The trial was centered around the sack of Athens, Alabama, an incident that occurred in the wake of the costly Union victory at Shiloh. In mid-April, the Army of the Ohio pushed deep into enemy territory, occupying a number of small towns in northern Alabama. Among these towns was Athens, which had a population of roughly nine hundred and was thought to be pro-Union. On May 1, the First Louisiana Cavalry mounted a surprise attack on the Union garrison, inflicting heavy casualties and driving the Union soldiers out of town. During their retreat, the soldiers were allegedly cursed and spat upon by the residents of Athens, who were delighted by the rout. The Confederates "were greeted with cheers and a waving of hats and handkerchiefs by the citizen of the square," wrote a witness. "The ladies at the tavern brought to light a Confederate flag that hasn't seen the light in some time before, I guess." The same witness wrote that some citizens helped the rebel cavalry drive the Union forces from the town. If that were true, it was a foolish thing to do because the town was recaptured the very next day.

On May 2nd, the town was invaded by the 19th and 24th Illinois Infantry under the command of a Russian-born colonel named Ivan VasilovitchTurchinov, who was now calling himself John Basil Turchin. Colonel Turchin was educated in a Russian military academy and fought in the Crimean War. Like Sherman, he was a proponent of a relatively new strategy called 'total war.' Unlike Sherman, he encouraged lawlessness. When Turchin arrived in Athens, he marched into the town square and told his men to punish the townspeople. His exact words were, "I see nothing for two hours." Later, he would claim that he was just following orders and that Brigadier General Mitchel, his superior officer, had instructed him "not to leave even a grease spot" where Athens stood.

The Union soldiers were more than happy to obey their orders, and they proceeded to sack the town. Stores and homes were looted and "indecent and beastly propositions" were made to many women. During the rampage, a 14-year-old black woman was raped. Soldiers also fired inside the home of a pregnant white woman, causing her to miscarry and subsequently die.

When General Buell arrived in Huntsville, he ordered an investigation, which eventually led to Turchin's court-martial. Never one to mince words, Buell labeled the incident an "undisputed atrocity."

Turchin was unbowed and more than a little perplexed by the charges brought against him. On July 5, he wrote: "I was at the head of my brigade everywhere and always on duty. Instead of thanks, I received insults; therefore I respectfully tender my unconditional resignation."

Initially, Garfield was appalled by Mitchel and Turchin's actions, and, like Buell, he spoke out publically. Addressing the court, he said, "There has not been found in American history so black a page as that which will bear the record of General Mitchel's campaign in North America." Referring to Turchin's men, he declared that they had "committed the most shameful outrages on the country here that the history of this war has seen."

Turchin objected to this characterization. He told the court that his men had merely destroyed some fields and fences to secure the area. Granted, they had helped themselves to some food, drink and perhaps a few warm blankets, but that was the nature of war. "Since I have been in the Army," he said, "I have tried to teach the Rebels that treason to the Union was a terrible crime. My superior officers do not agree with my plans. They want the rebellion treated tenderly and gently." In a brazen attempt to sway public opinion, he added, "I have been hated everywhere by secessionists in Missouri, Kentucky, Tennessee, and Alabama, and I consider it to be a good recommendation for a loyal officer."

Playing to the public and the press paid off, even in the most unlikely places. During the trial, Lucretia Garfield wrote to her husband imploring him to consider "the court of public opinion" . . . "I hope you will find Col. Turchin guilty of nothing unpardonable," she wrote. "Severity and sternness should be turned to the punishment of rebels for the barbarities committed on our boys rather than to the punishment of our own." In closing, she added, "It seems very strange that as soon as a man begins to accomplish something in the way of putting down the rebellion he is recalled, or superseded, or disgraced in some way."

Lucretia's attempt to sway the court, or to be more exact, its chief judge, was successful. Despite his initial misgivings, Garfield changed his mind about Turchin, admitting that the defendant had "quite won my heart." Unfortunately for Turchin, Garfield was stricken with malaria and forced to resign from the panel before the trial ended. In the end, Turchin was found guilty on all but two counts. The official findings of the court-martial, as published by Buell on August 6, were as follows:

> [He] allowed his command to disperse and in his presence or with his knowledge and that of his officers to plunder and pillage the inhabitants. They attempted an indecent outrage on a servant girl . . . destroyed a stock of fine Bibles and Testaments . . . defaced, and kicked about the floor and trampled under foot. A part of the brigade went to the plantations and quartered in the negro huts for weeks, debauching the females. Mrs. Hollingworth's house was entered and plundered. The alarm and excitement occasioned miscarriage and subsequently her death. Several soldiers committed rape on the person of a colored girl. The court finds the accused guilty as charged and does therefore sentence Colonel J.B. Turchin to be dismissed from the service of the United States.

The oddest part of Turchin's trial was the aftermath. Although Buell ordered Turchin dismissed from the Army, President Lincoln set aside the verdict and promoted him to the rank of Brigadier General. General Buell was accused of harboring pro-slavery sentiments and was himself relieved of command in October. Turchin returned to active duty and fought bravely at the battles of Stone River, Chickamauga, and Chattanooga. He retired, due to wounds, in 1864, but the sack of Athens seems to have stayed with him. Late in life he became deranged and was sent to the Southern Hospital for the Insane. He died at the hospital on June 18, 1901.

Brigadier General Garfield recovered from his illness and was ordered to report, in person, to the Secretary of War, Edwin M. Stanton. Reaching Washington, he learned that the government was going to court-martial another officer. As was his habit, Stanton spent part of the meeting complaining about "reluctant warriors," but then he got down to business and came straight to the point. Garfield had been summoned to serve on the court-martial panel. This time the case was more complicated, and there were political overtones. The plaintiff, so to speak, was Major General John Pope, one of the most incompetent officers in the Union Army. Pope had been humiliated at the Second Battle of Bull Run, but he refused to accept responsibility for the defeat. Instead, he blamed a fellow officer, and now he demanded justice. On November 25, Pope convinced Stanton, a close personal friend, to issue an arrest warrant for Major General Fitz-John Porter, a West Point graduate and career Army officer. Porter would be charged with insubordination and misconduct in the face of the enemy. If convicted, it would mean disgrace, dishonor, and the end of a brilliant military career.

Fitz-John Porter was no ordinary soldier. He came from a distinguished military family, and several of his cousins were prominent Naval officers. David Dixon Porter would soon become one of the first U.S. Navy officers to hold the rank of Admiral; William D. Porter would be recognized for gallantry in battle on the Mississippi River; and David G. Farragut, another relative, would soon attack Mobile Bay, meet fierce resistance, and utter the immortal phrase: "Damn the torpedoes! Full speed ahead!"

As Garfield eventually discovered, Porter had quite an impressive resume himself. He had served in the Mexican-American War and was promoted to captain for bravery at the Battle of Molino del Rey. He repeated the same feat at Chapultepec, for which he received a promotion to major. At the start of the Civil War, he was promoted to colonel. Three days later, he became a brigadier general. In August 1861, he received division command in the Army of the Potomac, a promotion that would lead to disaster. At the time, the Army of the Potomac was led by General George B. McClellan, the most controversial and universally despised officer in the Union Army. McClellan was well on his way to becoming known as "the general who would not dare," and he was disliked by some very powerful politicians, including the Secretary of War. In fact, Porter's friendship with McClellan and his open criticism of Pope were the main reasons for his court-martial. Some were calling it guilt by association.

Garfield tried to remain impartial, but, as the trial proceeded, it became clear that Porter had been guilty of insubordination. According to his own testimony, he had openly complained about joining Pope's Northern Virginia Campaign. He had also criticized Pope personally, which he now admitted was a foolish mistake. The misconduct charge was more serious but also harder to prove. Pope told the court that during the battle he had ordered Porter to attack the flank and rear of "Stonewall" Jackson's wing of the Army of Northern Virginia. Porter chose to ignore the order, sending a terse reply that General Longstreet's forces had arrived on the battlefield and were positioned directly in front of him. A frontal assault would be suicidal, and Porter was not about to obey such an absurd command.

The Secretary of War, in what might be described as a "fatherly talk," reminded the panel that Porter's testimony was pure speculation. What if Porter had attacked in force and inflicted heavy losses upon the enemy? How many men would Longstreet have sacrificed? Would the rebels have retreated?

Pope chimed in, too, telling the court that the entire concept of military order was at stake. Even now, discipline was a problem on the battlefield—how much worse would it be if officers were allowed to disobey orders with impunity?

In the end, the court was sufficiently buffaloed by Stanton's concerns. On January 10, 1863, Porter was found guilty of disobedience and misconduct. He was dismissed from the army the following week, and he spent the remainder of his life trying to clear his name. In 1878, a special commission would exonerate him by finding that his reluctance to attack Longstreet probably saved Pope's Army from total annihilation.

It would be Garfield's successor, President Chester A. Arthur, who would reverse the sentence and support a special act of Congress restoring Porter's military commission. Two days later, vindicated but still bitter, Porter would resign from the Army. When asked about his court-martial, he would remind people that Stanton had handpicked the judges and that almost all of them had received a promotion after the trial.

CHAPTER THIRTEEN

There was a time when military commanders sought advice and deferred to the War Department on questions of strategy, but those days were long gone. A prolonged war had changed the tone of discourse, and now many generals dreamt of becoming the next Napoleon. Few, of course, had the ability or the brains, but that did not stop them from dreaming. Perhaps in defiance of these circumstances, the citizen soldier rose to the occasion and often performed as well as, or better than, the career soldier. When President Lincoln learned of Garfield's success in Kentucky, he remarked to an officer who was with him, "Why did Garfield do in two weeks what would have taken one of your regular officers two months to accomplish?" "Because he was not educated at West Point," was the answer. "No," said Lincoln, "that was not the reason. It was because when he was a boy he had to work for a living."

Indeed, Garfield had worked very hard during the last two months, pouring over volumes of military law as he struggled with the complicated questions before the court. The Porter trial had taken its toll on all of the participants but had addressed some very important issues: the rules of war, the situation of Porter's command previous to the battle, the duties of subordinate commanders, and the military possibilities of the situation.

It was odd, in a way, that Garfield was reassigned to the Army of Cumberland under the command of General Williams S. Rosencrans. Rosencrans, Buell's replacement, was brilliant but testy, and a devout Catholic, wary of "pious preachers." Apparently, he had heard that Garfield was a Campbellite preacher, college educated, and fond of theological debate. He had asked for a West Point man, but those "imbeciles" in Washington had sent him a Bible-thumper. The assignment could not have come at a worse time. "Rosey," as his soldiers called him, had just lost his beloved chief of staff, an unlucky fellow who had his head taken off by a cannonball. He was in no mood to train a replacement, but the War Department had insisted on Garfield's appointment and would not take "No" for an answer.

In truth, Secretary Stanton was worried about Rosencrans' violent temper and legendary obstinacy. The man was a brilliant strategist but completely unpredictable. If Garfield could restrain the general, there was no telling what he might accomplish on the battlefield.

A diplomat by nature and an officer possessed with great intelligence, Garfield was the right man for this kind of work. Only a patient man like Garfield would even consider such a task. He perceived, with a clarity rare among subordinates, that his fellow Ohioan understood war, and he was right. Rosencrans had graduated from West Point, ranked fifth in the famous class of 1842. Among his classmates were two men that Garfield had recently come to "know," General John Pope and General James Longstreet. After twelve years of service, Rosencrans had resigned from the Army and became president of the

Preston Coal Oil Company, in Cincinnati, Ohio. In his spare time he became an inventor, producing such products as odorless coal oil, a round lamp wick, and a revolutionary new method of manufacturing soap. When the Civil War broke out, he immediately rejoined the Army and quickly became a legend by defeating Robert E. Lee at Rich Mountain, Virginia. Sent west, he was placed in charge of two divisions of Grant's Army of the Mississippi at the Battle of Corinth. Although he performed bravely, he was criticized for being too "head strong" and second-guessing his superior officers. When he was reassigned to the Army of the Cumberland, Grant wrote:

> "I was delighted at the promotion of General Rosencrans to a separate command because I still felt that when independent of an immediate superior the qualities which I, at that time, credited him with possessing, would show themselves. As a subordinate I found that I could not make him do as I wished, and had determined to relieve him from duty that very day."

Rosencrans was delighted by the promotion, too. Finally, he was rid of timid commanders. Now he would show those bureaucrats in Washington how to win a war. Upon receiving a report that General Bragg was moving toward Nashville with a large rebel force, he ordered a direct assault, confronting the enemy at Murfreesboro. The battle was fought well, but proved indecisive. Still, Congress later accorded him the Thanks of the Nation. In time, however, this proved to be more of a curse than a blessing. The War Department demanded an "encore," and they began to press for a quick victory over Bragg. After six months of preparation, Rosencrans began the Tullahoma Campaign, an ingenious plan designed to drive the Confederates out of Tennessee. By strategically moving his army, he drove Bragg back to Chattanooga, losing only five hundred men during the entire campaign. All in all, it was an amazing feat, but the War Department was not impressed. The lack of recognition prompted Rosencrans to compose the following complaint to Secretary Stanton: "I beg in behalf of this army that the War Department may not overlook so great an event because it is not written in letters of blood."

Rosencrans gradually came to realize that he did not have many friends in the War Department and that he would never be able to please Secretary Stanton. He began to express his displeasure in writing, and as time went on, the tone of his correspondence became quite harsh. These were bitter dispatches, all of them, and they caused a great deal of consternation back East. The histrionics continued for several months, and it was only Garfield's intervention that saved the volatile general from being relieved of his command. Garfield, it seemed, was Rosencrans' editor, not just his confidant. Prior to sending a dispatch, the Chief of Staff would edit and revise, eliminating the most offensive sentences. Slowly, Rosencrans began to realize that in some ways, Garfield completed him. Whereas Rosencrans was hotheaded, high-strung, and unpredictable, Garfield was cool, calm and calculating. In a letter, written after the war was over, Rosencrans gave his subordinate a rare compliment:

> "When Garfield arrived, I must confess I had a prejudice against him, as I understood he was a preacher who had gone into politics, and a man of that cast I was naturally opposed to. However, I found him to be a competent and efficient officer, and earnest and devoted patriot, and a man of the highest honor."

It was perhaps a measure of Garfield's worth that he was highly admired by officers and enlisted men alike and was singled out for praise in the Annals of the Army of the Cumberland as follows:

> "With the selection of General Garfield, universal satisfaction is everywhere expressed. Possessed of sound natural sense, an excellent judgement, a highly cultivated intellect, and the deserved reputation of a successful military leader, he is not only the mentor of the staff, but his opinions are sought and his counsels heeded by many who are older, and not less distinguished than himself."

During his tenure as Chief of Staff, Garfield had to deal with a number of touchy issues, including the proper disposition of the negro population. Sometime in June 1863, his superior received a letter detailing a plan to promote universal insurrection of slaves throughout the South. The uprising was to take place on August 1, and the planners were hoping to enlist the support of the Army of the Cumberland. Rosencrans was not in favor of the plan, but, before he responded in writing, he wanted to know what Garfield thought. Should the Union Army be used in such a fashion? Garfield was totally opposed to the idea, describing it as a violation of the rules of warfare. How could the Army encourage war upon noncombatants? What would happen to the innocent women and children of the South? If the plan was carried out, the country would not only be overrun with war, but also with riot. Writing to President Lincoln, Garfield addressed the issue on behalf of his superior officer:

> "I am clearly of opinion that the negro project is in every way bad, and should be repudiated, and, if possible, thwarted. If the slaves should, of their own accord, rise and assert their original right to themselves, and cut their way through rebeldom, that is their own affair; but the Government could have no complicity with it without outraging the sense of justice of the civilized world. We would create great sympathy for the rebels abroad, and God knows they have too much already."

The slave revolt faded away, but Washington insisted that Rosencrans move against the enemy. Through Garfield, Rosencrans reminded the War Department that he had no cavalry, inferior arms, and a depleted number of troops. On his own, he demanded horses, arms, and artillery. He would not, under any circumstances, advance until his men were properly equipped. The dispatches from Washington became increasingly harsh, but the replies were even more venomous. Once again, Garfield stepped into the breach and tried to resolve the problem. But this time, he agreed with Stanton. The Army had to move south. At first, Rosencrans was immovable, but Garfield would not give up. Finally, on June 8, Rosencrans agreed to consult his seventeen commanders, asking each of them to present a written opinion of the situation. Every one of the seventeen opposed an advance. Garfield was dismayed, but, instead of accepting the outcome, he asked to present a written rebuttal. The request was granted, but Garfield was told that he was wasting his time. Nonetheless, he spent the next four days writing an opinion that many historians view as the most thoroughly brilliant analysis of the entire war. The paper covered nine main points.

Summing up the relative strength of the two armies, it said: "There will be sixty-five thousand one hundred and thirty-seven bayonets and sabers to throw against Bragg's forty-one thousand six hundred and eighty."

The simple truth was Rosencrans had no excuse not to advance. The rebels were also short of arms, ammunition, and artillery. Furthermore, they had lost more men at the Battle of Murfreesboro. The only thing holding Rosencrans back was stubbornness. Once he read the rebuttal, however, he began to rethink his position. In this uncertain environment, he came to the conclusion that he had nothing to lose. If he attacked and won, he would be a hero. If he did nothing, he would be relieved of command. It was better to force a fight than to be forced out.

There were, of course, dissenters. The most vocal of this group was General Thomas L. Crittenden, an extraordinarily incompetent officer. On the morning of June 23, he had the temerity to march into headquarters and confront the Chief of Staff. His words were recorded by an eyewitness: "It is understood, sir, by the general officers of the army that his movement is your work. I wish you to understand that it is a rash and fatal move, for which you will be held responsible."

And so, with a reluctant leader and the general officers in near revolt, the Army of the Cumberland began a painfully slow advance toward Chattanooga. Rosencrans did not reach his destination until mid-September. By then, Bragg had repositioned his forces south of the city. If Rosencrans had kept his army together, he might have scored a decisive victory. Thinking that Bragg was in full retreat, he split his troops into three columns, hoping to outflank the enemy. The columns were forced to march through dense forests and mountainous terrain. Much to Garfield's dismay, they were often twenty-five miles apart. The blunder was caused by misinformation from Confederate deserters and by a telegraph from Washington indicating that Bragg's army was retreating to reinforce General Lee. The fact was that Lee was reinforcing Bragg. Rosencrans had no way of knowing it, but his foe was about to be strengthened by two divisions from the vaunted Army of Northern Virginia.

Meanwhile, Bragg went on the offensive, hoping to isolate one of the Federal columns. The attempt to trap and crush the enemy failed, but only because Bragg's subordinates refused to obey his orders. The delay gave Rosencrans just enough time to pull his troops together. After a week of sparring, the two armies came face to face, meeting at West Chickamauga Creek near Lee and Gordon's Mill. The month-long game of cat and mouse was over, and now it was time to stand and fight.

The battle was fought in a picturesque valley filled with rocky hills, ridges, and a forest that was thick enough to conceal two large armies. The front line stretched for five miles, making it difficult to send or receive orders. For two days, the combatants engaged in a deadly chess game, moving back and forth through dense fog and smoke. On the morning of September 20, the second day of battle, General Rosencrans was erroneously informed that a large hole had opened in the center of his line. Instead of consulting his Chief of Staff, he issued a direct order to close the gap, which caused the withdrawal of an entire division. Suddenly there really was a gap, and as fate would have it, the opening was directly in front of General James Longstreet and his seventeen thousand Virginia veterans. Longstreet charged right through the Union line, splitting the Army of the Cumberland in two. The top half fled toward Chattanooga, discarding their guns, knapsacks, and blankets. The bottom portion fought on, unaware that they were now facing insurmountable odds.

When Rosencrans heard the news, he was devastated, but he did not panic. Turning to his Chief of Staff, he asked, "Garfield, what can be done?"

"One of us should go to Chattanooga," Garfield replied calmly. "Secure the bridges in case of total defeat, and collect the fragments of the army on a new line. The other should make his way, if possible, to General Thomas, explain the situation, and tell him to hold his ground at any cost, until the army can be rallied at Chattanooga."

"Which will you do?" asked Rosencrans.

"Let me go to the front," said Garfield. "It is dangerous, but the army and the country can better afford for me to be killed than for you."

Rosencrans thought it was a futile gesture, but he knew that something had to be done to slow the enemy advance. If Bragg and Longstreet were able to leave the battlefield they would surely march north and try to recapture Chattanooga. "As you will," he said to Garfield. "We may not meet again. Good-bye. God bless you!"

Garfield hastily gathered together three of his best riders and raced out of camp, galloping past a steady stream of dazed and wounded soldiers. The party made a wide detour to avoid the Confederates, but by taking a circuitous route they were forced to travel through eight miles of tangled forest. They emerged on Lafayette Road, but, before they reached the battlefield, they were ambushed by a contingent of rebel sharpshooters. The ensuing chaos was described by a war correspondent for the *New York Tribune*:

> A volley of a thousand Minnie-balls falls among them, thick as hail, wounding one horse, killing another, and stretching two orderlies on the ground lifeless . . . Garfield is mounted on a magnificent horse, that knows his rider's bridle-hand as well as he knows the route to his fodder. Putting spurs to his side, he leaps the fence into the cotton-field . . . He has been in tight places before, but this is the tightest . . . Up the hill he goes, tacking, when another volley bellows from out the timber. His horse is struck—a flesh wound—but the noble animal only leaps forward the faster. Scattering bullets whiz by his head, but he is within a few feet of the summit . . . . Garfield's horse has been struck twice, but he is good yet for a score of miles; and at breakneck pace they go forward, through ploughed fields and tangled forests, and over broken and rocky hills, for four weary miles, till they climb a wooded crest, and are within sight of [General] Thomas . . . . He has come out unscathed from the hurricane of death, for God's good angels have warded off the bullets; but his noble horse staggers a step or two, and then falls dead at the feet of Thomas.

Later that day, General Thomas rallied his forces on Horseshoe Ridge, preventing a complete rout and earning a place in military history. From that day on he was known as the "Rock of Chickamauga," a name that became synonymous with standing firm against overwhelming odds. General Rosencrans did not fare as well. He was blamed for the Union loss and relieved of his command, ending any important role for him in the war. Garfield was promoted to the rank of Major-General "for gallant and meritorious conduct at the battle of Chickamauga." The promotion marked the end of a brilliant military career and the beginning of a new struggle in the rough and tumble world of Washington politics. He had been the youngest man in the Ohio Senate, the youngest brigadier-general, and now, at the age of thirty-two, he was about to become the youngest member of the House of Representatives.

CHAPTER FOURTEEN

On April 3, 1865, Guiteau left the Oneida Community and went to Hoboken, New Jersey, to start a religious newspaper called *The Daily Theocrat*. After years of searching, he had found the "great mission" of his life. He would become a newspaper editor, following the path of Horace Greely, his boyhood idol. "Here at last," he had written to the Community, "was a splendid chance for some one to do a big thing for God, for humanity, and for himself." He had been chosen, supposedly, by God Himself. "God makes no blunders," he wrote. "The millions inhabiting the earth are before Him, and he selects the right man every time for the right place; and in this He always successfully check-mates the devil's moves."

In less than a week, Guiteau produced a prospectus for the *Theocrat*, declaring that the newspaper would be "what Christ wants and what the world needs." He went on to say, "The grand object of the paper would be to infuse into the public minds true ideas of God, of Christ, and of the spiritual world, and to establish a standard of righteousness by including the doctrine that the *fear* of the Lord is the beginning of wisdom."

In practical terms, he would provide a daily dose of salvation, albeit a strong dose. "Instead of person's spending one hour or two once in seven days in religious thought, we shall present them a theocratic daily each morning at their breakfast table, and thus introduce God into the practical affairs of life."

Due to a shortage of funds, the paper would begin as a weekly publication. As readership grew, it would become a daily. In size, it would resemble the *New York Sun*, but its overall look would be similar to the *Tribune*. The motto of the paper would be "PROMISE LITTLE, BUT DO MUCH." Obviously the *Theocrat* would be a "warm friend of the Bible," although "It may develop many new and strange biblical theories, differing widely from the teachings of popular theologians."

Under normal circumstances, Guiteau might have found a toehold, but there now followed a chain of events that overwhelmed his venture. On April 3, the very day he left for Hoboken, Richmond fell to Union troops. The capitol of the Confederacy was now in Northern hands! The news, of course, spread quickly. The Civil War, it seemed, was finally coming to an end.

Six days later, Lee surrendered to Grant, formally ending the conflict.

On the fourteenth, President Lincoln attended a cabinet meeting at which General Grant was present. Presumably the President was anxious to receive a firsthand account of the historic surrender. Later that evening, as publically announced, the President went to Ford's Theatre, and therein became the first American President to be assassinated.

The assassination shocked the populace and produced a climate of anger and fear that paralyzed the nation. Almost overnight, Guiteau developed a sense that he was doomed to fail. He was right. He soon ran out of funds and was forced to abandon his dream. Disheartened and broke, he wrote to John Humphrey Noyes begging for readmission to Oneida. "When I review the past," Guiteau wrote, "I marvel at the Community's patience and charity towards me and pray God for a true spirit of humility and repentance, and that I may become a Little Child, and loyally yield himself to the Community spirit, and to be a partaker of its life and love."

Surprisingly, Noyes allowed Guiteau to return, but he insisted that the self-described "little child" follow a strict and demanding regimen. The day would begin early, starting with morning prayers at six and ending with evening prayers at dusk. In between, Guiteau would be compelled to work at the trap factory, the place he despised the most. If he met his quota, he would be permitted to socialize, but he had to remain celibate. Under no circumstances would he be allowed to engage in sexual relations.

Guiteau probably did not know it, but his "upsets" had become a potential threat to a brand new program that was taking shape. In one of his darker moments, Noyes had concocted a eugenics theory, and he was about to introduce the Community to scientific propagation—the breeding of "perfect" children. He called the practice *stirpiculture*, a name derived from the Latin words *stirpis*, meaning race, and *cultura*, meaning culture. "We are opposed to random procreating," he wrote to a friend. "But we are in favor of intelligent, *well-ordered* procreation. The physiologists say that the race cannot be raised from ruin till propagation is made a matter of science."

In other words, if domestic animals could be bred, why not children?

Noyes was not unsympathetic to the concerns of his followers, but he was convinced that the Community would grow and prosper by adopting the practice of scientific propagation. His chief worry, as he reported to the elders, was twofold: First, that some ruffian might pollute the gene pool, (i.e., Guiteau) and second, that the outside world might view his noble experiment as another example of the sect's preoccupation with "free love." Manipulating Guiteau would be easy—or so he thought. The second concern would be harder to ameliorate. Much harder. When his intentions were discovered, the public was outraged. Noyes only fanned the flames by defending the incestuous nature of his program. "First," he told the press, "there must be, in the early stages, mating between very near relatives."

To no one's surprise, Noyes volunteered to "initiate" many of the teenage females—including his own niece. Later on, he would allow certain couples to mate, and their offspring, the *stirpicults*, would be housed in special quarters far removed from the Community at large. Noyes would justify the special treatment by declaring that "There can be no doubt that by segregating superior families, and by breeding them, superior varieties of human beings might be produced."

Writing years later, Noyes would reveal that the experiment involved 53 women and 38 men, each of them chosen by the founder himself or by committee. In the years between 1868 and 1879, 58 *stirpicults* were born. Nine of the children were fathered by Noyes himself.

For five difficult, wearisome months, toiling from dawn to dusk, and forced to restrain his sexual urges, Guiteau fought his demons to a draw. Then, on the evening of November 1, 1866, he packed his belongings and snuck out of town, leaving without a word of farewell.

When he arrived in New York City, he wrote to the Community hoping to explain his abrupt departure:

> My object in leaving clandestinely is two-fold: 1st, to obviate the necessity of a personal interview; and 2d, to go as quietly as possible, thereby sparing the feelings of all parties concerned. I, therefore, hope that you will look charitably upon the peculiar manner of my exit.

In the same letter, Guiteau also asked for the money he had previously donated to the Community. "In regard to a financial settlement, I have to request that you send me immediately a sight draft for seven hundred dollars."

The request was ignored, but Noyes did contact Luther Guiteau asking for his advice and guidance. A reply was promptly sent, and it shed a disturbing new light on Charles Guiteau's mental state:

> Perhaps it is useless for me to say that I was much grieved at the intelligence of Charles' desertion . . . there is evidently a species of insanity hanging about him, and it seems to me that this had been the case for a long time . . . . As to the question what is expedient and best for you to do about refunding any or all of what Charles claims, I hardly know what to say, I am quite sure of one thing that it probably would not be long before he would run through with the whole of whatever you might place at his disposal.

Noyes wrestled with the problem for a few days, and then in early December, he sent Charles fifty dollars, hoping to conclude the matter.

Guiteau quickly wrote back expressing his displeasure in no uncertain terms. "I regret that you should have troubled Father with my private affairs . . . I say now more emphatically if possible than heretofore, that I don't want to have any trouble with the Community, but I do want that money, and that too, as soon as possible."

For the second and, he hoped, the last time in his life, Noyes offered to pay a small portion of Guiteau's claim, but Guiteau would not accept partial payment. He demanded the full amount and not a penny less. Noyes was now convinced that Luther Guiteau was right. Charles was insane. The audacious whelp was nothing more than a "lascivious hypocrite" and a "greedy ruffian."

From this point on there were no more offers, but that did not stop Guiteau from pursuing his claim. He continued to write, and month after month, his correspondence grew increasing bitter. On February 8, 1868, he wrote:

> I write to ascertain if you *intend* to pay the claim. If it is not paid soon it will be bad for you and for your communities.

On February 19, he wrote:

> If you want to spend 10 or 20 years in Sing Sing and have your Communities "wiped out," don't pay it.

On March 2, 1868, he wrote:

> Again, I warn you, if you fall into the clutches of the law, you will not spend less than twenty years in State's prison.

Finally, on March 4, he penned his most angry letter, threatening the Community and its leaders. "Come on!" he wrote, "I am ready for a fight . . . Either the Oneida Community pays my claim or else it will be '*wiped out*.' He went on to declare that it was now "*war to the teeth*," and he demanded an immediate payment of nine thousand dollars—a sum arrived at by estimating a yearly wage of fifteen hundred dollars. Apparently, he had forgotten that he signed a waiver of compensation, or perhaps he didn't care. In Guiteau's troubled mind he had been a diligent worker, and by God, he was entitled to his wages. "When I get that money," he wrote his sister, "I am going to buy half a dozen Chicago lots, and let them grow."

Noyes, of course, had no intention of paying anything. Completely fed up, he referred the matter to his attorney, who in turn, threatened to sue Guiteau and put him in jail. Guiteau responded viciously, telling a reporter (a willing accomplice) that the Oneida Community had not been formed for a religious purpose but rather to satisfy the sexual needs of John Humphrey Noyes. Furthermore, he charged, "The girls that were born in the Community were forced to cohabit with Noyes at such an early period that it dwarfed them. The result was that most of the Oneida women were small and thin and homely."

As so often before when feeling battered and abused, Guiteau crossed the line of propriety and exposed himself to harsh retaliation. Noyes was incensed by the inflammatory remarks, and he instructed his attorney to go after Guiteau. They would accuse him of slander, and if that did not ruin him, they would charge him with extortion. One way or the other, he would pay for his sins. Meanwhile, Noyes had to clear his name, and in order to do so, he recruited Luther Guiteau. "I am sure," he wrote to Luther, "I have no ill will toward him [Charles].

I regard him as insane, and I prayed for him last night as sincerely as I ever prayed for my own son, that is now in a Lunatic Asylum." In truth, Luther did not need much convincing as he had come to the same conclusion about his son. Feeling a sense of shame and guilt, he wrote to the New York newspapers defending the Community and its "misunderstood" leaders. At Noyes's suggestion, he went on to attack his son, describing him as "lecherous," "frustrated," and "jealous."

Years later, when Guiteau was on trial for his life, a cross-examination showed him to be something much worse:

> A hypocrite, a swindler; cunning and crafty, remorseless, utterly selfish from his youth up, low and brutal in his instincts, inordinate in his love of notoriety, eaten up by a love of money; a lawyer who, after many years of practice in two large cities, had never won a case; a man who left in every state through which he passed a trail of knavery, fraud, and imposition.

In short, he was a moral monstrosity.

CHAPTER FIFTEEN

Four weeks after the battle of Chickamauga, Garfield came to Washington to report on the condition of the Army of the Cumberland. While he was in the capitol, he met with President Lincoln and was promoted to the rank of Major-General. The promotion came at an awkward time, as Garfield had recently won a lopsided victory for control of the Nineteenth Congressional District of Ohio. As both men knew, it had been a remarkable win. Unlike his opponent, Garfield had refused to campaign. In fact, he told his supporters, "I will take no steps whatever in the matter . . . Should the people of their own motion, without any suggestions from me, choose to nominate me for Congress, I should esteem it a mark of high favor."

In the end, Garfield was nominated without his knowledge, and he only accepted the nomination because he believed that the war would soon be over. He had received twice as many votes as his opponent, which was also remarkable considering that the Republican Party had been trounced in the October election, carrying only five of Ohio's nineteen Congressional seats.

Lincoln was pleased by the outcome but uncertain of Garfield's intentions. Did the general intend to resign his commission and take a seat in the Thirty-Eighth Congress?

Garfield was certainly tempted. "I would," he confessed, "rather be in Congress than the army, if there is to be no more active service . . . For I have no taste for the dull monotony of camp life."

Lincoln was pleasantly surprised by Garfield's admission, and he told him so. He had heard—probably from Secretary Stanton—that the general preferred to serve his country on the field rather than in the halls of state. After a few minutes of polite conversation, President Lincoln explained his own preference, and he did so in blunt language,

> The Republican majority in Congress is very small, and it is often doubtful whether we can carry the necessary war measures; and besides, we are greatly lacking in men of military experience in the House to regulate legislation about the army. It is your duty, therefore, to enter Congress, at any rate for the present.

So there it was, Garfield thought. Honest Abe had been painfully truthful, and now it was time to act. As if on cue, the general offered to resign his commission with the understanding that his rank would be restored if he desired to return to the army. Lincoln agreed, and on December 5, 1863, after three years of military service, James Garfield became a civilian. He now held the seat of Joshua Giddings, the staunch anti-slavery champion from the Congressional District of Ashtabula. In 1863, the district was comprised of the counties of Ashtabula, Lake, Geauga, Portage, and Trumbull. All told, it had a voting population of about twenty-five thousand. Most of the inhabitants hailed from New England and were, of course, Protestant.

Ironically, Giddings had been Garfield's boyhood idol. Prior to his death, in May 1864, Giddings had established himself as a leader of the "Radical Republicans," the political group that viewed the "peculiar institution" of slavery as a crime against liberty and humanity. Giddings came to Congress in 1838, when he was forty-three years of age, and he gave his first anti-slavery speech two years later. Never one to mince words, he caused a stir by referring to the war upon the Seminoles in Florida as a "slave hunt." One year later, he became embroiled in a slave revolt that shook the nation. In 1841, a brig named the *Creole*, sailing from Virginia to New Orleans, was seized by its slave cargo and forced to sail to the British port of Nassau, where, under British authority the slaves were granted freedom. Secretary of State Daniel Webster explained that the slaves were legal properties and demanded their return. By that time, slavery was illegal in Great Britain and her colonies, so the British ignored the claim. Seizing the high ground, Giddings introduced nine different resolutions arguing that Virginia state law did not apply to slaves outside of Virginian waters. The resolutions were widely denounced, and the House censured Giddings, who promptly resigned. Wounded by his colleagues' actions, he turned to his constituents and was re-elected by a large majority. He returned to Congress six weeks later and held his seat for the next twenty years.

Following in the footsteps of his predecessor, Garfield became an outspoken supporter of the war and a fierce opponent of slavery. Later, when it came to Reconstruction issues, he followed the lead of his fellow "radicals," eagerly waving the "bloody shirt" and never wavering from any civil-rights bill. Clearly he loved to debate, but his pedantic tone was somewhat annoying. His independent voting habits, also, alienated some powerful colleagues. On one occasion, Salmon P. Chase, the Secretary of the Treasury, warned his young protégé "that such antagonism to his party would better be indulged sparingly." As the record shows, Garfield got the message and moderated his views accordingly. From then on he rose steadily through party ranks and was soon appointed to the most important congressional committee of all, the Committee on Military Affairs. Consequently, he became involved with a number of difficult issues, including patent rights for the newly discovered anesthetic called chloroform, the confiscation of Confederate property, and most importantly, the great debate on the Thirteenth Amendment to the Constitution.

Oddly enough, the most vocal opponent of the "slavery amendment" was George H. Pendleton, a fellow Ohioan. It was Pendleton who argued that State institutions could not properly be interfered with by the Nation. "The right of a state," he declared, "was reserved in the spirit of the Constitution . . . Beyond recall, by the letter of that instrument."

In response to his colleague, Garfield took the floor and gave a stirring speech, eloquently denouncing slavery as an institution:

> Mr. Speaker, we shall never know why slavery dies so hard in this Republic and in this hall . . . With marvelous tenacity of existence, it has outlived the expectations of its friends and the hopes of its enemies. It has been declared here and elsewhere to be in the several stage of mortality—wounded, moribund, dead . . . It has sought in all corners of the Republic to find some hiding place in which to shelter itself from the death it so richly deserves . . . But now, in the hour of its mortal agony, in this hall, it has found a defender . . .

> We desire to follow it even there, and kill it beside the very altar of liberty. Its blood can never make atonement for the least of its crimes.

In the aftermath of Garfield's speech, fearing that the Emancipation Proclamation would be seen as a temporary war measure, the House of Representatives joined their Senate colleagues and ratified the Thirteenth Amendment, abolishing slavery everywhere in the United States. Lincoln signed the resolution on February 1, 1865, and two months later, the war ended.

Five days after signing the resolution, President Lincoln and his party went to Ford's Theatre. As the play, *Our American Cousin*, was drawing to a close, John Wilkes Booth entered the President's box, drew a Derringer pistol, and shot Mr. Lincoln in the head. The ball entered back of the ear, passed through the brain, and lodged just behind the right eye. The President lived for nine more hours, but he never regained consciousness.

Garfield was on his way from Washington to New York, and he did not learn of the tragedy until he reached his destination. The next morning, when the news reached the city, the public went wild. Large crowds began to gather and the mood quickly turned ugly. Two men shouted that "Lincoln ought to have been shot long ago." One of them was killed instantly and the other severely beaten and thrown in a ditch. Before long, there were fifty thousand people crowded into Wall Street, most of them armed to the teeth. The atmosphere was very tense. Suddenly from the balcony of the Exchange Building, Garfield appeared, waving his hand for silence. The crowd fell silent as he spoke in a clear, loud voice:

> Fellow citizens, clouds and darkness are round about Him! His pavilion is dark waters and thick clouds of the skies! Justice and judgement are the establishment of His throne! Mercy and truth shall go before His face! Fellow citizens! God reigns, and the Government at Washington still lives!

The effect, according to one eyewitness, was "tremendous." The crowd was mesmerized, and, when they recognized the speaker they began to cheer and applaud. "Who is he?" someone asked. "It is General Garfield from Ohio!"

Garfield's words had calmed the mob, and more importantly, they had prevented a riot. When asked to repeat his words to a reporter, he answered, "I cannot; I could not have told five minutes afterwards. I only know I drew the lightning from that crowd, and brought it back to reason."

When the Thirty-Ninth Congress met, in December 1865, Garfield resigned from the Committee on Military Affairs and became a member of the Committee on Ways and Means. The logic of this move was clear. Now that the war was over, the nation would be focused on matters of finance, a subject that was dear to Garfield's heart. Unlike most politicians, he was actually fascinated by the intricacies of tariffs, taxation, currency, and the public debt.

Alan Peskin, the author of *Garfield*, offers an analysis that seems both astute and credible:

"Some might regard these topics as dry, but not Garfield. To him, statistical tables were full of hidden romance, and economics, which many dismissed as the "dismal science," was capable of arousing his most intense passions."

At the first special session of the Forty-first Congress held in the Spring of 1869, Garfield spoke on his own behalf confirming Peskin's analysis:

> This is the age of statistics, Mr. Speaker. The word 'statistics' itself did not exist until 1749, whence we date the beginning of a new science on which modern legislation must be based, in order to be permanent . . . Statistics are State facts, facts for the consideration of statesmen, such as they may not neglect with safety. It has been truly said that 'statistics are history in repose; history is statistics in motion . . . The legislator without statistics is like the mariner at sea without the compass.

Generally speaking, Garfield favored a moderate protective tariff and a steady reduction of public expenditures and taxation. He was well aware that the war had damaged the nation's financial stability. In fact, the burden of debt was approaching three billion dollars. In addition, a great army was still disbanding, and they were about to be joined by four million recently emancipated slaves.

Then there was the South and the expensive headache of reconstruction. As one might expect, Garfield was generally unsympathetic to Southern grievances. During his first term, he pushed for a relentless prosecution of the war, and now, victorious, he was determined to extract his "pound of flesh." As a bona-fide radical, he advocated equal rights for the Negro, confiscation of rebel estates, and execution or exile for Confederate leaders.

It should be noted, however, that his "bitter medicine" did not prevent him from challenging the fairness of certain laws. In the first and most controversial case he ever tried, he went before the Supreme Court on behalf of some conspirators who had been tried by court-martial and condemned to death for treason. The defendants were obviously guilty, but they had been tried *after* the war was over in a section of Indiana that was not under martial law.

The legal questions were complex: Did any military body hold such power under the circumstances? Should the civil power be ignored in time of peace, or in sections of the country where martial law had not been proclaimed?

Despite his lack of legal experience, Garfield joined the fray, presenting a writ of *habeas corpus* to test the legality of the proceedings. His friends and supporters were perplexed. Why would a Civil War hero defend such men? What did he hope to accomplish?

The answer was simple; he firmly opposed the government's tendency to break all restraints of law in the exercise of its powers. In other words, he was worried that the federal government might become judge, jury and executioner.

After two days and nights of preparation, he presented his argument, and by most accounts, it was a thoroughly brilliant presentation. In closing, he spoke these eloquent words:

> Your decision will mark an era in American history. The just and final settlement of this great question will take a high place among the great achievements which have immortalized this decade. It will establish forever this truth, of inestimable value to us and to mankind, that a Republic can wield the vast enginery of war without

> breaking down the safeguards of liberty; can suppress insurrection and put down rebellion, however formidable, without destroying the bulwarks of law.

Garfield won the case and the defendants were set free. One of the lawyers involved called the presentation the greatest and bravest act of Garfield's life. "Like old John Adams," the lawyer gushed, "defending British soldiers for the Boston Massacre. Storms of obloquy and the sunshine of favor he alike disregarded for the sake of principle."

The newspapers called it something different—treachery. How could a certified radical betray his party and the nation? What had come over the general? Was he becoming one of those "gentle-hearted patriots" he so often derided? The answer, of course, was no. He was simply following in the footsteps of old John Adams, who had also tried an unpopular case, firm in the belief, as Adams had said, that no man in a free country should be denied the right to counsel and a fair trial.

Many years later, lying on his death bed, Garfield would defend the same proposition. Only this time he would be referring to his own assassin.

CHAPTER SIXTEEN

No one had worked harder or done more to alienate Congressional Republicans than Andrew Johnson, Lincoln's successor. By the end of his first year in office, the new president had become a lightning rod for congressional anger, openly challenging his own party. His performance as the wartime governor of Tennessee had suggested that he would take a hard line on Reconstruction issues, but once he became chief executive, he supported a "commingling between the citizens of the two sections." Even worse, he began to pardon the old leaders of the South, in effect, restoring them to power. When the Thirty-ninth Congress met, all of the Confederate states sent members, and, as one might expect, they received a less than warm reception. In fact, when Congress convened, the Republican radicals took the unprecedented step of locking them out of the chamber and removing their names from the House roll call. Kenneth D. Ackerman offers a clear-headed explanation of these events:

> The unrepentant all-white delegations included four Confederate generals, several colonels and lieutenants, and even Alexander

> Stephens, the Confederacy's vice president under Jefferson Davis. These recent warriors now expected coequal seats in Congress, as if an ocean of blood hadn't been spilled to squash their rebellion. To Union eyes, they were criminals, rebels with fresh murder on their hands and treason in their hearts.

Supposedly Garfield held no personal animus toward his defeated colleagues, but he was still adamantly opposed to readmitting any of the rebel states until they demonstrated, as he put it, "repentance." And as Allan Peskin notes, Garfield "feared that the process of reconciliation was proceeding with unseemly haste."

Garfield's uneasiness can best be understood by citing a speech delivered at Arlington Heights, issued over the graves of Union soldiers:

> If silence is ever golden, it must be here, beside the graves of fifteen thousand men, whose lives were more significant than speech, and whose death was a poem the music of which can never be sung . . . . We do not know one promise these men made, one pledge they gave, one word they spoke; but we do know they summed up and perfected, by one supreme act, the highest virtues of men and citizen. For love of country they accepted death.

In a passionate speech on the floor of Congress, Garfild reinforced his deeply held convictions:

> It was not one man who killed Lincoln; it was the embodied spirit of treason and slavery . . . When two hundred and fifty thousand brave spirits passed from the field of honor through that thin veil to

> the presence of God, and when at last its parting folds admitted the martyr-president to the company of the dead heroes of the republic, the nation stood so near the veil that the whispers of God were heard by the children of men.

Half-measures would not heal the wounds of the nation, Garfield knew. One way or the other the South would have to seek redemption, which meant that they would be forced to suffer some sort of humiliation. President Johnson would have none of it. Instead of seeking common ground, he began to pull away from the republicans, using the power of his veto to frustrate them at every turn. To his credit, Garfield warned his party that they might have to compromise a little to gain a lot.

Congress grew obstinate.

On January 22, 1866, the President delivered a "vulgar" speech in front of the White House, denouncing, by name, leading members of Congress and the Republican Party. In response, Garfield delivered a speech on the "Restoration of the Southern States." The speech reinforced Republican held views on recently freed slaves, but it did not directly challenge the President's authority. None the less, Johnson denounced the Congress as "an illegal body of traitors." In his view, the Republicans were "trying to break up the government." With these statements the president had, in Garfield's eyes, declared war on Congress and the American people.

Obviously, Johnson was more concerned with the South's resurrection than the safety of the republic. He had once declared that it was his intention to "punish traitors and to make treason odious," but now he was preaching forgiveness.

What neither Johnson nor Garfield nor anyone could have anticipated was how quickly the situation would deteriorate. In February 1868, Johnson "violated" the Tenure of Office Act by dismissing the Secretary of War, Edwin M. Stanton. The House promptly impeached him, setting the stage for a partisan, vindictive trial. In the end, the Radicals failed to convict by a single vote.

The debacle took a heavy toll on many in Congress, including Garfield. After months of bickering, he was emotionally and physically drained, and it showed in his correspondence to Colonel A.F. Rockwell. "My work during the last Congressional year has been harder than ever before," Garfield wrote.

> "I gave eighty days' hard work last summer and fall to the census. Then I spent forty days on the Gold Panic Investigation and Report. Then I gave three or four weeks' hard work to the Tariff Bill, and more than that amount to the Currency Bill. On the whole, I had done as much as I had any reason to hope I should."

Increasingly though, Garfield began to view his career in a different light, and what he saw did not please him. "Politics," he wrote, "where ten years of honest toil goes for naught in the face of one vote."

In another letter to Rockwell he speaks from the heart, holding nothing back. "I think of you as away, and in an elysium of quiet and peace, where I should love to be, out of the storm and in the sunshine of love and books. Do not think from the above that I am despondent. There is life and hope and fight in your old friend yet."

From the tone of Garfield's letter, it appears he was longing for a little peace and quiet. He had grown weary of Washington and was anxious to be, as he put it, "out of the storm." Unfortunately, there would be no chance to rest. The metaphoric storm was gaining strength, and before long, it would become a full-fledged hurricane.

Unquestionably, the Credit Mobilier Scheme was the low point of Garfield's political career. In the winter of 1872-73, the unblemished record of the much admired Ohioan was called into question, and it nearly cost him his job. Eight years earlier, the Union Pacific Railway stunned the nation by announcing that it intended to build a railroad extending from the Missouri River to the Pacific Ocean. To accomplish this great feat, tracks would be laid across the vast Midwestern plain, through the "alkali desert," and over the Rocky Mountains. To do this, the Union Pacific Railway partnered with several other companies, including the company that owned one hundred miles of land from Omaha west. This company was known as the Credit Mobilier of America.

The contract was executed in August 1867, and it contained an agreement to build a total of 677 miles of road. The cost was 47 million dollars, and as agreed, the national government would be the major financier. Hastily drawn, the contract left much to be desired. One of its major provisions placed all of the burdens and risks with the general government, shielding all of the companies and their private investors.

Sensing a golden opportunity, Oakes Ames, then a member of Congress from the state of Massachusetts, began to encourage private investment from the House and Senate. Ames was already a major investor, and by enlisting his colleagues, he hoped to defer any scrutiny. A Congressional investigation was the last thing he needed. Consequently, he began to offer Credit Mobilier stock, followed by a guarantee of a ten percent return on investment. Some paid cash for their shares, while others asked to be "carried" until they had the money. Garfield was thought to be among the latter group.

The fact was, the managers of the two companies had conspired to build the road for double its cost, bill the government, and pocket the profit. Eventually, due to greed and mistrust, the scheme imploded, sending shock waves through the Capitol. Almost overnight, reputations were destroyed and careers ruined. In the midst of all the chaos, Garfield wrote to President Hinsdale of Hiram College:

> The Credit Mobilier scandal has given me much pain. As I told you last fall, I feared it would turn and that the company itself was a bad thing . . . It has been a new form of trial for me to see my name flying the rounds of the press in connection with the basest of crimes . . . It is fortunate that I never fully concluded to accept the offer made me . . . I shall go before the committee, and in due time before the House, with a full statement of all that is essential to the case, so far as I am concerned.

On January 14, 1873, Garfield gave a statement under oath, testifying that "Mr. Ames never gave nor offered to give me any stock or other valuable thing as a gift." And he added, "I never owned, received, or agreed to receive any stock of the Credit Mobilier or of the Union Pacific Railroad, nor any dividends or profits arising from either of them."

Not content with denying the charges against him under oath, Garfield published a twenty-eight page pamphlet refuting the accusations that were besmirching his good name. Others might cower in the eye of a storm, but not Garfield. He proceeded to distribute seven thousand copies of his pamphlet. Every member of the Forty-Second Congress received a copy, as did many of his constituents and every major newspaper in the country. The report had its critics, but by and large it was accepted as truthful. "General Garfield's answer has been received by the American people as satisfactory," wrote a reporter from the *New York Evening Post*. "I would rather be beaten in right than succeed in wrong," Garfield said later. "If there be one thing upon this earth that mankind love and admire more than another, it is a brave man, a man who dares look the devil in the face, and tell him he is a devil."

Another charge brought against Garfield was that he had accepted a fee of five thousand dollars from a pavement contractor known as the De Golyer Company. At this time, Garfield was the chairman of the Committee on Appropriations, and it was charged that he took the money in exchange for his influence on the Hill. In truth, the fee was paid for legal services rendered, and it had nothing to do with influence peddling. As Garfield himself testified, paving appropriations were made by the Board of Public Works, a District entity, not by Congress. Once again, there was smoke but no fire.

Most politicians would have crumbled under such intense scrutiny, but Garfield grew stronger and wiser with each passing trial. As Garfield stated at the time:

> "It has been the plan of my life to follow my conviction. I have represented for many years a district in Congress whose approbation I greatly desired; but though it may seem, perhaps, a little egotistical to say it, I yet desired still more the approbation of one person, and his name is Garfield. He is the only man that I am compelled to sleep with; and eat with, and live with, and die with."

These were wise words, and they would soon be tested on the national stage.

CHAPTER SEVENTEEN

"See two things in the United States, if nothing else," Richard Cobden, the Liberal statesman advised. "See Niagra and Chicago." The British observer had a good point. One represented the wonder of America and the other her achievement.

In 1868, with his money gone and the authorities breathing down his neck, Guiteau chose the latter. He came to Chicago after a brief stop in Freeport, broke, bitter, and badly in need of a new trade. Amazingly, he decided to study law, which was a most unusual choice, considering his animosity toward lawyers. Maybe he was willing to forgive and forget, or perhaps he was hatching another grand scheme? Whatever the reason, be it fame, fortune, or simply revenge, he had made a decision, and nobody was going to change his mind. God willing, he would finally have a chance to make something of himself.

Chicago was just the place to do it. The city was growing rapidly, and by 1868, it bore little resemblance to the stagnant bayou "discovered" by Joliet and Marquette. In fact, that bayou, commonly called the Chicago River, now flowed north and south, separating the fourth largest city in

America. It was hard to believe that only three decades earlier a grand wolf hunt had been held in the city and that one bear and forty wolves had been killed.

Nowadays 300,000 people called the city home, and it was one of the busiest ports in the Midwest. Shortly before the war, a miraculous feat of engineering had drained the water and raised the principal streets. Michigan Avenue, for example, was now fully paved and twelve feet higher than at first. Unfortunately, there were still slums and large sections of the city that were filled with rickety wooden structures. Chicago was far from perfect, Guiteau knew, but still a good place to make a fresh start.

As soon as Guiteau got settled, he contacted his sister Frances and asked her to help him obtain a position. Frances was married to George Scoville, a prominent attorney who had many contacts. Scoville had his doubts about Guiteau, but for his wife's sake, he agreed to intercede. Eventually Guiteau obtained a position in the law offices of Reynolds and Phelps, where, typically enough he was moody and unreliable. "I did well," he later bragged. "I was industrious and had no bad habits, and was active in getting business."

In truth, Guiteau had plenty of bad habits and very few clients. After he was admitted to the Illinois bar, he spent most of his time collecting bills and debts. When that proved unprofitable, he devised a scheme to enrich himself at his employer's expense. Simply put, he would collect a small down payment on an overdue bill and then tell the creditor that the balance was uncollectable. The down payment would then be kept for "payment of services," but there would be no effort to collect the remainder.

By coincidence, perhaps, Guiteau spent a great deal of time on Sangamon, Halsted, Lake and Monroe Streets—the streets that bordered the notorious Red Light district. In all likelihood, he was familiar with some of the district's inhabitants, including, Julie Johnson, a midget who was famous—or infamous—for her provocative exhibition at the Diddie Briggs Brothel.

Whatever the case, Guiteau was down and out when he met Annie Bunn, a librarian at the Y.M.C.A. Annie was eighteen years old, living on her own, and supporting herself. She had been born back east and raised by a prominent Philadelphia woman named Lydia Needles. The Needles had taken her in at eleven, shortly after her father's death. Despite her young age, she was, apparently, the mother of an illegitimate child. The child was probably given up for adoption, which might explain her abrupt departure from the City of Brotherly Love.

Guiteau was smitten by the young librarian but not quite ready to surrender his bachelorhood. Some time after they met, he began to pursue another woman, but this one wanted nothing to do with him. That did not stop Guiteau. He began to stalk her and he even had the audacity to show up on her front porch. After several unwelcomed visits, her father invited Guiteau inside, then locked him in a room and called the police. He managed to escape, but he returned a few nights later. This time, he was caught by a neighbor and severely beaten. It was the last they saw of him.

The following year, Guiteau was charged with stealing books from the Y.M.C.A. reading room. He was arrested and prosecuted, but acquitted of all charges. The incident caused some embarrassment, but not enough to interfere with his pursuit of Annie Bunn. After a brief courtship, Guiteau proposed and Annie gave her consent. They were married by the Reverend William Alvin Bartlett, pastor of the First Congregational Church, on July 3, 1869.

It was not a happy union. Not only did Guiteau continue his bill-collecting scheme, but he also insisted on bragging about it to his new bride. On one occasion, he became giddy boasting that he had just sold a worthless watch for twenty-five dollars. Apparently he had convinced an elderly pawn-broker that the watch was gold when in fact it was oroide. "I cheated that old Jew!" he announced triumphantly. "He had it coming."

Annie was beside herself. Why was he so gleeful? What sort of man did she marry? Years later, she would testify:

> "I lived in continual anxiety and suspense. I was constantly expecting that something would happen to him, during that time, because I knew how people felt toward him, and if he was late at mealtime or was out unusually late in the evening, I was in constant fear that something had happened to him. I became so sure of it that the least unexpected noise in the house or hall, would startle me, and I would think that perhaps he had been attacked or killed or injured in some way."

To a real extent, it was Annie who was in the most danger. As she soon discovered, it did not take much to rile her husband, and once he snapped, there was no turning back. The abuse was mostly verbal, but as time went on, he became increasingly violent. Incoherent lectures were followed by insults and threats, and then she would be forced to remain in the hallway for hours. Sometimes he would tie her hands to the stairway railing and make her sleep on the floor. If the neighbors complained, he would drag her inside by the hair and lock her in a dark closet. "I am your master!" he would shout. "You are to submit yourself to me!"

The police were seldom called, and when they did show up, they were reluctant to interfere with a domestic dispute. Knowing this, Guiteau would act contrite and promise to control his temper. He was a good actor, Annie explained. "He was able to explain satisfactorily all his questionable doings, and his manners were so pleasant and so agreeable to strangers that he was continually making friends."

During the marriage, Guiteau insisted upon living in a boarding house, ostensibly to avoid the cost of owning a home. The problem was that he never paid bills, which meant that he and his wife were forced to lead a nomadic life. Time after time they were ejected from their room, often without their luggage. On these occasions, Guiteau would sneak back at night and retrieve whatever he could or convince his wife to beg for their belongings. For Annie the shame was almost unbearable:

> "I remember one occurrence particularly. We were staying at a boarding house on Wabash Avenue . . . The woman became very tired of having us there . . . At last she notified Charles that he would have to find another place, as she needed the room for some one who would pay her cash every week . . . We had two or three trunks at that time, and when we came back to vacate she would not let us take our baggage along with us, and we had to depart without anything save what we were wearing . . . Charles said he knew the room in which the trunks were stored . . . that he would walk right into the house and into the room and have the trunks out before the woman could know anything about it."

"There is not one man in five hundred who would have attempted that," Guiteau said later. "They would be afraid they would be shot at. But not I; nobody will beat me, for I will be even with them in the end!"

As time would show, the end was very close. Back then, most of the buildings were made of wood or a combination of wood and brick. Many of the sidewalks were made from pine and hemlock. These materials were stored in lumber yards along the river, and by some estimates, the yards contained roughly 300 million feet of lumber. They also contained huge piles of lath and shingles, and an assortment of flammable liquids.

In addition, the entire South side was surrounded by furniture factories, carriage and wagon factories, and paint and varnish shops. These businesses produced many goods, and they also produced an abundance of wood chips, wood shavings, and sawdust. As one observer wrote, "It might be said, with considerable justice, that Chicago specialized in the production, handling, and storage of combustible goods."

Like most Chicagoans, Guiteau was oblivious to the dangers that surrounded him. If he had been more observant, he might have noticed that it was warm, unusually warm for early October, and very dry. During the past three months, only two and a half inches of rain had fallen. In prior years the average amount of rain had been closer to nine inches. The long dry spell had transformed Cook County into a tinderbox, but nobody seemed to take notice of the bare trees, parched lawns or dry wells.

Nobody noticed any of it until it was too late.

The first two fires were small, and they were quickly brought under control by the courageous work of the Fire Department. But then, on the evening of October 8, the O'Leary barn caught fire, and with the help of a strong south wind, the flames spread quickly. Around midnight, the fire jumped across the river and turned to the north, destroying everything in its path.

On Monday morning the inferno claimed the entire business district, including Guiteau's office on Randolph Street. The North Side was hit next, and shortly thereafter, the South Side.

The scene on Tuesday morning was one of utter devastation. The burnt area stretched north and south for nearly five miles, and in most sections, it was a mile wide. In less than twenty-four hours, the flames had swept across twenty-one hundred acres, killed three hundred people, and destroyed seventeen thousand buildings. Over one hundred thousand people, a third of the population, were now homeless.

Moreover, an entire city had been traumatized, many driven to despair and some scarred for life. Among the scarred were Guiteau and his wife. They had managed to escape without injury but now were left with nothing except the clothes on their back. Like thousands of others, they had lost everything, and their dreams had literally gone up in smoke.

CHAPTER EIGHTEEN

Only a fool would have gone back to New York, but Guiteau was desperate and had no desire to return to Freeport, Illinois. There were, of course, other options. Annie preferred Philadelphia, but her husband was not fond of Quakers and refused to live in a city that was so grand. No, he insisted, New York was the place to go. A clever fellow could make a lot of money in Manhattan.

He could also make a lot of mischief.

The war had taken a heavy toll on southern ports, but New York Harbor was thriving as it had become a smuggler's paradise. There were over one hundred and thirty piers in Lower Manhattan, and they were always busy, especially at night. The waterfront district contained three thousand rum shops, two thousand opium dens, and a score of gambling parlors. It also supported thirty thousand professional criminals, a majority of whom were extremely violent.

Nonetheless, Guiteau brought his wife to the Cortlandt Street Hotel, a seedy establishment on the west side, two blocks north of Trinity Church. They had ten dollars between them, but that did not stop Guiteau from renting a small office on Liberty Street or ordering business cards that read:

Charles J. Guiteau,
Attorney and Counselor-at-Law
of the Supreme Court

As brazen as ever, he began to solicit business, and, for a while, he made a decent living. Tormented by the thought of being robbed, he began to carry a small black cane with a large round head. The head was "loaded," as they said back then, and used for self-defense. When his wife asked why he carried such a deadly device, he answered, "Well, if I were to be attacked by anybody I could turn around and strike him and kill him, and I could disappear and no one would find out." Annie was alarmed. Did he really expect to be attacked? "I don't know but that one of these mean, dirty, low-lived whelps," as he termed his clients, "might try to get even with me, and it is best for a man to be on his guard, so that in case of an attack at night by any one, I can turn around and give him a hit that will kill him."

Before long, Guiteau became disenchanted with his quarters, and he began to withhold the rent. When confronted, he remained pleasant, but evasive. "I am very sorry to keep you so long," he told the landlord. "I appreciate your kindness. I expected money today, but didn't get it, but I shall probably be able to settle with you tomorrow."

Tomorrow never came, and as the new year commenced, Guiteau became increasingly annoyed by the audacity of his landlord, who was now demanding full payment—plus a carrying charge. "I will tell you what it is," he told his wife. "I haven't got the money to pay, and I presume I had better leave. I hate to be annoyed about board."

As always, the problem was how to sneak out without getting caught. The room they shared was on the second floor, in a corner of the hotel, facing the street. Guiteau thought it over, then told his wife to go downstairs and wait on the front porch. When nobody was looking, he would throw down their clothes. Annie was appalled, and she refused to cooperate. "You are a jackass!" he told her. "You have no sense. I had no business to have a wife anyhow; if I had not a wife I would have none of this annoyance about board bills."

Whether, in fact, they left with their belongings is not altogether clear, but they did escape without detection and without paying a penny. Their next stop was a "high toned" boarding house on 22nd Street. "Nothing but the best," Annie later recalled. "That was his great objective—always to be among them and to live at the most expensive places and to have the best accommodations; he was not satisfied to live in plain style anywhere."

Perhaps it was Guiteau's obsession of wealth that led to his next endeavor. In the summer of 1872, he became enthralled with presidential politics and the "inevitable" election of Horace Greely. "He talked of him continually," Annie wrote later. "He became infatuated with the idea of going into the canvass and doing everything he possibly could for the election of that gentleman."

Beginning in June, Guiteau wrote speeches for the candidate, and from time to time, they were actually used. In addition, he was allowed to address small audiences but only in the poorest sections of the city. It was, in all, a heady experience, but what appears to have pleased him the most was reading about himself in the newspapers.

When Annie complained that he was ignoring his legal practice, Guiteau replied:

> We will have to put up with these things for a while. After a time I will have a good position. There is no doubt that Mr. Greely will be elected; and as soon as he is elected, I shall see him and tell him of the work I have done, and shall ask him as a compensation for the services I have rendered, to appoint me to that [Chilean] foreign mission.

If Greely had won the election, he would have seen a lot of Charles Guiteau. As it turned out, he was soundly defeated by Ulysses S. Grant. Despite Greely's fame, he carried only six states and lost the popular vote by a wide margin. Sadly, that was just the beginning of his downfall. Shortly after the election, his wife died and he descended into madness and passed away before the electoral votes were cast.

Guiteau was devastated. He had come so close to achieving his dream of becoming a big man. In his view, life was so unfair. The melancholy that beset him was unrelenting, and it became even worse when he learned that his wife was pregnant. Now he would have another mouth to feed and another person to hold him back.

Typically, his frustration turned to rage, and Annie paid the price. By the time the baby came, she was battered, bruised and woefully malnourished. The baby died shortly after birth.

Afterwards, Annie became seriously ill, and it appeared as though she might die. Guiteau was badly shaken, and for the first time in his adult life he showed genuine compassion. In her "memoir" she wrote: "The only instance that he ever seemed really sensitive and interested in my happiness was immediately following a severe illness, when my life was despaired of and I was in profound grief at the loss of our only child, who died at birth, and whose death he knew was caused wholly by his brutal treatment of its mother."

She went on to say:

> "At the time he would occasionally display a spark of kindness by stroking my hair and pitying my thin, wearied appearance, and would study my comfort, and even bring me little delicacies and luxuries. He did at such times profess to regret his conduct, and promise, if I would only recover, never to act unkindly again."

But change was not Guiteau's strong suit. As soon as his wife was up and about he made a confession: During her illness he had succumbed to temptation and slept with a "lewd woman," who happened to be in the same boarding house. Even worse, he now had a venereal disease.

Annie was broken-hearted, but she did not have the will to leave.

> "In the summer of 1873, while I was living with him in New York City, he had a very long illness—resulting from his intimacy with improper women . . . I nursed him and took care of him through that sickness . . . . He was a very great sufferer and came very near dying . . . He was very much reduced on account of it, and in the worst stages of his illness he was entirely helpless . . . I was almost sure he would never recover from it."

As a matter of fact, he never did fully recover. Disease kept him in bed for three full months, and during that time he lost a considerable amount of muscle. He did recover most of his strength, but for the rest of his life he walked with a limp.

It was characteristic of Annie to put her faith in redemption, even when it came to her own brutal husband. All things were possible, she told herself. Charles had nearly died. Now he was back on his feet, struggling to make something of himself. Perhaps he would be grateful to her. After all, she had remained at his side, nursed him back to health, and forgiven his infidelity. What more could he ask?

Within weeks, she had her answer. What Guiteau really wanted—and needed—was someone to control. A person to humiliate. "You have such a terrible will," he told her. "Your will was never broken when you were a child, and the sooner you know that you are in subjection to me, why, the better it will be for you."

After several months of nursing, Annie was in no mood to take orders. As time passed, she began to display a small degree of independence. Naturally, this infuriated her husband, and one bad day followed another. By her own account, he became exceedingly cruel.

> Many times, while in such moods, when I have not knowingly offended him, he has taken hold of me suddenly, opened the door perhaps, wherever we might be boarding, and kicked me right out into the hall and fastened me there. It made no difference who was out there, or who was passing along the hall; it would have made no difference if I had fallen down-stairs from the kick or push. I do not think he would have opened the door to have seen whether I had fallen down and broken my neck or not.

At these times Guiteau seemed devoid of all reason, and he was capable of saying the most outrageous things. If she threatened to leave him, he would tell her, "Nothing would suit me better." With a smile he would add:

> "When you make up your mind to find other quarters, the better it will suite me, for you are not the kind of woman that I should have married any way. I want somebody who could help me. If I married a girl who had money—whose father, for instance, or some one belonging to the family had means, and could have helped me—it would have been a different thing. But you are poor; you have no one who can help you, who perhaps, could give you a meal if you wanted it, and I have no business with a woman like you. You are good enough and kind enough, but I made a great mistake when I married you."

These words had a chilling effect on Annie's heart, and she began to doubt herself. What if he were right? What if she was holding him back? Perhaps it was time to think about leaving. In the meanwhile, the abuse continued. "This conduct was repeated, time and time again. Until I became mentally crushed; my life was saddened; I got into the habit of constantly feeling so distressed, and so unhappy, that I would rather have died than lived. Existence was a perfect agony to me."

CHAPTER NINETEEN

The political predictability of Washington was shattered by the elections of 1874, which gave the Democrats control of the House for the first time since the beginning of the Civil War. When the Forty-fourth Congress convened, the Democrats chose a new speaker, new committee heads, and a radically new agenda.

They also stopped "waving the bloody shirt," which referred to the practice of politicians referencing the blood of martyrs or heroes in the Civil War.

Early in the session they began to debate a controversial proposal to grant amnesty to hundreds of Confederate leaders including Jefferson Davis, the "Father of the Confederacy." Understandably, the Republicans were outraged. The Republican party was filled with Union veterans, and they remembered the atrocities that characterized military imprisonment in the South. Most blamed Davis, not for condoning the torture, but for allowing it to happen under his watch. As the leader of the rebellion, he should have known about Belle Isle, Libby Prison, and Andersonville.

Others spoke, but it was Garfield who delivered the most reasoned condemnation of the proposal:

> I do not object to Jefferson Davis because he was a conspicuous leader. Jefferson Davis was no more guilty for taking up arms than any other man who went into the rebellion with equal intelligence. But this is the question: In the high court of war did he practice according to its well-known law—the laws of nations? Did he, in appealing to war, obey the laws of war; or did he so violate those laws, that justice to those who suffered at his hands demands that he be not permitted to come back to his old privileges in the Union?

In short, the House was faced with two main questions. Did atrocities occur in Southern prisons? If so, was the Confederate President responsible? Garfield knew for a fact that atrocities had occurred, and he was convinced that Davis was to blame. To prove his point, he presented a mass of evidence, much of it drawn from Confederate sources. In addition, he flooded the House with telegrams from Union veterans. Between cheers, he offered the following summation:

> Toward those men who gallantly fought us on the field I cherish the kindest feeling. I feel a sincere reverence for the soldierly qualities they displayed on many a well-fought battle-field. But there was a class of men referred to in the speech of the gentleman yesterday for whom I have never yet gained the Christian grace necessary to say the same thing. Do not, for the sake of the three hundred thousand heroic men who, maimed and bruised, drag out their weary lives, many of them carrying in their hearts horrible memories of what

> they suffered in the prison-pen—do not ask us to vote to put back into power that man who was the cause of their suffering—that man still unaneled, unshriven, unforgiven, undefended.

In effect, Garfield's speech had drawn a clear distinction between the Republican and Democratic parties, and his efforts were greatly appreciated by the current administration. As Peskin notes, "President Grant personally thanked Garfield on behalf of a presumably grateful nation, and the Republican National Committee printed literally millions of copies for use in the coming campaign." Reportedly, the Grand Old Party was in deep trouble, and it needed all the help it could get.

In the first of two four-year terms, Grant had failed to live up to expectations, and by the end of his second term he was seen as inept. Grant had remained honest, but as Garraty notes, he lacked the qualities that had made him a fine military leader. "When, for example, Congress failed to act upon his suggestion that the quality of the civil service needed improvement, he announced meekly that if Congress did nothing he would assume the country did not want anything done and dropped the subject."

For someone with so much common sense, Grant was remarkably naïve, and that contributed to him becoming the dupe of unscrupulous friends and schemers. During his eight years in office, his administration was linked to a number of scandals such as the Whiskey Ring affair, which implicated his private secretary, and the management of Indian affairs, which implicated the Secretary of War.

Against this backdrop, the Presidential election of 1876 took place. The leading contender on the Republican side was James G.

Blaine, the dynamic Speaker of the House of Representatives. Under normal circumstances, Blaine would have easily won the nomination, but these were not normal times. After eight years of scandal, the Republicans needed a squeaky clean candidate, and Blaine had recently been connected with some chicanery involving railroad securities. As a consequence, the party nominated Rutherford B. Hayes, the Governor of Ohio. The Democrats picked Samuel J. Tilden, the crime-fighting governor of New York.

In keeping with the times, the election ended in a bitter dispute as both sides claimed victory and refused to yield.

In truth, Tilden had won the popular vote by 250,000 votes, which seemed to give him 203 electoral votes to Hayes' 165. However, the Republicans had anticipated defeat and they were ready to steal the election. Accordingly, they telegraphed their henchmen to invalidate the Democratic ballots that had been cast in Florida, South Carolina, and Louisiana. The Democrats protested—and then they filed their own returns.

Now they had to recount the votes. But who was to do the counting? The House was controlled by the Democrats and the Senate by the Republicans. Neither would agree to allow the other to do the job. Finally, a month before Inauguration Day, Congress created the Electoral Commission to decide the case. The commission was comprised of five senators, five representatives, and five justices of the Supreme Court. The two parties were equally represented, and in order to break a tie they appointed one "independent."

On principle, Garfield opposed the commission and spoke against its creation on the floor of the House. "What, then, are the grounds on which we should consider a bill like this?" he asked his colleagues.

"The present good which we shall achieve by it may be very great; yet if the evils that will flow from it in the future must be greater, it would be base in us to flinch from trouble by entailing remediless evils upon our children."

Garfield had many questions about the commission's role, but his main concern was how the commission would affect the Electoral College. "In my view, then, the foremost question is this: What will be the effect of this measure upon our institutions?"

For Garfield, at least, the question was never fully answered. Nonetheless, the Electoral Commission was constituted by law, and Garfield himself was chosen to be a judge. He accepted, saying, "Since you have appointed me, I will serve. I can act on a committee when I do not believe in its validity."

On that promising note, the committee met, debated, and came to a decision. In the end, Hayes won by a vote of 8 to 7, but the Democrats refused to abide by the outcome.

Their candidate had won fair and square, and now they were being told that the election was flawed. Angered by such a blatant show of corruption, fifteen states called for volunteers to march on Washington. If Congress would not inaugurate Tilden, they would.

Fortunately, cooler heads prevailed, and the Compromise of 1877 was born. In essence, Southern Democrats agreed to accept Hayes in exchange for ending federal interference in their internal affairs. In addition, Hayes agreed to appoint a conservative Southerner to his Cabinet.

Seemingly, Hayes was the perfect man for the job. Unlike Tilden, he had modest ambitions and saw himself more as a caretaker rather than a leader. As one biographer wrote, "He had no intention of trying to be a President in the heroic mold." In contrast to Blaine, he did not enjoy or encourage controversy, and he hated to make difficult decisions. In the eyes of his contemporaries he was politically temperate, cautious, and utterly predictable.

Interestingly, he did not start out that way. In his younger days, Hayes had been more daring, even reckless. After the attack on Fort Sumter, he left his wife and family and volunteered for service. He fought bravely through nearly four years of war and was wounded at South Mountain on the eve of Antietam. After a brief absence, he served under Sheridan in the Shenandoah Valley campaign of 1864. As he often mentioned on the campaign trail, he had entered the army as a major and emerged as a major general.

Like many ex-soldiers, including Grant and Garfield, Hayes did not enjoy waving the bloody shirt, and that alone made him a perfect "compromise candidate." Reportedly, he wanted to focus on civil service reform, which suited the Democrats just fine.

There was just one problem. Like all compromises, this one had its share of flaws. Those "flaws" had a serious effect on the former slaves. John A. Garraty, author of *The American Nation*, describes the period following 1877 as "gloomy," but in reality it was far worse.

> "Forgotten in the North, manipulated and then callously rejected by the South, rebuffed by the Supreme Court, voiceless in national affairs, he and his descendants were condemned in the interests of sectional harmony to lives of poverty, indignity, and little hope. Meanwhile, the rest of the United States continued its golden march toward wealth and power."

By coincidence, 1877 marked the beginning of the Gilded Age. Most white Americans were optimistic; business was booming; and, the future looked bright. Day after day, there were reports of marvelous discoveries and wondrous new inventions.

One year earlier, an inventor named Bell began to experiment with a "speaking telegraph" that used electrified metal discs, acting like the drum of the human ear, to convert sound waves into electrical impulses and electrical impulses back into sound waves. The device was originally intended to aid deaf mutes in learning to speak, and at first, it was considered a clever gadget, or in the words of a competitor, an "electrical toy." Within three years the "toy" would become a fixture in 85 towns and cities, and one day it would become the cornerstone of the American Telephone and Telegraph Company.

Oddly enough, it would also be used to locate an assassin's bullet.

CHAPTER TWENTY

As time passed, Annie realized that Charles would never change and that, sooner or later, she would be seriously injured or even killed. She had hoped time would diminish his rage, but it appears to have had the opposite effect. If anything, he became meaner and more violent. As their marriage deteriorated, he began to flaunt his infidelity, amused by his wife's reaction. This essentially ended their union.

Annie finally left him, and, in the fall of 1873, she filed for absolute divorce on the ground of adultery. Guiteau did not contest the suit. In fact, he bolstered her case by sleeping with another prostitute and then bringing her to court to testify.

On April 4, 1874, Justice Calvin E. Pratt of Kings County, New York, issued the following decree:

DECREE OF DIVORCE

In the Supreme Court

Kings County.

Annie J. Guiteau, against Charles J. Guiteau Deft.	}	At a speical term of this Court held at the city of Brooklyn, April Pltf. 4, 1874 Present: Hon. C.E. Pratt, Justice.

This action having been brought on to be heard upon complaint herein and upon proof of the defendant's failure to answer, and upon the report of Levi A. Fuller, Esq., duly appointed referee in this action, from which it appears that the material facts alleged in the complaint are true, and that the defendant has committed the adultery charged therein, on motion of Warren G. Brown, plaintiff's attorney,

It is adjudged, That the marriage between the said plaintiff Annie J. Guiteau and the defendant Charles J. Guiteau be dissolved in pursuance of the statute in such case made and provided, and the same is hereby dissolved accordingly, and the said parties are and each of them is freed from the obligations thereof with fifty-one 55/100 dollars costs of this action to the plaintiff, and the privilege to her of applying to the court at such time as she shall be advised for a suitable allowance for her support in the nature of alimony.

And it shall not be lawful for the said Charles J. Guiteau to marry again until the said Annie J. Guiteau is actually dead.

Annie did not attend the proceedings, but she did get stuck with the legal fees after Charles refused to pay his share. Shortly thereafter, she returned to Chicago and began a new life. Without any constraints, Guiteau was free to resume his criminal career, and that is exactly what he did. Even as he gained a reputation as a "dead beat," he continued to collect bills, charged a commission of fifty percent, and, as often as not, failed to pay his client the balance. Needless to say, he made a lot of enemies, including James Gordon Bennett, the publisher of the New York *Herald*. As a result, he was soon exposed in print in an article titled "A Profitable Collecting Lawyer."

According to Guiteau, the article was written in a "sharp and witty" fashion and meant to be harmful. Not surprisingly, he demanded a full apology. He did not get one. The law editor refused to print a retraction and so did the managing editor. To this, Guiteau responded by suing the *Herald* for libel.

The motion was heard before a judge. During the hearing, Guiteau asked for a "modest" settlement of one hundred thousand dollars. He told the judge:

> Prior to the *Herald* publication I was doing well. I had clients and every prospect of success. After the *Herald* publication my clients got demoralized, and the newspapers talked about it a good deal at the time and it demoralized me, and, to make it brief, I got all rundown and run out.

At the same time he was not too "rundown" or "run out" to obtain a room at the fancy St. Nicholas Hotel. When the judge dismissed his suit, Guiteau tried to sneak out of the city, but he was caught by a hotel detective and arrested for "false pretense." The next thing he knew, he was back in court, only this time as a defendant. When he went to trial, he pleaded "not guilty," but six different landlords testified against him, virtually ensuring his conviction. Justice Sherman Smith, having heard the testimony on both sides, punished the defendant by sending him to the New York Halls of Justice and House of Detention—also known as the Tombs.

The place was truly hell on earth. Built in 1838, the prison resembled an ancient Egyptian mausoleum, and it was every bit as inviting. Inside, it was dark, damp, and crowded. In 1873, it accommodated about three hundred prisoners but often held twice that number. Due to overcrowding, the place reeked of urine and human excrement, but the worst odors came from the swampy landfill beneath the foundation. Those odors were thought to cause ague.

In a letter to a friend, Guiteau described his feelings about incarceration:

> I had no money and no relatives in the city, and I languished in prison for over five long and dreary weeks, hourly and daily expecting and hoping and praying for my release, as I knew my detention was wholly illegal. Finally it came, thank God! I was free again. Free to breathe the sweet air of heaven; free to go and come; free to do my own will; free to eat, drink, and sleep like decent people, and to associate with them. No one never imprisoned can realize the horrors of confinement. It is a lingering death.

After his release, Guiteau skittered from city to city, from scheme to scheme, finally landing in Chicago in the winter of 1876. While attending a revival, he ran into his ex-wife, but they did not speak. "I think he recognized me," Annie wrote later. "For as soon as he got a glimpse of me he turned directly around the other way." Days later, she got a surprise visit from Guiteau, and recorded her thoughts:

I was living with some friends, and one day, during the winter, I was informed that a stranger had called and wished to see me. When I entered [the parlor] Charles extended his hand and shook hands with me very pleasantly, inquired how long I had been there, and where I had been in the meantime.

> According to Annie, Guiteau talked in a very affable and amiable manner, but there was something odd about his appearance. "It was a very severe, cold day, one of the most bitter days of the winter, and I noticed as soon as I came into the room that he wore no overcoat and no gloves. I remember thinking that he certainly must be cold."

Only gradually did the conversation turn to Guiteau, and, when it did, the news was all bad. In short, the past twelve months had been hell. After a brief stint in the Chicago Municipal Prison, he went to visit his sister at her Wisconsin summer home, but the trip had ended on a sour note. According to Guiteau, Frances had become something of a nag. Had Annie known the truth, she would have probably called the police.

One afternoon, Frances asked Charles to cut some wood for the stove, but it was a very hot day and he did not wish to exert himself. Apparently, she had to raise her voice, which angered Charles and caused him to leave the house. Eventually he went to work. The more he cut; the angrier he became. When Frances came out to check on him, he raised the axe as if to strike her. "He looked like a wild animal," she would later testify. Luckily, he did not strike her, but that might have been because she ran into the house and locked herself in a room.

To Charles, the low point of the year was marked by a business failure. Earlier that fall, he had tried to buy the *Chicago Inter-Ocean*, a local newspaper that was doing quite well and far beyond his grasp. Nevertheless, he intended to retool the paper, making it the most influential daily in the West. All he lacked was funding. Nobody would lend him a dime, not even his own family.

Annie advised him not to dwell on the failure of the enterprise. There was more than one way to make a living. For instance, he still had his law practice.

"I have given up the law business," he informed her. "I am working now for the Lord." When pressed to explain, he said, "I am engaged to a lady of wealth. She is very good and very pretty, and beside all that, she is a devoted Christian woman." And then he added, "She and I are going to work together in this cause—working for the Lord."

Guiteau was reluctant to mention the woman's name, but he promised to introduce her when the time was right. From what Annie could tell, her ex-husband was still a troubled soul. In any event, she allowed him to visit and warm himself by the fire. He was always polite and well-mannered, and he never overstayed his welcome. In some ways, he seemed to be courting her, but she had no interest in that sort of thing. At this point she was stronger and wiser, and she had no intention of making the same mistake twice. Besides, she had met another man and was deeply in love.

When Guiteau heard of her relationship, he became silent. He managed a weak smile but could not muster the grace to wish her well. No matter, she did not expect him to be overjoyed. Charles had never been overly concerned about her happiness.

Still, she could not bear to see him so disheveled. On his last visit, she gave him a pair of gloves, but he seemed puzzled by the gift. "They are of no use to me," he told her. "Because I have no overcoat; I have no pocket to put them in."

Days later, she learned that Charles had been evicted by an irate landlord. His coat was still in the landlord's possession. Even stranger, he had not been staying at a hotel, but at a nearby boarding house. Before anything could be done, however, he disappeared as abruptly as he had arrived.

By the spring of 1878, Guiteau was back in New York, spreading the gospel and saving souls. In March of that year he traveled from Brooklyn to Newark, where he delivered a lecture at the opera house. Back then, Newark had 130,000 inhabitants, and it was the leading commercial and manufacturing city in the state. Like Brooklyn, it was also a city of churches and church-going people. Most congregants belonged to either the Reformed Dutch Church, which dated from 1663, or the first Presbyterian, which began in 1667. All in all, Newark was the perfect place to speak about Hell or, more precisely, the *possibility* of Hell.

After introducing himself as The Little Giant from the West, Guiteau gave a short, incoherent speech and then abruptly left the podium. The audience was flabbergasted, but after fifteen minutes of pure torture, they were convinced that Hell did indeed exist. The newspapers agreed. The *Newark Daily Journal* published the following review, under the headline, "Is there a Hell?"

FIFTY DECEIVED PEOPLE ARE OF THE OPINION THAT THERE OUGHT TO BE

The man Charles J. Guiteau, if such really is his name, who calls himself an eminent Chicago lawyer, has fraud and imbecility plainly stamped upon his countenance, and it is not surprising that his "lecture" in the Opera House last evening did not leave a pleasant impression on the minds of the fifty people who assembled to hear him . . .

His lecture was a wonderful production of genius. It consisted of the averment that the second coming of Christ occurred in the year 70 when Jerusalem was destroyed; interesting readings from the book of Genesis, and the prediction that the world would soon come to an end.

Although the impudent scoundrel had talked only fifteen minutes, he suddenly perorated brilliantly by thanking the audience for their attention and bidding them goodnight. Before the astounded fifty recovered from their amazement, or the half dozen bill collectors who were waiting for an interview with the lecturer had comprehended the situation, the later had fled from the building and escaped.

Attacks in the press were nothing new, and Guiteau had been long immune to criticism. He was completely convinced that he was doing the Lord's work, and he viewed his critics as little more than satanic pawns. As Rosenberg suggests, it's quite possible that Guiteau was unaware of his own shortcomings.

> I weave the discourse out of my brain as cotton is woven into a fabric. When I compose my brain is in a white heat, and my mind works like lightning. This accounts for the short epigrammatic style of my sentences. I write so rapidly I can hardly read it. I divest myself of all unnecessary clothing. I eat and sleep mechanically.

As time ticked away on the "pilgrimage," as he called it, Guiteau kept steadily at work, speaking about the devil and the path to salvation. Between lectures, he did some writing and began to hawk his theological tracts. In 1879, he came to Boston hoping to find a publisher for his new book. He remained in the city for several months, and then, purchased a steamship ticket only to become involved in one of the worst maritime disasters of the century.

CHAPTER TWENTY-ONE

On Wednesday, June 2, 1880, the Republican National Convention assembled in Chicago for the purpose of nominating a candidate for the Presidency of the United States. The convention was held in the immense hall of the new Interstate Industrial Exposition Building, one of the marvels of iron and brick that had sprung up after the *second* Great Fire swept through the city in 1874, destroying eighteen city blocks and consuming over six hundred houses.

Following tradition, the three main presidential candidates stayed away from Chicago during the convention, and although they may have been out of sight, they certainly were not out of mind. The most famous among them was Ulysses Grant. Despite having served two terms, he was the leading contender for the nomination. Senator Blaine, the leader of the reform-minded Half-Breeds, was second, followed by Treasury Secretary John Sherman, the young brother of Civil War legend William Tecumseh Sherman.

All three men were well represented by their friends and managers. Grant's main ally was Roscoe Conkling, the haughty senator from New York. "Lord Roscoe," as he was called, was the leader of the conservative Stalwart faction. He was tall, perfectly formed, and, in the words of one historian, "graceful in every movement, with the figure of an athlete, and the head of a statesman, surmounted with a crown of snow-white hair." Conkling not only looked the part, but as a speaker he had few equals. "His flute-like tones, modulated by the highest elocutionary art, his intensely dramatic manner, his graceful but studied gesticulation, united to call attention to the speaker as much as to the speech." By sheer coincidence, he had begun his political career in Oneida County, the home of the "free love" community. After serving as district attorney, he was elected as mayor of Utica, and then served in the House from 1859 to 1867. He was elected to the Senate a short time later, and he might have been a presidential contender if not for his strident persona, which was overbearing and condescending. Always ready for a good fight, he once summed up his political philosophy in a single sentence: "I do not," he wrote, "known how to belong to a party a little."

Neither did William E. Chandler, Blaine's combative manager. Prior to becoming a political operative, he had had a distinguished career serving as a New Hampshire State Representative, Judge Advocate General of the Navy Department, and First Assistant Secretary of the Treasury. Well educated—though not an independent thinker—he had supported all of Blaine's positions, including his proposal to amend the Constitution to prohibit the use of public funds by any religious school. The amendment was denounced as anti-Catholic, but it nearly passed, falling only four votes short of the required two-thirds majority in the Senate. As Chandler viewed things, it was not a defeat, simply a setback.

In contrast to Conkling and Chandler, James Garfield, Sherman's chief supporter, had an air of friendliness and cheer about him. "Garfield had a massive head," wrote a biographer, "but it rested more easily above the broad shoulders." And that was not the only difference. "His face lacked the lines of scorn traced on the other, and made a true picture of a benevolent good nature, a generous, kindly heart, and a great and wise intellect."

Conkling and Chandler were fond of tightly buttoned frock coats and fancy neckties. Sherman's manager wore a plain sack coat and a simple necktie. On the floor of the convention, Conkling and Chandler held court. Sherman's man had a habit of sitting with his leg swinging over the arm of the chair, and his manners, as described by his colleagues, were those of a big, jolly, overgrown boy. "In speaking he had a deep, rich voice, with a kindly accent. He was never sarcastic, though often grave. Socially, his manners were utterly devoid of restraint; he was accessible to everybody, and appeared to be on good terms with himself."

The most important trait of James Garfield was his determination to win. He may have been a stranger to the mysterious arts of the wire-puller and politician, but he believed in Sherman heartily. He was ready for war to the knife and knife to the hilt. Unlike his counterparts, he had not come to Chicago to enhance his own reputation or further his political career. There was no need for self-aggrandizement. The Ohio State Legislature had recently appointed him Senator-elect, a position previously held by Allen G. Thurman, the architect of the Compromise of 1877.

Even so, rumors began to circulate that Garfield wanted the nomination for himself, and the press, eager to sell papers, ran with the story. Garfield was outraged, but there was little he could do. As he indicated in his diary, he knew how the press worked. "It remains to be seen how far the reckless assaults of public journals can go in ruining public men. I am not sure but a friend of mine is right who says that the greatest danger this country has now to confront is the corrupt and reckless press."

Clearly, Garfield was there to win, and that became evident as soon as he sought and won the chair of the Committee on Rules. By winning this coveted spot he would now be in position to steer the convention toward the center and ensure fair play. Neither of these goals would have been obtainable without him.

Earlier, the delegates had skirmished over the "unit rule," a Stalwart scheme by which the delegates from New York, Pennsylvania, and Illinois would be irrevocably bound to Senator Conkling. They had also voted to seat the entire Illinois delegation, over riding Stalwart objections. Finally, adding fuel to the fire, they had removed the Convention Chairman, an ardent supporter of Grant. After three defeats, the Stalwarts were reeling, but they were not about to surrender. In fact, they had just begun to fight.

After four days and nights of caucusing, haggling, and speech-making, the convention finally began, chaired by Senator George F. Hoar of Massachusetts. Outside, as a correspondent noted, there was perfect harmony:

A more beautiful day in June probably never rose upon a Presidential Convention. The sun, the shade, the trees, the lake, the high facades of business buildings and palace hotels; the air cool, yet temperate; the well-dressed, energetic people, and the signs of prosperous business, uninfluenced even by such a convention, sent a hopeful, cheery feeling to the heart. The rageful features of the past day or two went into their tents at such sunshine and calm godliness of sky.

Inside, there was controlled chaos and a whole different vibe. No doubt there were some "moderates" who were uncomfortable to have as chairman the sharp-tongued Hoar. Judging by his opening remarks, they had good reason to be concerned:

> The Democratic party sees nothing of evil, except that a free man shall cast a free vote under the protection of the Nation. In Louisiana and Mississippi the Democratic party is the accomplice of the White League and the Ku-Klux. In South Carolina it took the honest ballots from the box and stuffed tissue ballots in their places. In New York it issued fraudulent naturalization papers, sixty thousand in number. In Maine its ambitious larceny tried to pilfer a whole State, and in Delaware it stood accomplice by the whipping-post.

After assaulting the opposition, the delegates got down to the business of choosing a nominee. On motion of Eugene Hale, a Blaine supporter, the roll of States and Territories was called, followed by the creation of four main committees: (1) Permanent Organization; (2) Rules; (3) Credentials; and (4) Resolutions.

The platform contained the core Republican planks; protective tariffs, strong federal powers, voting rights, civil-service reform, and immigration.

The immigrants in question were Chinese, and both parties were alarmed by the steady influx of these "cheap laborers." Many in

Congress were convinced that China intended to conquer Europe. In hindsight, this view seems a little silly, but it was a view that was held by some well-educated people—and some prominent politicians. In 1877, the *Wheeling Intelligencer* printed an interview with a well known Republican who had studied the subject at length. "The Mongolian race is capable of great personal prowess," Garfield told a reporter. "Being fatalists, they dare everything for the end they have in view."

He went on to say:

> Their food is simple, easily supplied and easily transported. Their endurance of fatigue is proverbial. Once organized and in motion they could swarm into Russia as irresistibly as the locusts of Egypt, and upon the Pacific coast of this continent as numerous and destructive as grasshoppers. Once started, where would they stop?

The real concern—both inside and outside of the convention hall—was the problem of assimilation. Garfield, his colleagues, and the Democrats felt threatened by the very uniqueness of the Chinese culture. "They have no assimilation whatever to Caucasian civilization," Garfield said.

> The negro wants all that we want. He adopts our civilization—professes our religion—works for our wages, and is a customer for everything that civilization produces. Hence (using a figure of physiology) we can take him up in the circulation of the body politic and assimilate him—make a man and a brother of him, as the phrase goes; but not so in the least degree with the Chinaman.

While the convention debated the various planks, Senator Conkling attempted to sneak in a controversial resolution which read:

> *Resolved*, That the delegates who have voted that they will not abide the action of the convention do not deserve and have forfeited their vote in this convention.

There had only been three dissenting votes (all from West Virginia), but Lord Roscoe was determined to punish anyone who dared to challenge his authority. Unfortunately for him, Garfield was one such man. Addressing the entire assemblage, he gave an impassioned defense of voting rights:

> There never can be a convention of which I am one delegate, equal in rights to every other delegate, that shall bind my vote against my will on any question whatever on which my vote is to be given . . . . I do not know the gentleman, nor their affiliations, nor their relations to candidates, except one of them. One of them I knew in the dark days of slavery, and for twenty long years, in the midst of slave-pens and slave-drivers, has stood up for liberty with a clear sighted courage and a brave heart equal to the best Republicans that live on this globe . . . . And if this convention expel him, then we must purge ourselves at the end of every vote by requiring that so many as shall vote against us shall go out.

Conkling was stubborn, but he was no fool. Sensing another defeat, he quickly withdrew his resolution. Sooner or later, he must have thought, he would get even with that meddling hayseed from Ohio.

Saturday was like Friday, dark and gloomy. The roll was called at noon, followed by committee reports and the adoption of the platform. Later that evening, the delegates reassembled to face "the inevitable hour" of triumph or defeat.

Williams Frye of Maine obtained the floor by consent and nominated his friend and colleague, James G. Blaine. A loud cheer went up, but it was surprisingly brief. Few spoke openly about Blaine, but many observers felt that he was just as arrogant and ambitious as Roscoe Conkling. "When I want a thing," he once said, "I want it dreadfully." President Hayes had described Blaine as "a scheming demagogue, selfish and reckless." As more than one senator noted, he had an inexhaustible capacity for making enemies.

Of course, Blaine had some assets, not the least of which was his enormous intellect. In the view of at least one historian, he also possessed "personal dynamism, imagination, political intuition, oratorical ability, and a broad view of the national interest." Lincoln himself had called Blaine "one of the brightest men in the House."

Even so, everyone knew that the "Plumed Knight" had serious flaws. He had openly sought the presidency in 1876, but a railroad-bond scandal helped cost him the nomination. Since then, he had made many speeches, but he still had a barren legislative record.

Of all the major candidates, Grant was the most beloved and respected, but even his name drew some awkward catcalls. When the cheers and hissing died down, Conkling climbed upon a reporter's table and waved his hand for silence. Then he roared, "When asked whence comes our candidate, our sole reply shall be, he hails from Appomattox with its famous apple-tree!" Suddenly the crowd went wild. The apple tree referred to the spot where General Lee waited to receive General

Grant's offer to meet and finalize the terms of surrender. Conkling, for his part, was only too happy to resurrect the image of a great warrior. In closing, he stayed with the theme of battle:

> Gentlemen, we have only to listen above the din and look beyond the dust of an hour to behold the Republican party advancing with its ensigns resplendent with illustrious achievements, marching to certain victory with its greatest Marshal at its head.

The Grant supporters on the floor and in the galleries went wild again, but this time it took over twenty minutes to restore order.

Now it was Garfield's turn to speak. He rose from his seat, climbed upon the table, and called for order. The crowd fell silent, and he began slowly, speaking in a loud, clear voice. "Mr. President," he said solemnly, "I have witnessed the extraordinary scenes of this Convention with deep solicitude. No emotion touches my heart more quickly than a sentiment in honor of a great and noble character. But now, gentlemen of the Convention, what do we want?

Later in his life, reminiscing in the White House, Garfield hinted that he had expected the delegates to shout, "Sherman!" Instead, somebody yelled "Garfield!" With that, the speaker seemed to blush. In accordance with his publicly declared aim of unity, Garfield then said, "How shall we do this great work? We can not do it, my friends, by assailing our Republican brethren. God forbid that I should say one word to cast a shadow upon any name on the roll of our heroes." All of the delegates stood. For the first time, they cheered as one group. Fortified by applause, Garfield spoke of Sherman's record. "You ask for his monuments. I point you to twenty-five years of the national statutes.

Not one great beneficent statute has been placed on our statute books without his intelligent and powerful aid." It remained to be seen if the delegates found this relevant. In closing, he said, "I do not present him [Sherman] as a better Republican, or as a better man than thousands of others we honor, but I present him for your deliberate consideration. I nominate John Sherman, of Ohio."

PRESIDENT JAMES A. GARFIELD

GENERAL JAMES A. GARFIELD

LUCRETIA GARFIELD

CHARLES JULES GUITEAU

CHESTER A. ARTHUR

ASSASINATION OF PRESIDENT GARFIELD—THE PRESIDENT, WHILE STANDING BESIDE SECRETARY BLAINE, IN THE BALTIMORE AND OHIO RAILROAD DEPOT AT WASHINGTON, JULY 3D, 1881, FATALLY SHOT BY CHARLES GUITEAU —A. Berghaus and C. Upham

HON. JAMES G. BLAINE

ROSCOE CONKLING

THOMAS C. PLATT

JAMES A. GARFIELD

CHAPTER TWENTY-TWO

The man who stood before Garfield on June 6 was a curious sight indeed. He was a large man, barrel-chested and thick at the waist. He had black hair and wore a moustache and goatee. People recognized him easily, even from a distance, and they were intrigued by his piercing dark eyes and olive toned skin. His name was Blanche Bruce, and he was the junior senator from Mississippi.

Born into poverty, Bruce had become a wealthy landowner in the Mississippi Delta. Prior to becoming a senator he had served as supervisor of elections, tax assessor, sheriff, superintendent of education, and sergeant at arms of the state senate. In the Senate, he had been a member of the Committee on Pensions, Manufacturers, and Education and Labor. Like many of his fellow Republicans, he supported desegregation of the army, protection of voting rights, and more human treatment of American Indians.

Initially, Bruce had been something of an outcast in Washington. Even his own party had treated him poorly. In fact, Mississippi's other Republican senator, James Alcorn, had refused to escort him to the front of the chamber to take the oath of office. Only Roscoe Conkling stood beside him, and together they completed the journey to the rostrum. Later in his life, Bruce would repay the kindness by naming his only son Roscoe Conkling Bruce.

A great deal had changed since that first unpleasantness. One year earlier, Bruce had presided over the full Senate, setting a historical milestone that no other senator, before or since, could claim: he had been born into slavery.

Before the convention was over, he would set another milestone by being nominated for Vice-President and receiving eight votes from his colleagues.

Bruce had cornered Garfield to tell him about a visit from colonel Fred Grant, the general's ambitious son. Colonel Fred, as he was called, wanted to know if he could count on the Senator's vote when his father's name came up.

The colonel must have been shocked by the senator's reply.

Bruce had promised his vote to Sherman, and he had no intention of voting for anyone else—not even Grant, a man he openly revered. He reminded the colonel that his word was his bond. The two shared a drink and supposedly parted as friends.

Despite his show of independence, Bruce was concerned that Sherman would lose, and in so doing, jeopardize negro gains. Garfield assured him that neither the Stalwarts nor the Half-Breeds had enough support to win the nomination, and he was right.

The first ballot came on Monday, June 7. As predicted, the front runners split the vote: Grant—304 and Blaine—284. Sherman received 93 votes, and the remaining votes were divided between the three minor candidates. Nobody had garnered the 379 votes that were needed to win, which was not too surprising. First-ballot victories were rare, especially when there was a large field of qualified candidates. Hayes, for example, had received the nomination on the seventh ballot in 1876. Ironically, Blaine had finished second in that ballot, too.

Winning a large majority would not be an easy matter. As the day wore on, the delegates cast vote after vote, eighteen ballots in all. Each ballot required a full roll call of the states and territories, and that alone was exhausting. But nobody came close to acquiring the magic number of delegates. After time out for dinner, they cast ten more ballots. When the votes were counted, it became clear that the convention was deadlocked. After twenty-eight ballots, and twelve long hours of arm-twisting, Grant's 304 votes had grown to 307, Blaine's 284 had shrunk to 279, and Sherman was down to 91.

No amount of tumult and shouting could disguise the fact that neither the Grant forces nor the Blaine forces could win unless the other side broke, and there was no indication that either side was ready to throw in the towel. That night, the exhausted anti-Grant leaders huddled together at the Grand Pacific Hotel, one of the first hotels that had opened after the Great Fire. During the meeting, the Sherman leaders demanded that the Blaine leaders surrender their delegates, but the Blaine faction refused, reminding Sherman's supporters that it was *their* candidate who held almost 300 votes.

The math meant little to the Sherman crowd. They insisted that Blaine drop out. After four hours of back-biting and bickering, the meeting broke up without having resolved anything.

The next morning, Garfield walked to the Exhibition Building with Governor Foster of Ohio. The convention had now been in session for five days, and both men were anxious to find a nominee.

"I think, Charlie," Garfield said at length, "we shall get through with this business of president-making today."

"Yes," Foster replied, "the delegates are all tired and want to go home."

"I am quite sure they will select a candidate before another adjournment."

"I hope it will be our man."

"Honest John Sherman will be nominated," Garfield said confidently. "And Ohio will be made proud."

"Amen," Foster said. "Let us take heart and work."

And that's precisely what they did. The voting resumed with the twenty-ninth ballot, and then the thirtieth, thirty-first, thirty-second, and thirty-third. Finally, on the thirty-fourth ballot, the Wisconsin delegation stunned the convention by casting sixteen votes for James A. Garfield.

Garfield was not pleased by the sudden shift. He jumped to his feet and asked to be recognized. "Mr. President," he shouted, "I rise to a question of order."

"The gentleman will state it," said the chair.

"I challenge," Garfield said, "the correctness of the announcement that contains votes for me. No man has a right, without the consent of the person voted for, to have his name announced and voted for in this convention. Such consent I have not given."

Chairman Hoar banged his gavel, over ruling the objection. "The gentleman from Ohio is not stating a question of order. He will resume his seat," Hoar announced. "No person having received a majority of the votes cast, another ballot will be taken."

The gentleman from Ohio took his seat, and a short time later, the thirty-fifth ballot got underway.

This time, Garfield received twenty-seven votes from Indiana, four from Maryland, and sixteen from Wisconsin. By the end of the roll call, the reluctant nominee had fifty votes.

Suddenly, the delegates had a compromise candidate—a dark horse. The thirty-sixth ballot began with Connecticut, which cast eleven votes for Garfield. Most of the Illinois vote followed, as did Indiana. "The storm at this point broke," said an eyewitness. "The people rose up and gave one tremendous cheer, and hats and handkerchiefs were tossed high, as they had so often before."

Iowa followed with twenty-two votes for Garfield, and then Maine, Blaine's home state, gave him fourteen more votes. Each vote stirred the crowd, and they began to cheer wildly. The chair called for order, but confusion reigned. "Order!" the chairman shouted. "Order on the floor!"

Sensing a tidal wave, Hoar stepped back, allowing the crowd to continue the boisterous display. The delegations of Maryland, Massachusetts, Michigan, Minnesota, and Mississippi insisted upon a roll call. When it was done, the Blaine and Sherman votes switched to Garfield. Ohio added forty-three more votes. Amidst the chaos, Vermont and Wisconsin weighed in, giving the dark horse candidate a total of 399 votes.

When the tally was announced, the crowd exploded. The roar was deafening. Flags and banners were unfurled, and the band began to play "The Battle-Cry of Freedom." Eight thousand people began to sing. Efforts were made to get Garfield out, but he was surrounded by the Ohio delegation. The celebration continued for a quarter of an hour, during which time Conkling remained in his chair without showing any emotion.

After a while, the ballot was verified by a re-reading of the votes and another long round of cheering. The changes in the vote by which the nomination was reached are shown in the following table:

REPUBLICAN PRESIDENTIAL NOMINATION

29th-36th Ballot

June 7 & 8, 1880

		29th.	30th.	31st.	32nd.	33rd.	34th.	35th.	36th.
Grant	...	305	306	308	309	309	312	313	306
Blaine	...	278	279	276	270	276	275	257	42
Sherman	...	116	120	119	117	110	107	99	3
Edmunds	...	12	11	11	11	11	11	11	-
Washburne	...	35	33	31	44	44	30	23	5
Windom	...	7	4	3	3	4	4	3	-
Garfield	...	2	2	1	1	1	17	50	399
Sheridan	...	-	1	-	-	-	-	-	-
Conkling	...	-	-	1	-	-	-	-	-

Surrounded by turmoil, Garfield sat down in an attempt to maintain his composure and to deal with the enormity of the event. He looked "pale as death," noted historian Kenneth D. Ackerman. "And he seemed to be half-unconscious." Only the Grant faction was unmoved. They sat silent and sullen in their seats, waiting for a cue from their leader. Conkling was bewildered, but he recovered nicely, rising to his feet and calling for order. "Mr. Chairman," he said loudly, "James A. Garfield, of Ohio, having received a majority of all the votes cast, I rise to move that he be unanimously presented as the nominee of the convention." There was a thunderous round of applause. Conkling acknowledged the ovation, then said:

> The chair, under the rules, anticipated me, but being on my feet I avail myself of the opportunity to congratulate the Republican party of the nation on the good-natured and well-tempered disposition which has distinguished this animated convention.

There were a few more speeches, and at half-past two, the convention adjourned for "consultation." The delegates returned at five o'clock, hoping to find an acceptable nominee for Vice-President. Many names were mentioned, but only one person attracted much attention—the six foot tall, sturdily built New Yorker with the bushy gray sideburns, Chester A. Arthur.

Arthur had been born in 1829 in the farming community of Fairfield, Vermont. After growing up in New England, he attended Union College before becoming a teacher and principal. Like Garfield, he was also an attorney. He had joined the Republican party at its inception and quickly rose to prominence, eventually becoming a confidant of Roscoe Conkling. In 1871, Grant appointed him Collector of the New York Customhouse, and as noted by a number of historians, "He [Arthur] presided over a patronage empire." In the view of some observers, Arthur not only tolerated, but actually encouraged, the illegal conduct that made the office a national scandal.

Nonetheless, many delegates found themselves in a mood to forgive and forget. Others were sympathetic for a different reason. Back in January, Arthur had lost his beloved wife, a soprano who often sang with the Mendelssohn Glee Club in New York. Mrs. Arthur had come down with a cold from waiting outdoors for a carriage following an evening concert. A frail woman, she soon developed pneumonia and died two days later, on January 12, 1880.

By some accounts, the nomination was a lifeline, a way to pull Arthur back into politics and give his life meaning. Others saw the nomination as a "peace offering" to Conkling. Whatever the case, Arthur won the vice-presidency on the very first ballot, receiving 468 votes, more than the rest of the field combined.

There was a great deal of joy and relief when Chairman Hoar banged his gavel at 7:25, signaling the end of the Republican National Convention. Not everyone was happy, but the longest convention in history was finally over. The Republican party had a solid ticket. As for the candidates, they were sorely in need of a good night's sleep. The convention had drained them physically and mentally, but what neither man could have known in June 1880 was that this was the easy part.

Now they had to face the Democrats.

Still, if one believed in omens, the future looked bright. During Garfield's absence, his Washington residence was occupied by George W. Rose, his private stenographer. Mr. Rose kept a diary, and in June he made the following entry:

On the day of the general's nomination for President, at about the very moment of absolute time that the nomination was made, allowing for the difference in longitude between here and Chicago, a magnificent bald eagle, after circling around the park, swooped down and rested on the general's house . . .

Before the eagle rose from its strange perch a dozen people noticed it and commented upon it. An old Roman would have seen in this an augury of the most inspiring character. But we Americans are free from superstitions, and so it was a mere 'coincidence.'

CHAPTER TWENTY-THREE

Charles Guiteau had spent the past two years in Boston, trying, unsuccessfully, to sell insurance. If the time had shown him anything it was that he was not cut out to be a salesman. "I didn't have any success in doing business," he later explained. "Boston is a very stupid place for life insurance." Apparently, it was also a stupid place to peddle books. In 1879, the Chicago firm of Donelly, Gassette&Loyd published a small volume of essays and lectures by "Charles J. Guiteau, lawyer, theologian, and lecturer." The book was titled *The Truth, a Companion to the Bible.* A short preface boldly declared, "A new line of thought runs through this book, and the author asks for its careful attention to the end that many souls may find the Saviour."

The book's central revelation was the discovery that the Second Coming had already taken place in 70 A.D. in Jerusalem. By Guiteau's calculation, this was a unique discovery, but, in fact, John Humphrey Noyes had come to the same conclusion in his own book, *The Berean*, in 1847.

Wounded pride prevented Guiteau from acknowledging this fact, but as Peskin noted, "The *Truth* was simply a plagiarism on *The Berean*." Original or not, the book was unintentionally gloomy and decidedly pious. In his conclusions, Guiteau stated the following:

> All who died before A.D. 70 went to Hades, and remained there until that time, when they were resurrected and judged, the sheep passing into heaven and the goats into hell. All who have died since A.D. 70 have been detained in Hades, where they will remain until the final judgement.

After failing to sell any books, Guiteau turned to his family for help. John W. Guiteau had lived in Boston for many years, and, in polar opposition to his brother, he was a successful businessman and a pillar of the community. The older, well-established John looked down contemptuously on Charles as the black sheep of the family, somewhat disreputable and spiritually bankrupt. "I believe that my brother's case was one of demonism," he would later testify. "He was possessed with the devil."

A practical businessman like John Guiteau would not have invested much time or energy promoting the schemes of a person he deemed worthless. Therefore, a loan was simply out of the question. He did, however, offer to pay his brother's boarding bill.

By then, for good or ill, Charles was in a different state of mind. "I wish to live as Christ did," he told his brother. "I am working for God, and it is God, not myself, who is responsible for my board."

Angry though he was, John tried to reason with his brother. Did Charles understand that he was breaking the law? Did he know that he was acting crazy?

Abandoning his friendly tone, Charles became agitated, then violent. He shoved his brother against the wall and accused him of being a thief and a scoundrel.

In a fit of rage, John threw Charles out of the office and told him not to come back.

He never did.

On June 8, 1880, Guiteau saw the headline of the *Boston Globe* announcing that James Garfield had won the Republican presidential nomination. In November, he would face a tough fight, probably against Hancock, the hero of Gettysburg. Ensuring victory would take a special talent—someone prepared to work hard and engage the Democrats blow for blow, matching their dirty campaign tactics.

Sitting on a bench overlooking Boston Common, Guiteau began to envision a new mission—one that would entail the true purpose of his life. Perhaps he was destined to help Mr. Garfield win the election. God only knows the senator would need a man like Guiteau—someone who could write well and deliver a spellbinding speech. If Greely had lived, things would have been different. Grant would have been defeated and Guiteau made ambassador to Chile. In Garfield, however, the Lord had provided a second chance.

This time, though, the candidate was young and healthy. Nothing could stop General Garfield. During the war, he had faced the enemy on the battlefield, recklessly charging through their lines to lead his men to victory. He had returned to Ohio without a scratch. The man was practically bullet-proof.

Gazing across the Common, Guiteau might have thought about another politician named Hancock—John Hancock, whose flamboyant signature graced the Declaration of Independence. He, too, had spent some thoughtful moments on the Common. It was said that his cows were pastured on the acreage during the Revolution. Whatever the case, the city had banned grazing in 1830, and now it was the perfect spot to while away the hours.

But Guiteau had thought long enough. If he wanted to join the campaign, he had to move quickly. On Friday night, June 11, just three days after Garfield's nomination, he boarded the *Stonington*, an overnight steamer bound for New York City. In a few short hours he would be back where he belonged—back in the rough and tumble world of presidential politics.

Or so he thought.

As darkness fell, the *Stonington* eased out of her slip and turned west, heading into the Long Island Sound. The night was pitch dark, with a light rain falling, thunder and lightning, and a moderate wind. Although thick, heavy fog hung over the water, neither the captain nor the crew were overly concerned. They had made this trip a thousand times, and they were all old-timers, accustomed to wind, waves and poor visibility. On board, there were about three hundred passengers, most of them sound asleep. The well-to-do had state rooms or berths, and the rest slept on sofas and chairs in the saloon.

It was said that the *Stonington* was in a class by herself, but that was not exactly true. There was one other steamer that was nearly identical, and that was her sister ship, the *Narragansett*. Both ships had been built by William P. Williams, a prominent Boston merchant. They were put into service in 1868, and originally used to haul freight along the east coast. In 1870, they were purchased by the Stonington Steamship Company and converted to passenger ships. Like most steamers, they were built of wood and propelled by side wheels. Each carried a walking-beam engine of 800-horse power and two tubular boilers that allowed the ships to run at fourteen or fifteen miles per hour.

To relieve the boredom of travel, the owners had refitted both vessels with a main deck and a saloon deck, and each was richly furnished with ottomans, tete-a-tetes, easy chairs, and marble-topped tables. Light was furnished by gas from large chandeliers, and each state room had a gas-jet and an electric ball. On a moonless night—like June 11—the light must have been extremely comforting.

Shortly after the *Stonington* left Boston, the *Narragansett* pulled away from her pier at the foot of Jay Street, heading south toward Battery Park. When she reached the Sound, she turned east, heading toward her final destination, Stonington, Connecticut. Nobody aboard either ship was particularly alarmed about the dense fog, except perhaps for William Young, the captain of the *Narragansett.* Young had just replaced Captain S. D. Walden, and this was his maiden voyage on a passenger steamer. Bad weather was occasionally a bad omen, but hopefully not on this night. In keeping with tradition, he told his pilot to sound the fog-whistle every three minutes.

By now, both ships were running on points—so many minutes on a certain course by the compass and so many minutes on another. Similarly, both ships were running with the bow lights covered and their wheel-house darkened. Some of the passengers thought this was odd, but it was actually standard procedure. In thick weather, the lights could produce a blinding glare, making it difficult to distinguish objects that lay ahead.

Near midnight, the *Stonington* passed the Cornfield Point Lightship, a nautical aid that was 100 miles east of New York. Engulfed by fog, the captain ordered the whistle to be blown at half-minute intervals. The noise was loud and quite disruptive. Unable to sleep, Guiteau went outside to take a look around. By his own account, the night was "black and dark as tar. You couldn't see an inch before your face." By the time he turned to go, the *Narragansett* was directly in front of him, closing quickly. He could scarcely believe his eyes, but there was no time to react. There was a sudden, horrifying crash as the ships collided. Guiteau was thrown to the deck, but miraculously, he was not injured. When he looked up, he saw an amazing sight. The *Stonington* had pierced the *Narragansett's* hull, leaving her with a gaping hole on her starboard side. As he watched in horror, the *Stonington* was thrown into reverse, but the damage was already done. According to one eyewitness, the bow of the *Stonington* had penetrated the boiler of the *Narragansett*, scattering burning coals across her wooden deck. A moment later, vast volumes of scalding steam poured through the ship. When the lights went out panic ensued. Three hundred passengers made a mad dash for safety, clawing, climbing, and kicking their way over one another. Some were trampled and others seriously injured, but nothing could be done to stop the melee. Those who make it out faced further danger. The coals had set the ship ablaze, and flames were spreading rapidly, igniting everything they touched.

As Guiteau watched in disbelief, men, women, and children dove overboard, vanishing into the dark and chilly waters of the Sound. The lucky ones found a spot on one of the seven metal life-boats, but most were left to fend for themselves, with tragic results. Life preservers were strewn across the deck, but as one survivor testified, they had not straps.

Unrestrained by belts, the buoyant pads of cork were useless, and most were swept away by the current.

As pandemonium spread, some acted heroically while others behaved like cowards. For some, it was women and children first; for others it was every man for himself. Some plucked strangers out of the water and dragged them into the life boat; others would save only white people. One gentleman walked to the rear of the ship, calmly loaded a pistol, and blew his brains out.

Even for the moody Guiteau, such intense despair was alarming. He would later describe the tragedy to a reporter, but the most vivid accounts came from the survivors of the *Narragansett.* Mrs. E.M. Mulholland, a young married woman from Rhode Island, said:

> "We were in our state-room when the boat struck: the shock was terrible; the people screamed, and the lights went out. We rushed into the cabin where men were at work throwing down life-preservers from above; I got hold of one, and made my husband take it and buckle it around him. Then he got another and gave it to me; I held the child in my arms. I sprang off the deck first, and went down under the water . . . There were people all around us struggling and screaming and crying to God for help . . . The water swept over me, and I went down, holding on to the baby. I rose again . . . I lost my hold of poor little Dora, and the waves carried her off . . . I could see her hair drifting off, and couldn't reach it, though I struggled on insanely."

One of the most interesting narratives, revealing the brutality and cowardice of the male passengers, was told by Mrs. Purdy, a young woman from St. John, New Brunswick:

> "I didn't jump till I saw the fire coming. I leaped from the upper deck, and fell right alongside one of the life-rafters, and went down, down into the water, and thought I would choke before I came up. Gasping and confused, I tried to catch hold of the side of the raft, but the gentleman shoved me off, and wouldn't let me hold on. I never saw such cowardice among gentlemen. I was only trying to cling to the side, but they struck me on the hands and pushed me off."

Meanwhile, on the *Stonington*, Guiteau and his fellow passengers were beginning to worry about their own survival. The collision had badly damaged their steamer. As she backed out, it became evident that she had lost her bowsprit and about three feet of her stem. Still dazed, the captain ordered the lifeboats lowered, but they, too, were of little use. The crew did not know how to handle the oars, and, incredibly, they had forgotten to plug the water holes.

By the time the boats were rigged and manned, the *Narragansett* was nearly gone. Eventually she burned to the water's edge and sank some two miles out from Cornfield Point in thirty feet of water.

By sheer luck, the *City of New York*, a cargo steamer, happened to be in the vicinity and was able to render aid and assistance. Captain A.C. Lamphear was in the pilot-house on his way east from New London, Connecticut, to New York City. He had seen the first flash of light, and two or three minutes later, the steady glow of a fire. He knew that something was terribly wrong, but he was not prepared to find a burning vessel, surrounded by hundreds of screaming passengers. Immediately, six lifeboats were put into the water, guided on their mission only by the cries for help from the drowning men, women, and children. To keep up the courage of those who were struggling in the water, the crews of the boats began to shout to the passengers: "We'll save you!" "Keep up!" "We are here!"

Unfortunately, these were the last words that many of the passengers ever heard. Hundreds were saved, but somewhere between 30 and 50 people were lost. The *Narragansett's* manifest went down with the ship, so the number of dead could only be estimated.

Regardless, it was an event that neither Guiteau nor his fellow passengers would ever forget. Many would be scarred for life, but a few would find a mystical explanation for the tragedy.

> "Eighteen months later, in December 1881, on trial for his life, pleading insanity, claiming in his defense that God had made him His instrument and directed his actions, Guiteau would point back to his deliverance on the high seas that night of the great marine disaster of the *Stonington*. It was an early sign, he would say. God had important plans for him. He had saved his life for a purpose."

CHAPTER TWENTY-FOUR

In late June, Guiteau came up with the idea of revising an old speech he had written for Horace Greely. He changed the title to "Garfield against Hancock," added a few compliments about the candidate, and had hundreds of copies printed. Captivated by the prospect of stumping for Garfield, he descended upon Republican Campaign Headquarters at the Fifth Avenue Hotel. Under his arm he carried copies of his speech, which he handed out to anyone who looked important. Although he was constantly mingling with dignitaries and politicians, he was considered a nuisance. Nobody thought much of his speech.

Whatever merit "Garfield against Hancock" may have had, it was not, by any means, pivotal to the campaign. In fact, the whole document consisted of just three pages, much of it filled with clichés and hackneyed observations. The speech began with a review of the great figures of the Republican past—leaders like Wendell Philips, Henry Clay, Horace Greely, Daniel Webster, and of course, Abraham Lincoln. Each received a colorful and somewhat trite description. Philips was called "the silver-tongued orator of Boston," Clay "Of matchless eloquence," Greely "the great, good Horace," Webster "the great defender of our national constitution," and President Lincoln "the immortal Lincoln."

As for Garfield, he wrote, "He was born in poverty and obscurity, and has attained his present position under Providence by his own efforts. He is a high-toned, conscientious, Christian gentleman."

"This is the issue," he declared toward the end. "A solid North against a solid South. The North conquered the South on the field of battle, and now they must do it at the polls in November, or they may have to fight another war." After this dire warning, he offered a triumphant conclusion:

> Ye men whose sons perished in the war! What say you to this issue? Shall we have another war? Shall our national treasury be controlled by ex-rebels and their Northern allies, to the end that millions of dollars of Southern war claims be liquidated? If you want the Republic bankrupted, with the prospect of another war, make Hancock President. If you want prosperity and peace, make Garfield President, and the Republic will develop till it becomes the greatest and wealthiest nation on the globe.

After failing to impress anyone at Republican Campaign Headquarters, Guiteau traveled upstate to Poughkeepsie and Saratoga. He had hoped to deliver his speech but he could not find an audience. In Poughkeepsie, on July 2, he tried to charge admission, but nobody was willing to pay twenty-five cents to attend a political meeting. The leading Republicans thought his mind was unsound and would have nothing to do with him. In Saratoga, on July 10, he tried the same thing, and once again, nobody showed up. Frustrated, he "skipped" his board bill and left town without paying for his room, the hall, or the advertising. The *Saratogian* wrote about the affair and called Guiteau a "fraud" and a "rattle-headed" fellow.

Guiteau's reaction was awkward, to say the least. Without being asked or encouraged, he continued to write speeches, hoping to show them to one of the party bosses. He pleaded with Chairman Jewell of the National Committee, Chairman Arthur of the State Committee, and President Manierre of the Republican Central Campaign Club to send him out as a campaign speaker. He even sent them two or three speeches as an example of what he could do. They were, in the words one participant, "wild and disjointed and showed the man to be incapable of making a speech." Accordingly, his services were rejected.

But the worst was yet to come. On the twenty-first of the month, Luther Guiteau died, leaving behind a wife and six children. We will never know how Guiteau took the news, but in all likelihood, he was more relieved than distraught.

To say that Charles Guiteau had an unpleasant childhood would be an understatement. Luther had been a strange and violent father, and he had subjected his son to many whippings and a torrent of verbal abuse. Not once had he expressed any affection or appreciation for young Charles. In a letter to John Guiteau, his eldest son, he confessed that he thought Charles "capable of any folly, stupidity, or rascality. The only possible excuse I can render for him is that he is absolutely insane and is hardly responsible for his acts."

Tellingly, it was John Guiteau who would offer the following "obituary" to the *Boston Herald*:

Luther W. Guiteau was born in Utica, N.Y., March 2, 1810, and was the youngest and eleventh child of Dr. Francis Guiteau and his wife, Hannah Wilson Guiteau, of Charlotte, Vt. He died at Freeport, Illinois, July 21, 1880, at the age of 70, the oldest age attained by any member of his father's family. He became an earnest Christian in early life, and died in the faith, having lived a consistent and conscientious life, honored and loved in the community where he lived and died.

If Guiteau was upset, he hid it well. After barely acknowledging his father's death, he resumed his quixotic mission. Day after day, for the rest of the summer and well into the fall, he stalked the halls and corridors of the Fifth Avenue Hotel, cornering anyone connected to the party. Overbearing and rude, he soon became the laughingstock of the campaign, but not everyone was amused by his antics. On one occasion, he had the audacity to sneak into General Grant's suite and confront him with a request for a political appointment. The general later recalled the incident with regret:

I met Guiteau in the Fifth Avenue Hotel at the close of the last Presidential campaign. He wanted me to sign a paper recommending him as a proper person to appoint as Minister to Austria. I knew nothing about him; but Col. Frederick Grant, my son, told me that Guiteau was a lawyer in Chicago, and was supposed to be half crazy. I subsequently heard that he had delivered some speeches in favor of the election of Presidents Hayes and Garfield. Guiteau evidently believed that he was a man of great importance to the Republican party, and the defeat of his aims must have unbalanced his mind. He told me that he was engaged to a young woman worth one million dollars, and that he should obtain the appointment he was looking for if I would join Henry Ward Beecher and others in seeking it for him. I refused to sign his paper. I told my servant not to allow him to enter my parlors. He subsequently forced his way in one day, but I refused to talk with him and dismissed him speedily. I regret this sad occurrence from the bottom of my heart.

Looking back, it seems odd that General Grant—the most famous living American—would be so vulnerable. One would think that a man of his stature would be better protected. After all, eleven public servants had been killed during his administration, and nine others had been attacked.

Somebody should have questioned the small, shabby man with the catlike walk, but nobody did. He was simply ignored.

In early August, Gutieau heard a rumor that Garfield was coming to New York to hold a political pow wow with the Stalwarts. The party bosses were calling it the "Fifth Avenue Summit," and from what they were saying, the conference would make or break the fall campaign. Roscoe Conkling would run the show, but everyone would get a chance to speak, including New York party leader Thomas C. Platt, banker Levi P. Morton, and Chester A. Arthur, the Vice-Presidential candidate. Presumably even Blaine would attend, which was bound to produce some fireworks.

All these dignitaries, together with the nominee himself, was enough to excite any man, and Guiteau knew that it was a golden opportunity. "Garfield against Hancock" would be his calling card, and they were bound to be impressed by its brilliance. "I gave or sent this speech to all the leading men at that conference," he later bragged. "This was my first introduction to them. Afterward, as I met them, I introduced myself and called their attention to that speech. They seemed to be highly pleased with it, and that was the beginning of my personal acquaintance with them."

During the conference, Guiteau presented his speech to Chester A. Arthur, Senator Conkling, General Logan, Senator Cameron, and a host of lessor known politicians. He then confronted Marshall Jewell, the former governor of Connecticut, offering to "take the stump" for Garfield. The governor turned him down—again—ostensibly because he did not have a national reputation. "So, as a matter of fact," he later admitted, "I only delivered the speech once, and that was at a colored meeting, I think, on Twenty-fifth Street, one Saturday evening."

Ultimately, Guiteau would come to believe that it was his speech that enabled Garfield to win the election. Amid all the celebrating in November, he would find time to drop the Presdient-Elect a congratulatory note:

> We have cleaned them all out just as I expected. Thank God!
> Very respectfully,
> Charles Guiteau

There is no evidence that Garfield ever saw the note, but even if he had, he would not have known who Guiteau was or what he was after. Those answers would come later in Washington, D.C.

CHAPTER TWENTY-FIVE

General Winfield S. Hancock of Pennsylvania, the hero of Gettysburg, won the Democratic Presidential Nomination in late June. He would prove to be a formidable candidate, a man admired by Northern voters and respected in the South for his moderate administration of Louisiana and Texas during Reconstruction. Unlike Garfield, he had shunned politics, but his relative obscurity was actually an asset. As one historian noted, "Without any political experience, he was without enemies."

The same could not be said of Garfield. Most of his enemies were in his own party, and they called themselves Stalwarts. Led by Roscoe Conkling, they were obsessed with the issue of patronage, the corrupt system that enabled them to retain control of the party. If Grant had won the nomination, the status quo would not be in jeopardy; however, Garfield was reform-minded, sympathetic to the Half-Breeds, and completely unpredictable. The Stalwarts were willing to support his campaign, but only if the spoils system remained in place. This, therefore, was the reason for the summit meeting at the fashionable Fifth Avenue Hotel in August.

For the Stalwarts, there were three main questions: Where did Garfield stand on the patronage issue? Would he be a wild-eyed reformer like Blaine or move cautiously like Hayes? Did he or did he not intend to destroy the spoils system?

It was these tough questions that drew the Republicans together on August 5, 1880. Surprisingly, there were some holdouts, most notably Roscoe Conkling, the man who had requested the meeting in the first place. "Lord Roscoe" simply disappeared, most likely because Blaine was present. In his absence, bargaining authority passed to the Stalwarts triumvirate of Thomas C. Platt, Levi P. Morton, and Chester A. Arthur. They were joined by New York Congressman Frank Hiscock, Richard Crowley, and Joseph Warren.

No one knows exactly what transpired at the meeting or what deals were struck, but most historians agree that the "Treaty of Fifth Avenue" favored Garfield. He seems to have emerged stronger than ever, untainted by political corruption and credited with uniting the party. In hindsight, the questionable arrangements involved financiers as opposed to politicians. In a private meeting, Garfield persuaded Levi Morton to head a special committee to raise money for the campaign. In return for calling on some of his wealthy Wall Street friends, Morton was promised a top position in Garfield's administration. Though never stated publicly, it was widely assumed that the position in question was Treasury Secretary.

Jay Gould, the owner of the Western Union Telegraph Company and the Union Pacific Railroad, wanted a guarantee that the Supreme Court would not interfere in his railroad business.

In exchange for this guarantee, he agreed to finance the entire campaign. Obviously each party needed the other, but it remains unclear how far Garfield was willing to bend. He remained deliberately ambiguous during the fall campaign, and in his diary, he wrote, "No trades, no shackles and as well fitted for defeat or victory as ever."

Garfield's ambiguity may have saved the day at the conference, but it would come back to haunt him after the election. The Stalwarts had left the meeting believing that he was firmly on their side. When they met with Conkling, they assured him that the patronage system was safe. Nobody knows how the message became so garbled, but as Allan Peskin noted, it was "a misunderstanding that was compounded by Garfield's deliberate ambiguity, the circus-like atmosphere of the conference and, to a degree, the wishful thinking of the Stalwarts themselves."

To almost everyone's surprise, Conkling accepted the terms of the "treaty" without speaking directly to the Republican nominee. A few days later, he wrote to Levi Morton that he was anxious "to read up and get ready for the campaign." In order to fulfill his part of the bargain, he agreed to speak at a number of political rallies and meetings, and, in the view of many historians, he played a crucial role in the fall campaign.

As the race began, the field was crowded, and there was no front runner. Besides Garfield, there were four other candidates: General Winfield S. Hancock, nominated by the Democrats, James B. Weaver of Iowa, nominated by the Greenback party, Neal Dow of Maine, nominated by the Prohibitionists, and John W. Phelps of Vermont, nominated by the anti-Masons.

As with most Gilded Age campaigns, there was plenty of partisan vituperation, mudslinging, and chicanery. Early on, the Democrats lowered the bar by dredging up the Credit Mobilier Scandal and the DeGolyer transaction. These issues failed to arouse the public, but their next trick was more successful. On October 21, a New York City newspaper called *Truth* published a letter purporting to have been written on January 23, 1880, to one H.L. Morey, of Lynn, Massachusetts. The letter was written on House stationary, and it implied that Garfield favored unlimited Chinese immigration.

Dear Sir:

Yours in relation to the Chinese problem came duly to hand. Individuals or companies have the right to buy labor where they can get it the cheapest. We have a treaty with the Chinese government, which should be religiously kept until its provisions are abrogated by the action of the General Government, and I am not prepared to say that it should be abrogated until our great manufacturing interests are conserved in the matter of labor.

The "Morey letter," as it came to be known, represented the undisputed low point of the campaign, and when Garfield refused to challenge its authenticity, it became a serious threat. If left disproven, it could cause irreparable damage, especially on the West Coast. At the very least, the Republicans would lose California, Oregon, and Nevada, the three states where restrictionist sentiments ran the highest.

Republican Chairman Jewell begged Garfield to issue a clear and speedy denial, but the candidate hesitated, reluctant to "roll around in the mud" of political slander. On October 22, he wrote:

I will not break the rule I have adopted by making a public reply to the campaign lies, but I authorize you to denounce the so-called Morey letter as a bold forgery, both in its language and sentiment. Until its publication I never heard of the existence of the Employer's Union of Lynn, Massachusetts, nor of such a person as H.L. Morey.

The letter had, in fact, had been forged by Democratic operatives, and a subsequent investigation revealed that no such person as H.L. Morey lived at or near Lynn, Massachusetts. In order to clear his name, Garfield took the newspaper to court, and a certain Kenward Philip, a contributor to *Truth*, was charged with forgery and arrested. A long trial followed, and during the proceeding the identity of the forger was revealed, as well as his motive, which as everyone suspected, was purely political. The prosecution failed to convict the publishers of the *Truth* of criminal libel, but as John Clark Ridpath noted, the country rendered the old Scotch verdict of "guilty—but not proven."

The backlash may have cost the Democrats the election, which proved to be extremely close. In fact, one of the closest in history. In the end, 9,200,000 votes were tallied, and Garfield's margin of victory was only 7,368 votes, or less than one-tenth of one percent of the total vote cast. As far as the electoral vote, Garfield received 214 votes and Hancock 155.

Technically, Garfield now held three different offices: He was still a member of the House of Representatives in the Forty-sixth Congress; he was United States Senator-elect for the state of Ohio; and thirdly, he was President-elect of the United States. On November 10, he resigned his seats in the House and Senate, and for the next four months he became Citizen Garfield.

On February 29, 1881, Garfield left his home in Mentor, Ohio and traveled east to Washington to be inaugurated. All along the route, he was met by large, cheering crowds. The train carrying the President-elect and his family reached the Capitol on the evening of February 29, and, as one reporter noted:

> The General looks travel-tired and weary, although the excitement keeps him well stimulated, having something of the effect of rich-living. He says that when once his Cabinet is settled, and he begins home-life at the White House, he will have a comparative freedom from worry. He does not sleep excellently well. Probably no man ever did while engaged in making up a Cabinet.

Garfield had every reason to worry. He was about to step into the lion's den, and after many years in Congress, he knew it would be difficult to survive. Before he even arrived in Washington, the Stalwarts made their first demand. In accordance with the "Treaty of Fifth Avenue," they insisted that Levi P. Morton be named Secretary of the Treasury. The appointment was particularly important to Roscoe Conkling, but only because it would remove Morton from the upcoming Senate race in New York. Garfield balked, telling the Stalwarts that Morton's appointment "would be a congestion of financial power at the money centre and would create jealousy at the West."

The essential message to the Stalwarts was clear: Garfield would be his own man, regardless of the consequences. This is not to say that he would be ungrateful, but he was not about to turn over the fifteen hundred patronage positions in the Treasury Department. In his heart, he knew that the department was too important to use as a feeding trough. It would be hard to think otherwise. As Justus D. Doenecke stated:

Its tasks ranged from collecting revenue to regulating the currency, and it daily enforced laws dealing with specie resumption, war debts, and the tariff.

Within its jurisdiction lay the collectorship of the Customhouse of New York, a most important patronage position, because that city's harbor handled more imports and collected more revenue than all other ports of entry combined. It dealt with up to 75 percent of the nation's customs receipts, and $840 million passed through the collector's office during a single year.

In short, Treasury was a political plum, and the Stalwarts would never forgive Garfield for giving it away. They were even more incensed when they learned that Blaine had been chosen for the State Department. What was Garfield thinking? Nobody trusted Blaine, not even the people who were closest to him. Even the President-elect had his doubts. In April 1880, he had written, "I like Blaine, always have, and yet there is an element in him which I distrust."

As Garfield soon learned, opposition to Blaine's appointment was remarkably intense, especially among New Yorkers. Hamilton Fish, who had served as Secretary of State under Grant, spoke for many when he called Blaine "valiant and irrepressible when in assured position and power, reckless in a crisis, but vacillating and timid in emergencies of which the issue is uncertain."

Despite the criticism, Garfield was determined to reward his old friend, and, by extension, Blaine's supporters, the very group that had delivered the greatest bulk of votes at the Chicago Convention. If Blaine had been more tactful, the controversy might have died down, but on December 30, he journeyed to New York City to convince attorney

Chauncy Depew to run for the Senate against several rival Stalwart candidates. The move infuriated Conkling, who was now convinced that Blaine intended to destroy his political machine.

Hoping to sabotage the appointment, Conkling traveled to Mentor, but Garfield stood firm. Some saw the meeting as "much ado about nothing." Others thought it marked a turning point. One thing was certain: Garfield was making a lot of new enemies—and very few friends.

CHAPTER TWENTY-SIX

The morning of March 4, 1881, was dark and gloomy and completely unfitting for a presidential inauguration. Snow and ice covered the streets and avenues of the nation's capital, and, if the "weather clerk" was right, more bad weather was on the way. Nevertheless, at 10:15, the presidential party, consisting of President Hayes, President-elect Garfield, Vice-President elect Arthur, and Senators Bayard, Pendleton, and Anthony, entered two carriages at the Executive Mansion and drove to Pennsylvania Avenue, accompanied by the First Cleveland Troop.

Garfield looked weary, and, according to at least one keen-eyed observer, "the effect of sleepless nights and deep anxiety was plainly visible on his countenance." Tired or not, there was still the matter of being sworn into office, and that was no easy task. Mainly due to the weather, it took more than an hour to reach the Capitol, but once the entourage pushed through the crowd, things went smoothly. The Senators and Senators-elect were seated on the left side of the chamber, and by tradition, the President-elect's family sat in the front seat of the gallery, opposite the Vice-President's desk.

Soon General Hancock, the Democratic candidate for the Presidency, came in, accompanied by Senator Blaine. "Hancock was dressed in Major-General's full uniform," Ridpath wrote. "Looking in splendid condition, and conducted himself in a manly, modest fashion, which called forth warm applause, and commanded the respect of all spectators."

Shortly before noon Vice-President elect Arthur took the oath of office, and a few minutes later, the Senate of the Forty-sixth Congress adjourned *sine die*. At 12:40, the doors of the Rotunda were thrown open, and the members of the Supreme Court—escorted by Frederick Douglass—led Garfield outside. A great platform had been erected in front of the Capitol building, and directly in the center stood several chairs, including one that was rather old and worn, which tradition, if not history, claimed was occupied by George Washington at his first inauguration. The President-elect, clearly moved by the size of the crowd, sat in the historic chair, surrounded by his family and an assortment of dignitaries. At about a quarter of one, he rose from his chair, walked to the front of the platform, and delivered a thirty-five-minute Inaugural Address.

"Fellow citizens," he said at length, "We stand today upon an eminence which overlooks a hundred years of national life, a century crowded with perils, but crowned with triumphs of liberty and love."

The speech covered a lot of ground, which was customary and expected, considering the nature of the ceremony. Garfield was, of course, speaking to the nation, and for that reason, he touched upon a variety of subjects: the Constitution, the Civil War, Emancipation, monetary policy, Mormonism, and civil-service reform.

The address was delivered in a deliberate, forceful manner, and when Garfield finished speaking, he received a polite ovation. The oath of office was administered by the Chief Justice, and when it was completed, James A. Garfield, the twentieth President of the United States, turned and kissed his wife and mother. By now, the public was well aware of Garfield's affection for both women, but what they may not have known was that Eliza Ballou Garfield was the first mother to witness the inauguration of a son.

Exhausted but elated, Garfield rode to the White House and spent the next two hours reviewing the long procession that marched down Pennsylvania Avenue. Afterward, he met with the Williams College Alumni Association, and in the evening, he attended an elaborate inaugural ball. The ball was enhanced by "one of the most superb efforts of the pyrotechnic art," but the loudest display came from the Germania Orchestra of Philadelphia, a one-hundred-piece ensemble led by John Philip Sousa.

On March 5, Garfield sent the Senate a list of cabinet nominations, which raised some eyebrows in certain factions of the party: Secretary of State, James G. Blaine; Secretary of the Treasury, William Windom; Secretary of War, Robert T. Lincoln; Secretary of the Navy, William H. Hunt; Secretary of the Interior, S.J. Kirkwood; Attorney-General, Wayne MacVeagh; and Postmaster-General, Thomas L. James.

It soon became apparent that the Stalwarts were unhappy with many of the nominees, but, in fact, the cabinet represented all of the disparate wings of the party. Blaine was the recognized leader of the Half-Breeds; James and Windom were offerings to Senator Conkling; Hunt was a gift to the South; Lincoln an overture to the Midwest, and MacVeagh and Kirkwood were admired by the President himself.

All in all it was a remarkably well balanced Cabinet, although it fell far short of suiting Roscoe Conkling. Blaine was too close to the throne, and if the truth be told, Conkling wanted to control Federal patronage so that he could punish the New York delegates who had deserted him at the Chicago convention. In his mind, these men were traitors, and they had to pay for their treachery. Naturally, this put him at odds with the Administration.

Unlike Conkling, Garfield detested patronage, and he had good reason to fear its negative influence. In the estimate of one nineteenth century historian, the President controlled 100,000 positions that attracted 500,000 applicants. This meant that it would be necessary to offend 400,000 men and their friends—at least a million people.

To apportion out these 100,000 offices amounted, therefore, almost to a special revolution; and incurring the enmity of a million men meant danger, great danger. It would produce a diseased political atmosphere; the atmosphere of discontent, that any moment might discharge some thunderbolt to do an ineffaceable national damage.

In some ways, the damage had already been done, but it was about to get a lot worse. On March 20, Conkling was summoned to the White House to confer on the topic of appointments. During the meeting, the President told Conkling that he intended to reward the New York delegates who had supported him at the Chicago convention. The Senator strenuously objected, but he did not challenge the President's authority. What Conkling did not say, but what is crucial in understanding his strategy, was that the real prize was the New York Customhouse, with its staff of fifteen hundred workers. The meeting ended amicably, and

Conkling returned to the Senate believing that he would be consulted before the position was filled.

On March 22, Garfield sent to the Senate for confirmation the names of Stewart L. Woodford and Asa W. Tenny to be United States Attorney for the Southern and Eastern District of New York, respectively. In addition, he nominated Lewis F. Payne to be United States Marshal for the Southern District of New York, Clinton D. McDougall for the Northern District of New York, and John Tyler to be Collector of Customs at Buffalo. Levi P. Morton, who had lost the Treasury position, was nominated to become Minister to France. Significantly, each and every one of these men had been pre-approved by Senator Conkling.

The next pick, however, belonged to Blaine, and he chose the man who had spearheaded the break in the New York delegation at Chicago. This was a man the Stalwarts hated above all others, Judge William H. Robertson.

On thc following day, March 23, Garfield nominated Robertson for Collector of the Port of New York. Needless to say, the Stalwarts viewed the nomination as in insult to their leader. Conkling was furious. The President had broken his promise. Even worse, he had nominated a scoundrel. Had the man lost his mind?

Whether or not Garfield had intended it, Robertson's nomination was a declaration of independence. He had never approved of "Senatorial Courtesy"—the custom whereby the Senate will refuse to confirm any presidential appointment if objections are raised by a Senator from the state to which the appointment applies. Now he had an opportunity to end that foolishness once and for all.

Whatever Garfield intended by the nomination of Robertson, Senator Conkling treated it as a declaration of war. Together with

Thomas Platt, the junior Senator from New York, he fought the nomination on every front. Despite their best efforts, they had few supporters. Even the New York State Senate (of which Roberston was the presiding officer) came out against them and passed a resolution in support of the Administration. If the Senators had taken the time to read the resolution, they would have seen that it contained some salient points: First, that it was the President's constitutional right to nominate; second, that they had overstepped their Congressional prerogative; and third, that the office of Collector of the port was a national office, free from local patronage. President Garfield, said one able writer, used political weapons to combat politicians in the matter of the New York Custom House. But he achieved much by doing so.

"For the first time since 1876 we have a Republican party in New York distinct from the close corporation that has controlled the organization there these recent years. A nucleus has been established around which all shades of Republican opinion can rally with the good hope of destroying the despotism that has virtually ostracized the best Republicans of the State from influential participation in national politics. The nucleus is an administration part, which invites the cooperation of all who would liberalize the organization. With the overthrow of "machine" control, as it has existed in New York and Pennsylvania, and the old would-be dictators remanded to their proper place, a great advance had been made towards that purer condition of political and public affairs that all honest men favor."

There were many who did not share this enlightened view, but much to his credit, Garfield held his ground. In his view, the issue would settle the question whether the President was a registering clerk of the Senate or the Executive of the United States. Meanwhile, the Republican Senatorial Caucus sent committee after committee to the White House, hoping to induce the withdrawal of Robertson's name. Even Vice-President Arthur begged the President to give Robertson a different post. Garfield remained intransigent, but he reminded the Vice-President that he was standing up for the prerogatives of his office, and, in some small way, curbing the Senate's power. Some day Arthur himself might benefit from this principled stance.

After all, there was always a chance that he could inherit the highest seat in the land.

CHAPTER TWENTY-SEVEN

According to the *New York Herald*, the winter of 1881 was the coldest winter in half a century. From December to February there had been eighteen snowstorms, and, even now in early March, the weather was frigid. Throughout the city, contagious diseases were spreading, and, in the first three months of the year, there was a sharp increase in diphtheria, scarlet fever, and smallpox—diseases that, along with the measles, typhoid fever, and "winter cholera," killed three out of five children in the city before their first birthday.

God only knows how Guiteau survived without an overcoat, but survive he did. On March 5, the day after Garfield's inauguration, he boarded a train and traveled south to Washington, D.C. After studying the lay of the land, he found lodging at a modest boardinghouse on Twelfth and G streets, just six blocks from the White House. Acting in fear that the best consulships would be awarded first, he got right to work writing to a long list of dignitaries. Back in November, he had sent his first letter to Williams Evarts, the outgoing Secretary of State:

Dear Sir,

I wish to ask you a question. If President Garfield appoints Mr. A to a foreign mission does that supersede President Hayes' commission for the same appointment? Do not all foreign Ministers appointed by President Hayes retire on March 4 next? Please answer me at the Fifth Avenue Hotel at your earliest convenience. I am solid for General Garfield, and may get an important appointment from him next spring.

Very truly,

Charles Guiteau

On March 8, he made his first trip to the White House, joining a large group of well-wishers and office seekers who had lined up to meet the President. After waiting a few hours, they were told that the President was in a meeting, and that he would not have time to meet with anyone. Kenneth D. Ackerman, the noted historian, describes what happened next:

"Guiteau walked across the lawns and past the Treasury Department to the prestigious Riggs House on Fifteenth Street. He [Guiteau] had discovered that he could arrange to receive his mail here at Riggs, sit in its library to read the daily newspapers, and use its stationery for his letters."

The first person he wrote to was President Garfield. "I called to see you this A.M.," he told the president, "but you were engaged."

On March 11, he wrote to Secretary Blaine. "In October and January last I wrote General Garfield touching the Austrian Mission, and I think he has filed my application and is favorably inclined. Since then I have concluded to apply for the Consul-Generalship at Paris instead of the Austrian Mission, as I prefer Paris to Vienna." Immodest as ever, Guiteau enclosed a copy of his "famous" speech, then wrote, "I will talk with you about this as soon as I can get a chance. There is nothing against me. I claim to be a gentleman and a Christian."

Blaine loved intrigue, but this was highly unusual. Most troubling was the tone of familiarity. Who was this impudent fellow? How did he have the gall to write to the Secretary of State?

On the 25th, Guiteau sent another letter:

> I vote in Chicago, although I have been in New York for nearly a year. I was running the canvass with the National and State committees last fall. I asked Gen. Logan to sign my applications and he said he had already signed so many applications for consuls that he did not think it would do any good; but, he added: "I have no objection to your having the Paris consulship."
>
> This is the only office I ask for myself or friends, and I think I am entitled to it.
>
> I ask it as a personal tribute . . .
>
> I am very glad that the President selected you for his Premier. It might have been some one else.

The vast bulk of Blaine's mail consisted of routine job applications, so he was probably puzzled but unconcerned by Guiteau's correspondence. Then again, he may have thrown the letters in a special folder, as Garfield did, designated "the eccentric file." As Peskin states, "This was crammed with messages from unhinged patriots." In later years, after sad experience, all such threats would be taken very seriously, but now they were regarded merely as amusing tidbits for the delectation of clerks and passing journalists."

Less amusing were the cranks and crackpots that showed up at the White House, which in 1881, was still open to the public. These were the people that troubled Joe Stanley Brown, the president's private secretary who had an office upstairs on the second floor. Brown had the pleasure of meeting Charles Guiteau in mid-March, when, incredibly, he introduced the disheveled visitor to the President of the United States. Describing the meeting, Ackerman wrote:

"Guiteau was startled for a moment on entering the private office. The famous figure of James Garfield, large, husky, and full-bearded, taller and more athletic than himself, stood before him, close enough to see the lines of weariness around the President's eyes, the gray patches in his beard, the heaviness in his step."

Garfield was puzzled by the intrusion, but he waved Guiteau forward and introduced his other guests, General Tyner and Levi P. Morton. When Tyner and Morton left, Guiteau stepped forward, introduced himself, and handed the president a copy of "Garfield against Hancock." He had written his name and the words "Paris consulship" on the front cover, hoping that Garfield would make the connection later on.

In a scene that can only be described as surreal, Garfield sat down and began to read the speech. Guiteau sat, too, directly across from him. Neither man spoke, but as Guiteau recalled later, the president seemed interested in his writing. In any case, he had nothing negative to say. After a minute or two of awkward silence, Guiteau stood up and quietly left the room. He did not tell the president that he was leaving. He just walked out.

Guiteau returned a few days later, anxious to know if the president had approved his appointment. He was told that his papers had been sent to the State Department, which was customary for a consular appointment. That was good enough for Guiteau. He would now pressure Blaine, the second most power man in Washington.

At first all went well. Almost every day Guiteau walked the six blocks from his rooming house to the State Department to press his claim for the Paris consulship. Occasionally he got to see Secretary Blaine, who was "exceedingly cordial," but always absorbed in the affairs of state. Later, on the witness stand, Blaine would recall seeing the small, wild-eyed man. He would remember not only his persistence but also his shabby appearance. Unlike other office seekers, he wore no socks, and his coat collar was turned up to conceal his ragged shirt. Still, as Ackerman noted, "Blaine saw no reason to act harshly toward a well-meaning if misguided fellow like Guiteau. He spoke with him, always said good day, and tried to be polite, even if he never had news about the Paris consulship."

In spite of his best efforts, Gutieau made no progress with the State Department or the White House. Had he been more alert, he would have noticed that the new administration was preoccupied with a growing scandal in the Post Office. For the present, Garfield and Blaine had to worry about keeping their own jobs.

Having been called to the presidency almost by accident, Garfield had never anticipated that he would have to deal with so much corruption so soon. Nor had he expected his campaign manager to be named as the ringleader of a criminal enterprise. Nonetheless, by early April, the administration was overwhelmed by scandal.

Stephen Dorsey was not your average crook, and the Star Route scheme was not your average crime. Both were bold, brazen, and exceedingly controversial. Prior to becoming Garfield's manager, Dorsey had served as a United States Senator from Arkansas, but he was much more than a politician. In the words of one historian, he was one of the West's most outlandish characters. He was a carpetbagger, cattle baron, mining speculator, wheeler-dealer, and the respondent of countless lawsuits.

Shortly after becoming involved in a railroad scheme in Arkansas, he was compelled to move to New Mexico, where in 1878, he began construction on the "Dorsey Mansion," a lavish Victorian structure completed in 1880. The amenities of Dorsey's home included an art gallery, billiard room, library, 60-guest dining room, and the very first indoor bathroom in the state.

Not surprisingly, the mansion was built on a vast but fraud-ridden land grant. Even worse, it had been financed by the Star Route Frauds, a lucrative scandal whereby United States postal officials received bribes in exchange for awarding postal delivery contracts in southern and western areas. The contracts were leased to the lowest bidder willing to guarantee faithful performance, and the bids for this service became classified as "celerity, certainty and security bids." For the sake of brevity, they were designated in the mapbooks by three asterisks, or stars, which became known as star routes.

Dorsey was smart enough to know that one of the biggest problems connected with the rapid expansion of the Far West was the establishment of adequate means of communication. On the importance of mail delivery, J. Martin Klotsche wrote, "So important had the "star service" become that by 1890 the total annual transportation amounted to over 75,000 miles." By the time Garfield became aware of the scandal, there were nearly 10,000 start routes, costing the federal government nearly six million dollars a year to maintain.

In April, the president forced the resignation of Thomas Brady, the second assistant postmaster general. When Dorsey was confronted, he stoutly denied any involvement with the Post Office, but as Peskin wrote, "this was an unblushing lie. Dorsey was up to his ears in star route contracts, and so were his brother, his brother-in-law and numerous friends and relations."

All of a sudden, the new administration was in danger of being labeled "corrupt." Already there were whispers that Garfield was following in the footsteps of another beleaguered general, Ulysses S. Grant. Some reformers said that Garfield's administration was simply an extension of the corruption-riddled administrations of Grant and Hayes.

As usual, Garfield decided to face the problem head on. Thomas James, the Postmaster General, was ordered to investigate the matter. He was told to pursue all leads, regardless of where they led and who was involved. For the time being, the administration would concentrate on restoring trust, and in so doing, ignore Charles Guiteau, who presented more of a serious danger then anyone imagined.

CHAPTER TWENTY-EIGHT

May had arrived. The weather was unseasonably warm, but nobody in Washington seemed to mind. The winter of 1881 had been a hard one, but now in late spring, the cold was just a memory. Throughout the city, there was a feeling of joy mixed with the dread of an early heat wave. Faced with the prospect of a long, hot summer, Guiteau continued to write the President. The letters started arriving back in March, and they became more intense with each passing month.

"I called to see you this A.M.," Guiteau wrote on March 8. "What do you think of me for Consul General for Paris?"

"I think I have a right to press my claim for the Consulship at Paris," he wrote on the twenty-sixth.

"I have practiced law in New York and Chicago," he wrote on April 6. "I have been here since March 5, and expect to remain some little time, or until I get my commission."

On April 29, he had the audacity to give the President some advice about strategy.

I wish to say this about Robertson's nomination. Would it not be well to withdraw it on the ground that Mr. Conkling has worked himself to a white heat of opposition? Mr. Conkling feels you ought to have consulted him about the appointments in his own State, and that is the reason he is so set against Mr. Robertson; and many people think he is right. I am on friendly terms with Senator Conkling and the rest of our Senators, but I write this on my own account and in the spirit of a peacemaker.

If Guiteau thought his letters were helping his cause, he was wrong. More annoying were his frequent visits. "Most of his time was spent on the benches in Lafayette Square," wrote Rosenberg. "When not in the park, he visited the White House or State Department, sent his card each day and badgered the secretaries with demands for attention." Nobody took him seriously, and in fact, he became a source of some amusement. In the words of one Washingtonian, "He was a kind of butt, sent around from place to place, his own egotism sustaining him."

In early May, the President was distracted by a far greater problem, but this time it was literally a matter of life and death. The malarial atmosphere of Washington had been a problem for years, but, for some reason, the politicians had never taken any action to combat the disease. The Analostan marshes, south of the Capitol, provided a perfect breeding ground for mosquitoes, but so did the swampy area directly behind the White House. During the Civil War, an entire regiment—the Eighth Maine—had camped behind the Executive Mansion, and within weeks, every soldier had malaria. Nothing had been done to rectify the situation, and with all the warm weather and rain it was only a matter of time before somebody got sick.

That somebody was Lucretia Garfield.

Her husband had previous written:

"Do you know that it frightens and unmans me to know that you are sick. Your health is the continent, the solid land on which I build all my happiness and hope. When you are sick, I am like the inhabitants of countries visited by earthquake. They lose all faith in the eternal order and fixedness of things. Your sickness is my earthquake."

One can only imagine how Garfield felt when he learned that his wife had been diagnosed with the most malignant form of malaria. Even as he rushed to her side, her condition grew worse. Over the weekend her fever climbed to 104 degrees, and she began to exhibit signs of cerebrospinal meningitis, commonly called "brain fever." Strangely enough, this was the very disease that had killed Charles Guiteau's mother. "She [Mrs. Garfield] twisted painfully through the nights in sweat-soaked sheets," wrote Ackerman. "In the morning, she found her pillow covered with clumps of hair that had fallen from her head."

Dr. Boynton, her family physician, was hastily summoned from Ohio. When he arrived at the White House, he found Mrs. Garfield in critical condition, very close to death. He immediately administered a massive dose of quinine, and he insisted that Mrs. Garfield remain in a room on the north side of the White House. Moving the First Lady may have saved her life. If Mrs. Garfield had returned to her room on the south side of the building, she would have been exposed to the miasmic breezes from the marshes by the river. In her weakened state, the foul-smelling air could have proved fatal.

Hour after hour and day after day, the President remained by her side, caressing her forehead and seldom sleeping. Little by little her condition began to improve. Meanwhile, with the Senate in turmoil, the Star Route Scandal growing, and the Robertson nomination coming to a head, Guiteau continued to bombard the White House with his bizarre letters.

On May 7, he wrote, "I am sorry you and Senator Conkling are apart, but I stand by you on the ground that his friends Morton, James, Pearson and the rest of them have been well provided for, and Mr. Conkling ought to have been satisfied."

On May 10: "I have got a new idea about '84. If you work your position for all its worth you can be nominated and elected in '84."

P.S.—I will see you about the Paris Consulship tomorrow, unless you happen to send my name to-day."

Finally, on May 13, he wrote:

"I hope Mrs. Garfield is better. Monday I sent you a note about the Paris Consulship; Tuesday, one about 1884. Your nomination was a providence, and your election a still greater providence. May I tell Mr. Blaine to prepare the order for my appointment to the Paris Consulship?"

On Friday the 13th the day he sent his regards to Mrs. Garfield, he was officially banned from the White House. Joe Stanley Brown had been instructed to end all contact with the strange little man in the rumpled suit. He would no longer be allowed to enter the building, leave his card, or pester the secretaries. The very next day, he ambushed Blaine, demanding to know the status of his application. This time, however, the Secretary was not so polite. He stuck his finger in Guiteau's face and told him, "Never speak to me again about the Paris consulship as long as you live."

Enraged and frustrated, he wrote one final letter to the President. In light of the tragedy that followed, it seems prophetic:

General Garfield—I have been trying to be your friend. I do not know whether you appreciate it or not, but I am moved to call your attention to the remarkable letter from Mr. Blaine, which I have just noticed. According to Mr. Farwell, of Chicago, Blaine is a vindictive politician and an evil genius, and you will have no peace till you get rid of him. This letter shows that Mr. Blaine is a wicked man, and you ought to demand his immediate resignation; otherwise you and the republican party will come to grief. I will see you in the morning if I can, and talk with you.

Very respectfully, Charles Guiteau.

As the days passed by, Guiteau spent hours alone by himself in Lafayette Park, directly across from the White House. As Rosenberg wrote, "Charles was coming to the end of his path, his life increasingly unrelated to others. He had no source of income, no lecturing, no books to sell, no bills to collect; he had no family; he had never had any friends." What else could possibly go wrong?

Just one thing.

Roscoe Conkling and Thomas Platt had been fighting the Robertson nomination for several months, and despite a growing chorus of criticism, they had no intention of backing down. Nobody, especially "that man from Ohio," would dictate terms to the leader of the Stalwarts. In a last ditch effort to sabotage the nomination, Conkling convinced the *New York Herald*, the nation's most widely read newspaper, to print an "expose" about Garfield's double-dealing against the New York Stalwarts. The entire story was dictated, anonymously, by Conkling himself, and the goal, according to Kenneth D. Ackerman, was simple: "By Roscoe Conkling's calculation, the story would shock the Senators and stop them in their tracks. Robertson's nomination would be doomed, along with the president who had made it."

The Senators read every word, but, by now they had heard it all before, and they were hardly shocked. Too late, Conkling discovered that his colleagues were sick and tired of arguing over one "inconsequential" nomination. The vast majority were willing to bow to the President, but not "Lord Roscoe." He refused to concede and vowed to fight the nomination when it reached the Senate floor. Thomas Platt, New York's junior senator, had a better idea. Why not resign in protest, embarrass the President, then run for re-election?

The idea sounded crazy, but with help from the *Herald*, it just might work.

On May 16, Vice-President Arthur handed the Reading Clerk of the Senate a small sheet of paper containing these words:

Sir:

Will you please announce to the Senate that my resignation as Senator of the United States from the State of New York has been forwarded to the Governor of the State. I have the honor to be, with great respect, your obedient servant,

Roscoe Conkling

When the clerk finished reading, the chamber fell silent. After a while, some incredulous Senators demanded a second reading. The clerk obliged, and when he was done, the Vice-president handed him a second note. He hesitated for a moment then read it aloud:

Sir:

I have forwarded to the Governor of the State of New York my resignation as Senator of the United States for the State of New York. Will you please announce the fact to the Senate?

With great respect, your obedient servant,

T.C. Platt

A showdown with Conkling and Platt had been inevitable, but nobody thought that it would come to this. Nevertheless and not surprisingly, the Senate had work to do, and they were not inclined to call a recess just to satisfy their unhappy colleagues. Within minutes, the Senate resumed its business as though nothing had happened.

When Garfield heard the news, he predicted that the resignations would "be received with guffaws of laughter," and he was right. As Doenecke noted, "Hayes claimed that Conkling was suffering from "monomania on the subject of his own importance." Platt henceforth had to live with the nickname "Me Too."

The New York Senators were undoubtedly shocked when, two days later, Judge Robertson was unanimously confirmed as Collector of the Port of New York. Time would tell if Conkling and Platt would ever return to the Senate, but for now, one thing was clear. In the city of Washington, the President reigned supreme.

Guiteau had reason to be worried, for he had alienated the two most powerful men in government. Garfield and Blaine would not see him, and the White House and the State Department were now off-limits. Whatever plans he had for a consulship would not come to fruition—not with the present administration running the show. From Guiteau's standpoint that could mean only one thing. Despite his misgivings, it was time to consider the unthinkable.

CHAPTER TWENTY-NINE

The police were not looking for Charles Guiteau, but they did want to talk to him about an unpaid boardinghouse bill. Mrs. Lockwood, the proprietor of the Twelfth Street House, was very upset. She was owed two weeks' rent, but her border was gone. He had vanished in the middle of the night, and she had no idea where to find him. For all she knew, he might have gone back to New York City.

Actually, Guiteau had found himself a second, cheaper boardinghouse on Fourteenth Street.

Poor Mrs. Lockwood was nearly beside herself. She had disliked Guiteau from the start, which is why she had given him an out-of-the-way room. There was just something about him that made her uncomfortable, and she was not the only one who felt that way. "He appeared to have a cat-like tread," said one of her tenants, "and walked so easily that he was always up alongside persons before they knew it."

He had also been a rude tenant. He was so rude, in fact, that some of his fellow borders refused to sit next to him at the dinner table. Strangely enough, he had taken the time to send Mrs. Lockwood a note stating that he was expecting a six thousand dollar position and would soon pay his bill. The position was a good one—Minister to France.

On the evening of May 18, Guiteau retired early, depressed and exhausted by the events of the past few days. Lying in bed unable to sleep, he began to have some very dark thoughts. As his mind continued to wander, an "impression," as he later described it, came over him that if the President were out of the way, everything would go better. At first the idea startled him, but the more he thought about it, the more it made sense. "With Garfield removed," Ackerman wrote, "Chet Arthur would become President. Arthur would set things right—for Guiteau, for his friends, for the country."

Guiteau expressed a similar sentiment in his "autobiography":

> At first this was a mere impression. I kept reading the papers and kept being impressed, and the idea kept bearing and bearing and bearing down upon me that the only way to unite the two factions of the Republican Party, and save the Republic from going in to the hands of the rebels and Democrats, was to quietly remove the President.

To Guiteau, in his weakened state of mind, quietly meant no bombs, the favorite tool of European assassins. Killing a man with explosives was cowardly, and, as history showed, there were always innocent victims. Such was the case in March when, three days before Garfield's inauguration, Czar Alexander II had been murdered by a trio of "nihilists," as they were called in Europe. Unlike the President, who had rejected the idea of posting uniformed guards at the White House, the Czar was well aware of the dangers of holding public office. Before the March attack, he had been the target of three other assassination attempts, which had forced him to travel in a bulletproof carriage accompanied by Cossack guards. Still, he remained vulnerable. As his carriage drove over the Pevchesky Bridge, a young nihilist tossed a bomb under the horses' hooves, killing one of the Cossacks and seriously wounding the driver and people on the sidewalk. The Czar emerged shaken but unhurt. Suddenly a second bomb was thrown, but this one landed at the Czar's feet, exploding with enough force to knock down twenty people. Alexander was taken by sleigh to the Winter Palace, where he was given Communion and Extreme Unction. After he died, the Romanov family learned that there had been a third assassin in the crowd, and he too had brought a bomb—just in case the first two bombers failed.

Over the next few days, Guiteau's "impression" took on a spiritual tone, evolving into a divine inspiration. "I never had the slightest doubt as to the divinity of the inspiration," he said later. Even a blind man could see that he was the right man for the job. "I had the brains and the nerve to do the work."

Meanwhile, on May 20, the Senate adjourned in an orderly and peaceful manner. Later that same day, Dr. Boynton announced a slight improvement in Mrs. Garfield's condition. That evening, her fever fell to 101 degrees, down significantly from just twenty-four hours earlier. Days and weeks would pass before she could leave her bed, but, for now, the shadow of death was lifted.

Four days later, Conkling and Platt arrived in Albany, New York, accompanied by their close friend and colleague, Chester A. Arthur. The triumvirate had returned to the State Capitol to reclaim the two senatorial positions they had recently surrendered. In order to accomplish this goal, they would have to win a special election in the state legislature, which was thought to be a minor obstacle. After all, these were the leaders of the Stalwarts, the most powerful men in state politics. How could they lose?

Both chambers of the State Legislature—the Senate and Assembly—would participate in the exercise. The 60 combined members would vote as one body. In accordance with the rules of the Legislature, 81 votes were needed to win. The first roll call was taken on May 31, but, surprisingly, none of the leading candidates won enough votes to declare victory. "From here on," Ackerman wrote, "the law required the legislators to meet every day, six days a week, to cast ballot after ballot until someone prevailed. It would be a long, hot summer in Albany."

Back in Washington, Guiteau began to envision himself as a tool of the Lord, locked in a deadly struggle against the unholy influences of the federal government. "Two weeks after I conceived the idea," he wrote, "my mind was thoroughly settled on the intention to remove the President." In addition to doing the Lord's work, he now had an opportunity to enrich himself and spread the gospel.

"I sent to Boston for a copy of my book. I cut out a paragraph, and a line, and a word, here and there, and added one or two new chapters, put some new ideas in it, and I greatly improved it. I knew that it would probably have a large sale on account of the notoriety that the act of removing the President would give me, and I wished the book to go out to the public in proper shape."

The next step would lead him to George C. Maynard, a distant relative. On June 8, Guiteau borrowed fifteen dollars from Maynard, ostensibly to pay his boardinghouse bill. Instead of paying his rent, he went to John O'Meara's gun and cutlery store at the corner of Fifteenth and F Streets. O'Meara would later testify that Guiteau had come into his shop twice, once on the sixth of June and again on the eighth. On the sixth, he spotted two "British Bulldog" revolvers in a display case: a snub-nosed five-shooter with an ivory handle and a similar model with a wood handle. Unlike most Mid-Westerners, Guiteau knew nothing of firearms and had a difficult time deciding which gun he liked most. The wooden-handled model would be less expensive, but the one with the fancy grip would look much better displayed in the museum case it was destined to occupy. He examined the ivory-handled pistol carefully, inquired about its accuracy, and then left, telling O'Meara that he would call again in a few days. He returned on the eighth, anxious to take another look at the Bulldog.

O'Meara told him that the revolver sold for ten dollars and that, in his opinion, it was worth every penny. There were a number of .44 caliber guns on the market, but none as accurate and reliable as the Webley& Scott Bulldog. Despite its thick frame, it could be carried in a coat pocket, and when fired correctly, it had a range of somewhere between 15 and 20 yards. At a closer distance, it could kill a horse.

Maybe so, but ten dollars was a hefty sum to pay for a "pocket gun." On the other hand, it was quite imposing, almost scary. "I looked at it as if it was going to bite me," Guiteau later wrote.

Sensing Guiteau's discomfort, the wily shopkeeper placed another revolver on the counter. "You might like this Smith & Wesson," O'Meara said. "The *Schofield* is a popular pistol. In fact, it's the personal favorite of Jesse James."

Guiteau made a face. He had no use for a weapon that was used by a common outlaw. He nudged the *Schofield* aside and lifted the Bulldog, aiming at an imaginary target. He guessed its length to be somewhere between two and three inches. The weight was difficult to judge, but it felt comfortable in his hand. When he hesitated, O'Meara lowered his price to nine dollars, asking an extra dollar for small penknife and several boxes of cartridges.

Guiteau jumped at the offer, and a helpful customer showed him how to load the revolver. O'Meara advised him to keep the pistol in his pocket. There were laws against carrying a loaded weapon within city limits, and even though the laws were only enforced against drunks, it would be wise to be discreet.

Later that evening, at the end of a particularly hot and sultry day, Guiteau placed the gun in his pocket and walked down to the foot of Seventeenth Street. When he reached the muddy banks of the Potomac River, he took out the gun and fired ten shots into the water. The purpose, as he later explained, was "just to get used to the outward act of handling a weapon."

Guiteau had never handled firearms before, and, as he later confessed, they actually frightened him. Yet here he was standing on the bank of the Potomac River, firing away within earshot of the White House. At first he was startled by the deafening noise and the unexpected recoil, but then he realized that both were part of the Bulldog's "charm." O'Meara was right, he told himself. The powerful gun could kill a horse.

The truth, it happens, was that Guiteau began to stalk the President less than forty-eight hours after buying a gun. On Sunday, June 10, the President and his family attended services at the National City Christian Church on Massachusetts Avenue. "Guiteau had watched the president there before," Ackerman wrote. "This time, he walked in and stood at the rear door, his revolver in his pocket, and noted in his mind the exact spot where the president sat—in a pew near an open window with his family at his side." Nobody noticed the short, unkempt man with his hands in his pockets, but he noticed a few things. For instance, he thought it would be easy to shoot the President through the open window. He also noticed that there were no guards or policemen outside. When the time came, he would simply run up to the window and shoot Mr. Garfield in the head. "I intended to shoot him through the back of the head and let the ball pass through the ceiling, in order that no one else should be injured." The noise would scare the devil out of everyone, and with any luck, he might avoid capture—or a lynch mob. "I made up my mind that the next Sunday I would certainly shoot him if he was in church."

Later that week, the *Washington Evening Star* reported that the President and his wife—still recuperating from her illness—planned to leave for Long Branch, New Jersey on the morning of June 18th. Guiteau was pleased beyond measure. The Baltimore and Potomac Railroad Station would be an ideal spot to "remove" the President. Early on Thursday, June 16, he composed an "address to the American people." Hoping to clarify his motive, he wrote,

"I conceived of the idea of removing the President four weeks ago. Not a soul knew of my purpose. I conceived the idea myself. Ingratitude is the basest of crimes. That the President, under the manipulation of his Secretary of State, has been guilty of the basest ingratitude to the Stalwarts admits of no denial. In the President's madness he has wrecked the once grand old Republican Party; and for this he dies. I had no ill-will to the President. This is not murder. It is a political necessity."

Guiteau arrived at the depot at 9:00 on Saturday morning, his personal papers in one pocket and his revolver in the other. As he expected, the President and his party arrived a few minutes later. To Guiteau's surprise, the president and his wife were traveling with their three youngest children, Mollie, Irvin, and Abram—as well as cabinet secretaries Windom, Hunt and James, and their wives. In his autobiography, Guiteau would describe the scene in chilling detail.

"He [Garfield] got out of his carriage. I stood in the ladies' [waiting] room, about the middle of the room, watching him. I was all ready; My mind was all made up; I had all my papers with me; I had all the arrangements made to shoot him and to jump into a carriage and drive over to the jail."

Guiteau followed the President to the platform, fully prepared to kill him, but when he saw how frail and weak Mrs. Garfield had become, he hesitated. She "looked so thin and she clung so tenderly to the president's arm," he later wrote, "that my heart failed me to part them, and I decided to take him alone."

The President and his party climbed aboard their train, anxious to breathe the "bracing and invigorating salt air" prescribed by Dr. Boynton. Their final destination was the Hotel Elberon, one of the finest beach resorts on the Jersey shore. They would spend ten days together, enjoying a family vacation that none of them would ever forget. During the daytime, Mollie, Irvin and Abram engaged in horseplay and swam in the ocean while the President and the First Lady toured the town in a horse-drawn carriage. In the evening, they dined lavishly and mingled with some prominent well-wishers including a former president named Grant.

One fine day followed another, and with each passing day, Mrs. Garfield grew stronger. The salt air was a big factor, but she also ate well and got plenty of rest. By the end of the month she was able to write, "I had a splendid sleep last night, more natural than any since my illness and was more sleepy at eight this morning than when I was in bed, and am feeling very well this morning."

By the time Garfield read these words, he would be back in Washington, hours away from the worst nightmare of his life.

CHAPTER THIRTY

Back in Washington, Guiteau began to make his final preparation to "remove the President to paradise," as he later put it. On June 24, he decided to visit the District of Columbia Jail, figuring that it would be a good idea to inspect the cell he would have to occupy in the near future. In an act that whiffed of insanity, he strolled up to the front door of the jail and asked the deputy warden if he could take a short tour of the facility. The deputy warden must have shaken his head in disbelief. In any case, he declined the request and told Guiteau to go away. Before he left, Guiteau peeked inside and declared that it was "a very excellent jail."

When the President returned from New Jersey on the 27th, Guiteau was waiting for him at the depot, ready to complete his mission. He later wrote:

> "I noticed in the papers that he [Garfield] would be back the first of the week. I watched the papers very carefully to see when he would return. The following Monday [June 27th] was a terribly

> hot, sultry day. I remember I suffered greatly from the heat, but notwithstanding that I prepared myself again, and I went to the depot again on Monday with my revolver and my papers, but I did not feel like firing on him."

Instead, Guiteau decided to cool off in the ladies' waiting room. "I was watching for the President all that week," he explained. "I got up one morning at half-past five, thinking that I might get the President when he was out horseback riding, but he did not go out that morning."

On Tuesday or Wednesday, Guiteau read that the President would soon be leaving on a long trip to New England. Barring an emergency, he would be gone for most of the summer. Reports indicated that Garfield would be traveling with his wife, his older sons, Harry and James, and his daughter, Mollie. The younger boys, Irvin and Abram, would be staying with relatives in Ohio. The high point of the trip would be a stop at Williams College in Massachusetts, where the President would attend a commencement ceremony at his alma mater. The rest of his itinerary was spelled out in detail, including the exact date and time that the President would be departing—Saturday, July 2, at 9:25.

As it was, Guiteau saw his situation to be so precarious that the only choice was to act immediately. On Thursday evening, June 30, he decided to ambush the President as he rode by Lafayette Park in his carriage.

"In the evening, after dinner, at five o'clock, I went up to my room and got my revolver out and carried it in my pocket. I was in Lafayette Park opposite the White House watching for him, and about half-past six the White House carriage drove up. They drove out the entrance nearest the Treasury Building and passed right along the east side of Lafayette Square toward Arlington."

The carriage moved quickly, and Guiteau had no chance to fire. "I hung around the park about half an hour or so," he later added, "and they did not return, and it was very warm, and I concluded to let the matter drop for that night, so that, after sitting in the park for some time, I went as usual to my home and went to bed."

On that very same day, two other strange events occurred, one in Albany, New York, and the other inside the White House itself. In Albany, a "Mrs. Baldwin" walked into the fancy Delavan House Hotel and checked herself into room 113. About an hour later, former senator Thomas Platt surreptitiously entered the same room, closed the door, and locked it. Unfortunately for Platt, the hotel was filled with political rivals, and when they discovered the liaison, they closed in for the kill.

Ackerman described the scene as follows:

> "Within minutes, half a dozen of them [Half-Breeds] had congregated in the hallway outside room 113. They waited, and when no one came out after a long while, someone got the idea to pull over a stepladder to peek through a small window over the door. Suffice to say that the couple were scantily attired and were caught in *flagrante delicto* one of them later told reporters."

When the story broke, Platt became a national joke. In a moment of weakness, he had ruined his reputation and squandered all hope of reclaiming his Senate seat. Even worse, he had tarnished the reputation of his friend and colleague, Roscoe Conkling. After this escapade, "The

Great Quarreler" was openly mocked and ridiculed. He would remain in politics a while longer, but he would never serve in the Senate again.

Inside the White House, Garfield had a different sort of encounter, but one that was almost as strange. Following a cabinet meeting, he asked Robert Lincoln, the Secretary of War, to recount the night his father was assassinated at Ford's Theatre. The Secretary thought it was an odd request, but he politely obliged. Apparently Garfield was mesmerized by the firsthand account of the terrible event. Months later, Secretary Lincoln would learn that Garfield had actually been concerned about his own mortality. For many years Garfield had believed that he would not live to be older than his father was and that he would die in a sudden and violent manner. He had been quoted as saying that the feeling was wholly involuntary on his part, and that it haunted him most when he tried not to think about it.

> "I think of my father and how he died in the strength of his manhood and left my mother to care for a large family of children, and how I have always been without his assistance and advice, and then I feel lit so strong upon me that the vision is in the form of a warning that I cannot treat lightly."

Even after Garfield reached the age of his father at death, he was convinced that he would die violently in one of two ways—either by falling between the cars of a train or in the simple act of traveling with his family.

And now, in less than 36 hours, he would be traveling by train—with his sons Harry and James—to Long Branch, New Jersey.

On Friday morning, July 1, Guiteau snuck out of Grant's boarding house and checked into the fashionable Riggs House at Fifteenth and G Streets. Later that evening, he walked to Lafayette Park and took his usually spot on a park bench facing the White House. At about 7:00, the President walked out of the White House alone and unguarded. "I had not been there a minute before I saw the President walk out," he recalled. "Now, I thought to myself, I have got a splendid chance at him; he is all alone; there isn't any one around him."

The President walked along the east side of Lafayette Square and made his way down H Street, never once looking back. Guiteau got up from his bench and followed. "I walked along the opposite side of the street from him. The pistol was in my hand and in my pocket." Having waited long enough, he was just about to cross the street when Garfield entered a large brick house—the home of his Secretary of State, James G. Blaine. Cursing his bad luck, Guiteau ducked into an alley. "I went into the alley in the rear of Mr. Morton's house and got out my revolver and looked at it, and wiped it off and put it back into my pocket." Thirty minutes later, Garfield and Blaine came out together and walked arm in arm to the White House. Guiteau followed from a safe distance, but after standing in the alley for half an hour, he felt "tired and wearied from the heat." He held his fire, but their open display of friendship left a lasting impression in his mind. "They seemed to be in a very hilarious state of mind," he observed dryly. "This scene made a striking impression on me; it confirmed what I had read in the papers, and what I had felt for a long time, to wit, that the President was entirely under Mr. Blaine's influence, and that they were in perfect accord."

Guiteau concluded that it would be perfectly natural to remove such a weak man. Who could blame him for acting boldly? After all, he was acting under Divine authority and serving the best interest of the American people. In time, the public would understand his motive and history would judge him kindly. One day he would be known as Charles Guiteau, the great American patriot.

Later that evening it dawned on Guiteau that he was running out of time. Tomorrow morning the President was leaving for Long Branch.

Like it or not, he had only one more chance to accomplish his mission. The time had come to act. There could be no more excuses and no turning back.

Sitting alone in his room at the Riggs House, he composed two final letters. The first was a feeble attempt to explain his motivation for removing the President:

> The President's tragic death was a sad necessity, but it will unite the Republican Party and save the Republic. Life is a fleeting dream, and it matters little when one goes. A human life is of small value. During the war thousands of brave boys went down without a tear. I presume the President was a Christian, and that he will be happier in Paradise than here.
>
> It will be no worse for Mrs. Garfield, dear soul, to part with her husband this way than by natural death.
>
> He is liable to go at any time anyway.
>
> I had no ill-will toward the President. His death was a political necessity. I am a lawyer, a theologian, a politician. I am a Stalwart of the Stalwarts. I was with General Grant and the rest of our men in New York during the canvass. I have some papers for the press,

which I shall leave with Byron Andrews and his co-journalists at 1440 N.Y. Ave, where all the reporters can see them.

I am going to the jail.

Charles Guiteau

The second letter was addressed to General William Tecumseh Sherman, General of the Army. Most historians agree that it was written as an afterthought, intended to reduce the possibility of a lynching:

To Gen. Sherman:

I have just shot the President. I shot him several times as I wished him to go as easily as possible. His death was a political necessity. I am a lawyer, a theologian, and a politician. I was with Gen. Grant and the rest of our men in New York during the canvass. I am going to jail. Please order your troops and take possession of the jail at once.

Very respectfully, Charles Guiteau

The letters were sealed in separate envelopes, and both were placed in his suit pocket, where the police could easily find them. Now only one chore remained. He cleaned his revolver, checked the firing mechanism, and carefully loaded the cylinder with five rounds of ammunition.

Finally, after weeks of planning and several false starts, Charles Guiteau, the great American patriot, was ready to save the Republic.

CHAPTER THIRTY-ONE

When James Garfield awoke on the morning of July 4, 1881, he discovered that he was drenched in sweat, but the pain and nausea were gone. During the night someone had moved his bed closer to the window, and if he tried, he could hear the comforting sounds of summer. He had spent the last three days drifting in and out of sleep, and for a while, he had been extremely close to death. Miraculously, his pulse and temperature were back to normal and holding steady. Even his appetite had begun to improve.

The public was elated, almost delirious, by what they read in the newspapers. "The President himself is full of splendid courage," one reporter wrote. "His nerve is remarkable, and has done much to sustain him. His grasp is as strong as ever. His eyes are bright, and he talks to those about him cheerfully. Sometimes he contrives to joke with the doctors, but he realizes very clearly the straits that he is in."

In truth, Garfield had little to laugh about. For one thing, it was unbearably hot and humid. The breeze that came up from the Potomac rustled the window draperies, but the air itself was tainted by the foul-smelling swamp near the river. A correspondent from *The New York Times* described the situation in vivid detail. "The night [July 6th.] was very warm, the thermometer at one o'clock this morning registering 84°. A very slight breeze was blowing, but it came from the north, and did not penetrate to the President's room. He was constantly fanned by those in attendance on him, however, and if he suffered any inconvenience from the heat, he made no complaints, and certainly no evil effects followed."

Suggestions for cooling the sick-room poured in from every corner of the globe, but in the end, the problem was solved by scientist Simon Newcomb and a group of Navy engineers who invented and installed what may well have been the world's first air-conditioner.

The brilliant Newcomb was a revered astronomer and mathematician, best known for his work on recalculating the major astronomical constants and measuring the precise speed of light. He had met the President in 1863, shortly after Garfield won election to the House of Representatives. At the time, Newcomb held a position at the Naval Observatory. He remembered Garfield as a "man of classic culture, refined tastes, and unsurpassed eloquence." Years later, he would describe the President as the "only truly honorable" politician he had ever known.

A week after the shooting, Newcomb and his engineers constructed a box-like structure containing cloths [bed sheets and blankets] saturated with melted ice water and a fan that blew hot air overhead. The contraption lowered the sick-room temperature by 20 degrees Fahrenheit. It also consumed half a million pounds of ice in two months' time.

Unfazed by the minor detail of ice, Newcomb went on to speculate that it might be possible to locate the bullet in Garfield's back by the process of electrical induction. The idea was met with a great deal of skepticism, but there was one person who thought it might work—a Scottish inventor named Alexander Graham Bell.

Bell wired Newcomb to say that he was prepared to rig up an "induction machine"—an apparatus that could generate an electrical field around a man. "With such a machine," Bettyann Kevles wrote, "an operator could pass an exploring coil over someone, like a divining rod seeking hidden water: The moment the coil passed over metal it would trip a mechanism to signal its find."

At this point, Garfield began to show intermittent signs of recovery, but he still ran a small fever and was never entirely free from discomfort. Small doses of morphine helped him sleep, but it was evident that the wound was not draining properly. Something had to be done before the area became infected, and to the doctors, that meant one thing: finding the ball.

Bell arrived in Washington bursting with confidence, certain that he would find the "mysterious missing bullet," as it was now being called in the press. As the President lay in bed, sipping iced champagne, Bell went to work, scavenging parts from all over the town. In a relatively short time, he was able to accumulate an impressive array of equipment: huge induction coils, Bunsen elements that were used to ignite gas lamps, and an electric motor from the Western Union Telegraph Company.

A description of the newfangled device was published in the newspapers, and despite being couched in scientific language, it proved to be of great interest to the public.

> The instrument consisted of two circular primary coils of insulated copper three inches in diameter and half an inch in thickness, the

one being constructed of No. 19 wire, and containing between seven and eight ohms of resistance, forming the primary coil, and the other of No. 28 or 30 wire, giving more than eighty ohms of resistance, forming the secondary coil, the two being connected in separate metallic circuits. In the circuit with the former there was placed an electrical battery and a spring vibrator, so adjusted as to make a very rapid series of "breaks" of the circuit, sending a hundred or more electrical pulsations over the circuit and around the primary coil of wire per second. A hand telephone only was placed in the circuit with the secondary coil. The batteries being connected, and the vibrator set in motion, the secondary coil was placed so as to cover the primary, and the operator having the telephone at his ear, hears the pulsations of the primary current sent through the vibrator.

Finally, on August 1, almost a month after the shooting, Bell and his colleagues were ready to use the "metal detector" on the President.

The patient was bolstered up in bed, and he watched the proceedings with mute interest. His physicians stood around. Professor Bell stood with his back toward the President, holding the telephone to his ear, while Mr. Taintor, Professor Bell's assistant, moved the coils over that portion of the abdomen where the leaden ball was thought to be imbedded. When the sensitive centre of the instrument was immediately over the black and blue spot that appeared shortly after the President was wounded, Professor Bell said: "Stop! There it is."

As it turned out, Bell was wrong. The source of the clicks was not the lead ball, but the metallic springs inside the presidential hair mattress. Undeterred, Bell tested the device again, but once more the results were inconclusive. Still, the bulletins and newspaper accounts touted the experiments as a success. Bell himself published his finding as *A Successful Form of Induction Balance for the Painless Detection of Metallic Masses in the Human Body.*

What Bell failed to realize was that even without the mishaps, he would never had found the ball because, like the doctors, he was looking in the wrong place. As they would later learn, the elusive bullet had actually turned left—180 degrees away from the estimated path—and was, in fact, lodged to the *left* of the vertebrae near the pancreas.

By the end of August, Garfield had lost over one hundred pounds and had become so weak that he could barely wave to visitors. His doctors feared that the heat and malaria of Washington might kill him, so they decided to move him to Elberon, New Jersey, near Long Branch. The President was more than willing to leave, so in early September, the Pennsylvania Railroad Company laid a special track to the White House and another track to the seaside cottage of New York financier Charles G. Franklyn.

The removal of the President took place on September 6, under the respectful gaze of several thousand well-dressed spectators. At 5:45 a.m., he was carried out of the White House and placed in a horse-drawn wagon. Slowly, the wagon was led to a special train that had been modified to keep him safe and comfortable. Back in Altoona, the seats had been ripped out to make room for an ingeniously designed bed that floated on heavy-duty box springs. To keep the car cool, boxes of ice were placed beneath the bed, and, to assure a constant temperature, a false ceiling was installed to allow for the circulation of air.

Onlookers craned their necks, hoping to catch a glimpse of their beloved President, but those who saw him were shocked by his appearance. The once robust Garfield looked pale and gaunt, and his beard was cropped short. The prominent moustache was gone. To many he looked like a corpse, and some said that it would be a miracle if he survived the wagon ride, much less the two-hundred-mile train trip.

In spite of the obvious difficulty, the President handled the trip well, but doctors could not predict how long he would be incapacitated even if he recovered. Vice-President Arthur had passed the summer in his New York home on Lexington Avenue, and like everyone else, he was waiting anxiously to see if the fresh salt air would be beneficial. Clearly, he was not looking forward to the alternative. "My heart is full of deep anxiety," he wrote in late July. "May God in his infinite goodness bring us safely out of this great peril; and my faith is strong that He will."

For a while, it seemed like Arthur would get his wish, but then, on the morning of September 15, the President began to sink once more. The relapse brought on chills, fever, vomiting, and an irregular pulse. Even worse, the wound began to discharge a large amount of pus. On the 17th the President sank still lower. During the day his pulse shot up to 120, the vomiting increased, and he fell into a raging delirium.

The absent members of the Cabinet were telegraphed to return to Elberon immediately.

But Garfield was not ready to go just yet. Somehow, despite the pain and suffering—and the onset of pneumonia—he lived for two more days. The last official bulletin was issued on September 19 at 6:00 and stated the President's condition as follows:

> Though the gravity of the President's condition continues, there has been no aggravation of symptoms since the noon bulletin was issued. He has slept most of the time, coughing but little and with ease. The sputa remains unchanged. A sufficient amount of nourishment had been taken and retained. Temperature, 98.4; pulse, 102; respiration, 18.

At ten o'clock that evening, Dr. Bliss took Garfield's pulse and discovered it was very weak. He expressed his concern to General David Swaim, the President's close friend and personal attendant. Swaim knew that the end was near, but all he could do was watch and wait—and pray that the President passed peacefully. After Bliss stepped out of the room the President awakened and stirred slightly. "How it hurts here!" he whispered, pressing his hand to his heart. "Oh, Swaim. I am in terrible pain here . . . Swaim, can't you do something for me?"

Swaim sent for Mrs. Garfield and the doctor, who had just begun work on his daily report. Bliss ran into the sick-room and immediately surmised the gravity of the situation. "My God, Swaim!" he said. "The President is dying!"

Mrs. Garfield arrived an instant later. She turned pale when she saw Bliss massaging her husband's limbs. "What does this mean?" she demanded to know. Swaim tried to comfort her, but her complete attention was focused on her husband, who lay motionless on the bed, barely breathing, a slight tremor in his hands and feet. "Oh! Why am I made to suffer this cruel wrong?" she moaned.

Bliss frantically searched for a pulse in the President's wrist, then his neck, then placed his ear over Garfield's heart. He heard a faint heartbeat, but it was clear that the President was slipping away. He grabbed a hypodermic needle from his case and administered a dose of stimulants, but it was too late. The raspy breaths came farther and farther apart, and at 10:35 p.m., they ceased altogether.

Bliss placed a hand on the President's chest and said softy, "It is over."

Lucretia Garfield had remained calm and composed throughout her husband's long ordeal, but now that the end had come, she could restrain her tears no longer. She sat in a chair, shaking convulsively, with tears pouring down her cheeks. After a little while, she stood, took her husband's hand, and began to stroke his arm. Young Mollie, standing on the other side of the bed, sobbed uncontrollably.

By strange coincidence, Garfield died on the anniversary of his promotion to Major-General, for brave deeds in the battle of Chickamauga. It was during this battle, in 1863, that Garfield had ridden his horse through a gauntlet of rebel guns to reach Generals Rosencrans and Thomas. The strange part was that Garfield had told a few close friends that he was certain that when he died, he would die on the anniversary of this important event.

General Mussey had told Lucretia Garfield about the prophecy on August twenty-seventh. "He will not live; but he will not die until the nineteenth day of September."

"Why do you make that statement?" she had asked.

"Because it was on the nineteenth day of September, 1863, that General Garfield was made Major-General for gallantry in the battle of Chickamauga, and he has often told me that when he died, he thought he should die on the anniversary of his promotion."

CHAPTER THIRTY-TWO

Chester Alan Arthur had had over two months to prepare for the inevitable, but when the news reached him later that night, he buried his head in his hands and began to weep. "I hope—my God, I do hope it is a mistake," he said on hearing about the President's death. But there was no mistake.

Arthur was now the de facto head of the federal government. The telegram from Elberon was signed by all of the cabinet members present, a somber reminder that even in times of grief the continuity of the government had to be preserved. "It becomes our painful duty to inform you of the death of President Garfield and to advise you to take the oath of office as President of the United States without delay. If it concur with your judgement we will be very glad if you will come on the earliest train tomorrow morning."

Arthur's first inclination was to take the oath in Washington, D.C., but after conferring with his friends, he decided to proceed without delay. Two judges of the State Supreme Court—both Democrats—were brought to his residence on Lexington Avenue, and shortly after 2:00 a.m., Chester A. Arthur became the 21st President of the United States.

The ceremony was held in the front parlor, the oath administered by Judge John R. Brady, the first judge to arrive. At precisely 2:15 a.m., Arthur raised his right hand and placed his left hand on a bible, then said, "I, Chester Alan Arthur, do solemnly swear, that I will faithfully execute the office of the President of the United States, and will to the best of my ability preserve, protect and defend the Constitution of the United States. So help me God."

The following morning, September 20, President Arthur climbed aboard a special train that took him from New York City to Elberon, New Jersey. There he joined Mrs. Garfield and cabinet members who were bringing Garfield's body back to the Capitol. During the ride, he had ample time to reflect on his own career, which was truly admirable, even in comparison to his predecessor.

Like Garfield, Arthur was a Protestant, but his roots were Irish. William Arthur, his father, hailed from Ballymena, County Antrim, in Northern Ireland. William was a graduate of Belfast College, and after he emigrated to America, he became a renowned minister. From 1855 to 1863, he served as pastor of the Calvary Baptist Church, marrying an American, Malvina Stone, who bore him a family of two sons and five daughters.

Chester A. Arthur was born in Fairfield, Vermont, October 5, 1829. (Out of vanity, he claimed to be born in 1830.) After extensive home tutoring, he entered Union College, and despite his young age—he was just fifteen years old—he excelled in all of his studies and graduated near the top of his class in 1848. After two years of law school, he became an educator, accepting the position of principal at the North

Pownal Academy in Bennington, Vermont. In 1852, he moved to New York City and was admitted to the bar, and within months, he became embroiled in the most contentious issue of the day—slavery.

One of his very first cases was the celebrated Lemmon Slave Case, a legal battle that generated plenty of publicity and death threats from both sides of the Mason-Dixon Line. In November of that year, Jonathan and Juliet Lemmon, Virginia slaveholders, intending to relocate to Texas, arrived in New York City to make a steamship connection. In addition to their luggage, they brought along eight black slaves—a man aged eighteen, two women of about the same age, each with a young infant, and three children. Louis Napoleon, a free black man residing in New York City, discovered their presence and asked Arthur to petition the court for a writ of habeas corpus. Arthur obtained the writ, arguing that the slaves were free under the terms of a New York law that automatically emancipated any slaves brought into the state.

Four years later, he became involved in another controversial case, and this one also had a racial component. Lizzie Jennings, a "colored woman of excellent character," was thrown off a Fourth Avenue street car because she was black. She brought suit against the railroad company that owned the line, then hired Arthur to represent her in court. The jury would award the plaintiff five hundred dollars in damages, and more importantly, the railroad company issued an order to permit colored persons to ride on their street cars.

When the Civil War began, Arthur was given the important post of Quarter-Master-General of the Second Brigade, New York State Militia. Had he been so inclined, he could have used the post to enrich himself, but he adamantly refused to accept all gifts. Unlike other men, he left his post poorer than when he began. "So zealous was he of his integrity," wrote a friend, "that I have known instances where he could have made thousands of dollars legitimately and yet he refused to do it, on the ground that he was a public officer and meant to be like Caesar's wife—above suspicion."

Arthur's own words best illuminate his true character—and his behavior during the war. "If I misappropriated a cent, and in walking down town saw two men talking on the corner together, I would imagine that they were talking of my dishonesty, and the very thought would drive me mad."

After the war, Arthur returned to his law practice and made a small fortune collecting war claims. Much of his income was spent on lavish parties, held at his luxurious brownstone under the watchful gaze of his beloved wife, Nell. The parties attracted many of the movers and shakers of the Republican Party, and it was through these connections that Arthur was appointed to the lucrative and politically powerful post of Collector of the Port of New York. He served in that capacity until 1878, when he was removed by Rutherford B. Hayes, the new president, who was determined to reform the federal patronage system in New York.

Ironically, Arthur would soon embrace the cause of civil-service reform by advocating and enforcing the Pendleton Civil Service Reform Act—the act that was to become the centerpiece of his administration.

As the train rolled south, then west, Arthur had plenty of time to reflect on the events that had brought him to the highest seat of power in the nation. Some were sad, others puzzling, but each had played a small part in the grand scheme of things.

On January 12, 1880, his wife died of pneumonia.

On June 10, 1880, while attending the Republican Presidential Convention in Chicago, he was nominated for Vice-President—despite the fact that nobody had won the presidential nomination.

In the fall of 1880, his Democratic foes raised doubts about his U.S. citizenship, alleging that he was born in Canada, not Vermont. The charge, if true, meant that Arthur was ineligible to ever serve as president, since the U.S. Constitution stipulated that only a "natural-born citizen" could hold that office.

Arthur never dignified the attacks by publicly addressing the allegation, but that did not stop the Democrats from pursuing the matter. According to Thomas C. Reeves, a biographer of Arthur's, the Democrats hired a New York attorney named Arthur Hinman to explore the rumors and make a report. Hinman got carried away and claimed that Arthur was born in Ireland—and was brought to America as a teenager. The allegation was laughable, and later played a role in the presidential campaign—which the Republicans won by fewer than 2,000 popular votes.

After the election, Arthur had tried—unsuccessfully—to persuade Garfield to fill certain cabinet positions with his fellow New York Stalwarts. The rebuke had caused a serious rift between the two men, exacerbated by Arthur's statement—a month before inauguration day—that Indiana, a swing state, had been won by illegal voting.

Finally, on May 16, 1881, New York Senators Conkling and Platt resigned in protest of Garfield's continuing opposition to the Stalwarts.

Soon rumors began to swirl that Arthur might resign. Of all the absurd charges leveled at Arthur, none was more hurtful than the accusation that he was somehow hindering the investigation of Garfield's shooting. The implication was clear; perhaps Charles Guiteau had not acted alone. Maybe the Vice-President was involved in a Stalwart plot to seize control of the White House. *The Washington Post*, engaging in the worst form of "yellow journalism," often reminded the public of Guiteau's first statement after his capture: "I am a Stalwart of the Stalwarts . . . Arthur is President now!"

On July 9, 1881, one week after the shooting, the *Post* published an article with the following headline: GARFIELD RECOVERING, VP ARTHUR HINDERS INVESTIGATION. This was just the first of numerous articles that employed fictional sources, dramatic headlines, and outright lies. In an effort to sell newspapers and smear the Republican Party, the newspaper had convinced its readership that Arthur was part of a dark conspiracy—and could be arrested.

The following, published in the Early Edition of the *Post*, is an excerpt from one of their vitriolic articles:

Reports have come in from our trusted sources within the police department that Vice President Chester Arthur has refused to aid police investigating the possible ties between the Vice President and the Stalwart Conspiracy . . . According to our sources, the police have received warrants to search the houses and offices of Vice President Arthur, as well as former Senators Roscoe Conkling and Thomas Platt, in an attempt to uncover other would be assassins within the Stalwart faction of the Republican Party . . . Arthur, Conkling and Platt have all refused to allow any inspection of their private correspondence or homes, stating that such an intrusion would violate their Fourth Amendment rights.

A lesser man might have struck back, if for no other reason than to salvage his reputation, but Arthur ignored the personal vendetta of the press. Even so, they continued to whip up public sentiment against the Vice President. In time, the daily barrage wore him down, as evidenced by his own words, written in a letter to his sister on September 2, 1881:

"My dear Mary, why have I been vilified in this manner? What have I done to deserve such a fate? I spend every waking hour hounded by members of the press . . . I have nothing left to say to the vultures who so swarm over my ever step. I have stated innocence more times than I care to remember and have taken every possible action to relieve them of their suspicions. President Garfield has made statements to the public, assuring them that I had no part in the assassination attempt. Even that [obscenity] Guiteau had admitted he acted alone . . . The fact that such lies are spread about by my enemies have given me great cause for concern. I lie awake at night, fearing that someone may take matters into their own hands . . . I fear that my only course of action may be to tender my resignation and do away with this nonsense."

Arthur would remain in office and become a competent honest President. Not only would he take on the Stalwart faction in regard to appointments, but he would also lend his full support to the Pendleton Act of 1883, which said that people could take civil-service exams for a number of positions, and keep those positions no matter who was elected.

According to Barbara Holland, author of *Hail To The Chiefs*,

"This upset all the key people, because handing out jobs had been a good way to make friends, and get presents and votes and surprising envelopes full of money, and pay people for favors and so on."

The atmosphere in Washington would remain poisonous, and soon, for the first time in American history, both houses of Congress would propose some startling new policies concerning security.

Prominent members of Congress would now be escorted to and from their homes to the Capitol Building, and it was suggested that Secret Service Agents from the Treasury Department should provide round-the-clock security for the President.

The political world was changing quickly—and it was all because of a deranged assassin named Charles Guiteau.

CHAPTER THIRTY-THREE

Eighteen years before his death, Garfield had made his famous ride from General Rosencrans to General Thomas, galloping through a gauntlet of Confederate guns, his two aides and their horses being shot at his side. During the summer of 1881, when the President's physicians had abandoned all hope that he would recover, General Mussey, a former military colleague, had predicted that Garfield would die, but not until the nineteenth day of September. When asked to explain his prediction, General Mussey repeated a statement that he'd made earlier to Mrs. Garfield:

Because it was on the nineteenth day of September, 1863, that General Garfield was made major-general for gallantry in the battle of Chickamauga, and he has often told me that when he died, he thought he should die on the anniversary of his promotion. I claim nothing for his prophecy, but only repeat what he told me several times with an earnestness I shall never forget.

The last "official bulletin" was issued at Elberon on the evening of the nineteenth at 11:30 p.m. It stated that the President had died at 10:35 p.m. After taking nourishment, Garfield fell into a quiet sleep for about half an hour before his death, and while he was sleeping, his pulse rose to 120. At ten minutes after ten o'clock, he awoke, complaining of severe pain around his heart, and almost immediately, he became unconscious and stopped breathing twenty-five minutes later. The bulletin was signed by the attending physicians, D.W. Bliss, Frank H. Hamilton, and D. Hayes Agnew.

Early the following morning, September 20, a message arrived at the home of Mrs. Mary Larabee, President Garfield's sister. The message was addressed to Eliza Garfield, who was living with her daughter in Solon, Ohio. It read:

> To Mrs. Eliza Garfield:
> James died this evening at 10:35. He calmly breathed his life away.
> D.G. Swaim

On Wednesday morning, September 21, while the nation wept, President Garfield's funeral cortege left Elberon for Washington, accompanied by the new President, Chester A. Arthur, Ex-President Ulysses Grant, and all the members of the Cabinet. The train was met by a contingent of eight officers from the Second Artillery. They lifted the body of the slain President from the car and carried it through the main room of the Baltimore & Potomac Railway Station, passing the very spot where the assassin had shot him in the back. Outside, the coffin was placed on a hearse, the troops coming to attention as the Marine Band played *Nearer, my God, to Thee.*

The procession, led by President Arthur, moved down Pennsylvania Avenue and came around the south wing of the Capitol, to the front entrance, where Garfield had been inaugurated a few months before.

As thousands watched, the coffin was brought into the Rotunda and placed on a catafalque—the same platform that had been used for President Lincoln. In accordance with custom, the body was left in the Rotunda to lie in state, guarded by a detail of the Capitol and Metropolitan police.

The next day, the public was allowed to view the casket, and the line of visitors stretched a quarter of a mile outside the Capitol entrance. Thousands more returned on Friday, the 23rd, to catch a glimpse of the funeral services. The service began at three o'clock in the afternoon, opening with the hymn *Asleep in Jesus* and concluding with a prayer by the late President's pastor.

At the close of the services, the casket was taken from the Rotunda and placed on the hearse. A long cortege of troops and dignitaries followed the horse-drawn wagon to the railway station, then watched in solemn silence as the body was carried aboard the funeral car.

At about five o'clock, the train moved off, bound for Cleveland.

All along the route—in cities, towns, villages, and hamlets—throngs of people gathered, eager to pay their respects. At the Baltimore station, the line of mourners stretched for over a mile. In Pittsburgh, the train was met by five thousand citizens. When the train entered Ohio, the passengers discovered that nearly every house in the state was draped in mourning. Nobody had ever seen anything like it before—not even when Lincoln had died.

The funeral train rolled into the Cleveland depot at 1:00 p.m. on Saturday, draped from end to end in black crape. An estimated crowd of fifty thousand were in attendance, and many were moved to tears when they saw the train arrive. Once again, the President's casket was transferred to a hearse, but this time it was brought to a large outdoor pavilion that had been erected in Monumental Park.

The pavilion, where Garfield lay in state for the next three days, was an imposing structure. The floor on which the burial platform rested was forty-five feet square and five-and-a-half feet high. It was reached by steps on the east and west sides. There were four arched openings on the sides, each facing a focal point. The columns at each corner were festooned with flags, and over each hung a large black banner.

The interior of the pavilion was decorated with magnificent floral arrangements, the most stunning, perhaps, a tower of balsams, tuberoses, begonia, and geranium leaves, surrounded by a broad base of ferns.

A simple wreath of flowers, a gift from Queen Victoria, was the only floral piece placed upon the casket.

For the rest of that afternoon, and all day Sunday, thousands of mourners passed around the casket, four abreast, disappointed that the President's face could not be seen, but glad to pay their respects to a man they truly admired.

Not surprisingly, Arthur's first public act as President was to proclaim Monday, September 26, the day that Garfield was buried, a national day of fasting, humiliation, and prayer.

After lying in state on Saturday and Sunday, the remains of President Garfield were solemnly committed to a tomb at Lake View Cemetery. The lot that was selected for the burial site was perched on the edge of a high ridge that offered a commanding view of Lake Erie. It had been Garfield's wish to be interred at this very spot, and his mother, speaking to the press, explained why it was appropriate.

"It is proper that he should be buried in Cleveland. It is the capital of the county in which he was born, and of the section where he grew into prominence. Mentor had been his home but a short time, although he had intended to spend the balance of his life there. Most of his years have been spent in Solon and Orange, and it seems best that his final resting-place should be near the places that he loved the best."

On the day that Garfield was buried, memorial services were held in many of the churches of the larger cities in England, Scotland, and Wales.

The Russian government expressed sympathy and condolence, and the newspapers published flattering obituaries, reminding their readers that their own Emperor, Alexander II, had recently been assassinated.

King Leopold, of Belgium, ordered his court to wear mourning clothing for eight days.

King Alfonso, of Spain, did the same.

The Parliaments of Australia and New Zealand issued unanimous proclamations of support.

A special mass was held in Paris and Rome, and the Pope himself telegraphed his condolence to Mrs. Garfield.

Words of sympathy poured in from every corner of the globe, but as one might expect, Garfield's eighty days of suffering were felt most keenly in his own country. In 1881, New York City was the largest city in America, but even the "great commercial metropolis" came to a standstill to honor the late President.

An article in *The New York Times* described the scene in graphic detail. "All classes participated in the sad celebration, and the ragged inhabitants of the tenement-houses of the lower part of the City seemed to feel as keenly and to lament as sorely the bereavement of the Nation as the denizens of the mansions of Fifth Avenue. The City was unusually quiet—more so, if possible, than it is on Sunday." Even the bustling harbor was tame. "The docks along the water-front, both in the North and East Rivers, were crowded with steamers and sailing craft, and all on board were aware of the solemnity of the occasion, which was fully recognized and its observance faithfully kept. The ensigns on all the vessels were displayed at half-mast, and foreign ships, as well as American, paid this tribute of respect to a Nation's sorrow."

In the aftermath of the funeral ceremony, some of America's greatest poets offered written tributes to Garfield. The list included Henry Wadsworth Longfellow, Julia Ward Howe, and John Greenleaf Whittier.

Oliver Wendell Holmes wrote a sweet poem titled, After The Burial, which was published in the *Boston Globe*. It concludes with the following stanza:

Farewell! the leaf-strewn earth enfolds
Our stay, our pride, our hopes, our fears;
And autumn's golden sun beholds
A nation bowed, a world in tears.

Alfred, Lord Tennyson, wrote the following to James Russell Lowell:

"We learned yesterday that the President was gone. We had watched with much admiration his fortitude, and not without hope the fluctuations of his health, these many days. Now we almost seem to have lost a personal friend. He was a good man and a noble one. Accept from me and my wife and family assurance of heart-felt sympathy for Mrs. Garfield, for yourself, and for your country."

In the end, however, it was Garfield himself who best captured the essence of his own character, and in so doing, left the nation a poignant epitaph for his incredible life. He wrote:

"I have sometimes thought that we cannot know any man thoroughly well while he is in perfect health. As the ebb-tide discloses the real lines of the shore and the bed of the sea, so feebleness, sickness, and pain bring out the real character of a man."

CHAPTER THIRTY-FOUR

The official autopsy on America's twentieth President had been conducted on Wednesday, September 21, the day that Eliza Garfield turned eighty years old. In addition to the corps of physicians who had been at the late President's side, the event was witnessed by Dr. Andrew H. Smith of Elberon, and D.S. Lamb, Acting Assistant Surgeon of the Army Medical Museum in Washington. The post-mortem lasted for three and a half hours and was performed by Dr. Lamb, who later wrote:

"It was found that the ball, after fracturing the right eleventh rib, had passed through the spinal column in front of the spinal cord, fracturing the body of the first lumbar vertebra, driven a number of small fragments of bone into the adjacent soft parts, and lodging below the pancreas, about two inches and a half to the left of the spine, and behind the peritoneum, where it had become completely encysted."

The immediate cause of death was secondary hemorrhage from one of the arteries adjoining the track of the ball. Nearly a pint of blood had escaped, rupturing the thin membrane that formed the lining of the abdominal cavity. The ruptured lining was believed to have been the cause of the severe pain in the lower part of Garfield's chest.

Dr. Lamb's report described the injury in graphic detail:

"An abscess cavity, six inches by four in dimensions was found in the vicinity of the gall bladder, between the liver and the transverse colon, which were strongly abherent. A long suppurating channel extended from the external wound between the loin muscles and the right kidney almost to the right groin."

As Dr. Lamb continued the dissection, surgeon J.J. Woodward recorded the observations that were made, and some of them were startling. The body was considerably emaciated, especially the limbs. The embalmer had injected preservative fluid into the left femoral artery—the large artery in the thigh—and the pipes used for the procedure were still in position.

The area over the sacrum was covered with bed sores, the largest of them measuring about half an inch in diameter.

Acute pustules—pus-filled blisters—were scattered across the shoulders, back, and buttocks. Hemorrhoidal tumors, some the size of a walnut, protruded from the anus.

No major abnormities were discovered in the stomach or intestines, but Lamb noted that the liver was larger than normal, weighing approximately eighty-four ounces. No evidence of bullet damage was found, and there were no abscesses in any part of the tissue.

The right kidney weighted six ounces, the left kidney seven, and both were normal in appearance and texture.

The heart weighed eleven ounces, which was normal, but the muscular tissues were soft and tore easily.

The physicians had unanimously agreed not to examine the President's cranium, but that did not stop the *New York Tribune* from publishing an article titled, "Garfield In The Light of Phrenology." The article first appeared in the August issue of *The Phrenological Journal*, and it purported to be a scientific analysis of Garfield's mental characteristics—from the phrenologist's point of view:

> The head, [Garfield's] which is twenty-four inches in circumference, seems to be very long from front to rear, and then the length seems extreme from the centre of the ear to the root of the nose; it is also long from the opening of the ear backward. The whole back-head is large, and the social group amply indicated, but the reader will observe the extreme length anterior to the opening of the ears, especially across the lower part of the forehead, in which are located the organs of the perceptive intellect, those which gather and retain certain knowledge, and bring a man into quick sympathy with the external world, and also with the world of facts as developed in science and literature.

Phrenology, as described in *The Phrenological Journal*, was the study of the shape of the human skull in order to draw conclusions about particular character traits and mental faculties. The theory, widely studied and debated in the 1800s, was developed at the beginning of the nineteenth century by the German physiologist Franz Joseph Gall. The theory was popularized in the United States by Orson and Lorenzo Fowler through their publication, *The Phrenological Almanac*, and other publications.

Modern neurology and physical anthropology would eventually refute the theory, but in 1881, there were plenty of people who believed that Gall and his followers were on to something. In fact, the idea of phrenology, that the shape and bumps on one's head could be used to determine one's mental type, would soon be applied to men such as Guiteau, in order to "prove" their moral deficiency and insanity.

The trial of the assassin was just about to get under way, and it appeared that Guiteau's lawyers might invoke the insanity defense, even though their client was vehement in his denial that he was legally insane. Even so, one of their major witnesses, a prominent physician, would flirt with the phrenological delineation of Guiteau's character by describing the abnormal shape of his head.

"If the man [Guiteau] only had the mean face," the witness would state, "I should say he might be a depraved man, but when I add to that the defective shape of his skull I am strongly of the belief—as strongly as science permits us to come to a conclusion—that he is a congenital monstrosity."

CHAPTER THIRTY-FIVE

If anyone thought that the days leading up to the most celebrated insanity case of the nineteenth century would be calm they were wrong—dead wrong. Eight days before the President died, Charles Guiteau was nearly shot by a member of Battery B of the Second Regiment of Artillery—the very unit that had been sent to guard and protect him.

On the evening of September 11, 1881, Sergeant James Mason joined three wagonloads of soldiers on a trip from the armory in Washington, D.C., to the jail where Guiteau was being held. Upon arriving, Mason threw his cape to one side and ran toward Guiteau's cell. As his fellow soldiers watched, he lifted his .45 caliber rifle, stuck it between the bars of the cell, and fired at the prisoner.

Guiteau just stood there, staring at the sergeant in stunned silence.

Mason then calmly walked over to his commanding officer and surrendered his weapon. Allegedly, he said, "Captain, I have tried to kill that dirty loafer in there. Here is my gun and bayonet. Take me in charge."

Miraculously, the ball-cartridge missed Guiteau by inches, and was later found embedded in a coat he had hung on the wall. Once again, he had cheated death, and just as before, against all odds. Sergeant Mason, the would-be assassin, was no raw recruit looking to make a name for himself. He was a "sober" 35-year-old soldier and a veteran of the Civil War. He had a wife and a child, and was well liked and well respected by all of the officers of his regiment.

And he was a skilled marksman.

Mason was later tried by a general court-martial on the charge of violating the sixty-second Article of War—attempting to kill a prisoner confined under the authority of the United States. After a short trial, he was found guilty, dishonorably discharged, and sentenced to eight years of hard labor.

The officers who rendered the verdict thought that the sentence was fair and stated that the question of Mason's intended victim should have no bearing on the case. In their view, the sergeant had set a bad example and committed an act that was "subversive of all discipline."

The public outcry was deafening. How could an American military court punish such a patriotic soldier? Eight years in prison was simply outrageous. The coward Guiteau deserved to be shot!

At first, the press was neutral, but then they began to publish sympathetic stories, focused on the fact that Sergeant Mason had a small baby boy and a wife that was almost destitute. The public response was overwhelming, culminating in a national campaign for "Pennies for Betty and the Baby." The campaign was followed by a benefit performance held at Ford's theatre in Washington, D.C.—the very theatre in which Lincoln had been shot.

Money poured in to a special account earmarked for Mason and his family. The account was administered by the Riggs Bank—of Riggs Hotel fame, the very hotel where Guiteau had spent his last night as a free man.

Efforts to secure the sergeant's release led to the House of Representatives decrying the military court as unconstitutional, and in Chicago, 50,000 signatures were attached to a petition calling for a full pardon.

Eventually, 900,000 citizens would sign their names to various petitions, expressing their belief that Mason should be pardoned because of the "great and general indignation" felt by the American people. In another strange twist, the only prominent politician who opposed a pardon was Robert Todd Lincoln, the Secretary of War. Mr. Lincoln was roundly criticized for his stance, and even his most ardent supporters in the press began to describe him as "stony-hearted."

In the end, Mason would serve twenty months of his eight-year sentence—and leave Albany State Prison a rich man.

George B. Corkhill, Washington's District Attorney, had spent the summer doing what a prosecutor was supposed to do—interviewing witnesses, gathering statements and depositions, and carefully reconstructing the assassin's every move. All of the key players were easily located, and most of them were anxious to testify. The list included the hackman who was to drive Guiteau from the depot, the gun dealer who had sold him the Bulldog revolver, and the witness who had seen him shoot President Garfield in the back.

In some ways, Colonel Corkhill was the perfect man for the job. He certainly had a lot in common with the victim. Both men were from Ohio, devout Christians, members of the bar, and Civil War veterans.

Being the cautious sort, Corkhill announced that there would be no formal proceedings until the President either recovered or died. The decision raised a few eyebrows, but the District Attorney's motivation was based upon the belief that the prosecution faced a huge obstacle—proving that Charles Guiteau was not a madman. Clearly, this would be a difficult task, but if Guiteau was judged to be legally insane, then his crime might be seen as the random act of a lunatic. A sympathetic jury might hand down a lenient sentence. Justice would not prevail.

After the President died, the stakes grew even higher, and it soon became clear that Guiteau's trial would be the first important murder case in the United States in which the defendant's claim of insanity would be subjected to the modern legal test of whether or not the defendant understood that his actions were wrong.

In truth, the "insanity plea" was hardly new. The plea had been used for centuries in England, dating back to the 1400s, when it was made available to a person who was "deprived of thought and memory so as not to know what he [was] doing, no more than an infant, a brute, or a wild beast."

Later on, the M'Naghten rule was used to determine whether a person accused of a crime was sane at the time of its commission and, therefore, criminally responsible for the act. The rule, which had made its way into American jurisprudence, was named for Daniel M'Naghten, who, in 1843, tried to kill England's prime minister.

At the time of the Guiteau trial, the prevailing test of legal insanity was not whether or not the defendant knew that his or her actions were wrong, but whether or not the defendant knew that his or her actions were criminal. Therefore, even though a miscreant like Guiteau might be considered insane because he did not think it was wrong to shoot the president, he could still be convicted if the judge (and jury) determined that he understood the law made it illegal to shoot people.

Corkhill tried to shape public opinion on the subject by asking the *Washington Sunday Chronicle* (his former employer) to publish his "observations" about Guiteau. On July 9, he told a reporter:

> "He's no more insane than I am. And he scouts the idea of being insane himself; in fact, he gets indignant at any suggestion of that kind . . . . There's nothing of the madman about Guiteau: He's a cool calculating blackguard, a polished ruffian, who had gradually prepared himself to pose in this way before the world . . . . He was a dead-beat—pure and simple . . . . Finally, he got tired of the monotony of dead-beating. He wanted excitement of some other kind and notoriety, and he's got it."

The trial of Charles Guiteau, presidential assassin, began in the Supreme Court of the District of Columbia, before Judge Walter Cox, on Monday, November 15, 1881. Guiteau's lawyers were Leigh Robinson and George Scoville. Interestingly, Scoville was married to Guiteau's sister, Frances—the woman he had threatened with an axe. U.S. Attorney General Wayne MacVeagh, anxious to secure a conviction, named five lawyers to the prosecution team, but it was George Corkhill, the pre-trial strategist, who would lead the charge.

Guiteau had been imprisoned in Washington since July 2, the day he shot the President. During the past four and a half months, he had been indicted of willful murder by the grand jury of the District, arraigned before the court, acknowledged shooting the President, and entered a plea of "not guilty" upon the three grounds of insanity, malpractice, and lack of jurisdiction.

The actual indictment, which had been delivered on October 11, listed eleven different counts, all related to the charge of willful murder. Each count closed with the following formal charge: "And so the Grand Jurors aforesaid do say that the said Charles J. Guiteau, him, the said James A. Garfield, in the manner and by the means aforesaid, feloniously, willfully and of his malice afore-thought, did kill and murder, against the form of the statute in such case made and provided, and against the peace and government of the United States of America."

The arraignment took place on Friday, October 14, and was followed by the reading of the indictment. After the indictment was ready, Guiteau presented a paper to the court—an explanation of his "not guilty" plea:

> I plead not guilty to the indictment and my defense is threefold:
>
> *First*—Insanity, in that it was God's act and not mine. The divine pressure on me to remove the President was so enormous that it destroyed my free agency, and therefore I am not legally responsible for my act.
>
> *Second*—The President died from malpractice. About three weeks after he was shot his physicians, after a careful examination, decided that he would recover. Two months after this official announcement he died. Therefore I say he was not fatally shot. If he had been well treated he would have recovered.

Third—The President died in New Jersey, and, therefore, beyond the Jurisdiction of this court.

Guiteau continued to share his odd religious beliefs by stating, "I undertake to say that the Lord is managing my case with consummate ability and that He had a special object in allowing the President to die in New Jersey. His management of this case is worthy of him as the Deity, and I have entire confidence in his disposition to protect me and send me forth to the world a free and vindicated man."

In closing, Guiteau reiterated his belief that President Garfield would not have died had the Lord not wanted him to. Furthermore, he did not view his action as murder or an assassination. Garfield had been "removed" because it was God's will, not his, and in the end it was for the good of the American people.

The idea of an assassin being an instrument of God was not a new one, but the crime did raise an interesting question: Why had God allowed this to happen? In the court of public opinion—and in many pulpits across the nation—a general consensus began to emerge that Garfield's death had served to bring the nation closer together, negating sectionalism and healing the lingering wounds of the Civil War.

Needless to say, Corkhill and his team were alarmed by the suggestion that Guiteau had acted under divine pressure as an "agent of Deity." They refused to accept the premise, or even the possibility of divine inspiration. If that were the case, how could they portray the defendant as a cool and calculating killer?

Of course, this strategy was not without risk. By denying the possibility of divine inspiration they were also repudiating the Bible itself as an inspired work, thereby risking the wrath of the jurors.

Thus began what some were calling "the trial of the century," a hackneyed phrase that had been used to describe a number of high-profile cases. In this instance, public interest was heightened by the deportment of the prisoner, which was defiant, impertinent, blasphemous, and downright vulgar.

The court convened at ten o'clock in the morning, and when Guiteau was led into the courtroom, he discovered that the room was filled with spectators. He seemed to be delighted by the turnout believing that the spectators were there to support him. In any event, he put on quite a show, claiming the privilege of a licensed lawyer (which he was) and demanding that he be allowed to act as his own counsel and conduct the case as he saw fit. When Mr. Robinson asked for a postponement, Guiteau sprang to his feet and told him to stop making speeches and get on with the trial.

As so it went. Hour after hour, jurors were called into the courtroom, questioned by the defense and prosecution, and then dismissed for a variety of reasons. Many of the jurors were disqualified for expressing contempt for the defendant, and some went even further, articulating a desire to see him hang.

It took all of three days to select a jury, which as finally constituted, was made up as follows:

John P. Hamlin, restaurant keeper.
Frederick W. Brandenberg, cigar dealer.
Henry J. Baright, retired merchant.
Charles J. Stewart, merchant.
Thomas H. Langley, grocer.
Michael Sheehan, grocer.

Samuel F. Hobbes, plasterer.

George W. Gates, machinist.

Ralph Wormley (colored), laborer.

W.H. Brawner, commission merchant.

Thomas Heinlein, iron worker.

Joseph Prather, commission merchant.

As Guiteau looked on, appraising each juror, the following oath was administered to the twelve men chosen: "You and each of you do solemnly swear that you well and truly try and a true deliverance make between the United States and Charles J. Guiteau, the prisoner at the bar, whom you shall have in charge, indicted for the murder of James A. Garfield, and a true verdict give according to the evidence, so help you God."

After almost five months in jail, Charles J. Guiteau, the most hated man in America, was about to have his day in court.

CHAPTER THIRTY-SIX

Early on, Guiteau proved to be his own worst enemy, criticizing the defense team, interrupting the proceedings, challenging the judge, and providing the press with outrageous statements. On day four, November 17, he got into a shouting match with Judge Cox and demanded that Mr. Robinson, one of his lawyers, be removed from the defense team.

"May it please the Court," Guiteau said angrily, "I object to Mr. Robinson appearing in this case."

"Take your seat," Judge Cox ordered. "I wish you to understand distinctly that your labors as counsel in this case, as you claim to be, shall be confined to consultation with the associate counsel in the case. If you disobey, the court will be under the necessity of ordering your removal from the court-room and proceed with the trial in your absence."

"Your Honor," Guiteau shot back, "said I could be heard, and I have a speech."

"You cannot be heard till the close of the case," Judge Cox replied.

At this point, Guiteau began to tremble with excitement and wave his arms about. "I desire to be heard throughout the case," he proclaimed. "Your Honor has no right to cut me off; and I am going to make a noise to the country about it. When I want counsel I will notify your Honor."

"Counsel have been assigned to you," Cox said calmly. "And you must keep quiet."

After the deputy marshals forced the prisoner to sit, District Attorney Corkhill opened the case with a long speech, outlining the events that had preceded the assassination of the President. During his presentation, he produced five letters written by Guiteau, which revealed that the assassin had sought first to be appointed Minister to Austria, then Consul at Paris. When his requests were rejected, he began to plot his revenge, carefully planning his every move.

Without posing the question directly, Corkhill had cleverly introduced the central question that was on everyone's mind: Would a lunatic be capable of planning such an elaborate crime?

The first witness for the prosecution was James G. Blaine, the Secretary of State. The most riveting part of Blaine's testimony was his precise description of the actual assassination. He told a hushed courtroom that he had walked into the depot arm in arm with the President, who was on his left side. When they were about two-thirds across the ladies' waiting room, there was a loud explosion, followed by a second explosion that sounded like a pistol discharge. Just as Blaine began to lead the President to safety, Garfield threw up his hand and said, "My God, what is this?" When Guiteau ran by them, Blaine gave chase for about eight feet, then stopped abruptly when he saw that the assassin had been caught. By the time he got inside, the President was on the floor, vomiting and barely conscious.

Corkhill produced a diagram of the depot and asked Blaine to indicate the positions occupied by the President and himself at the time of the shooting. Then he turned his attention to the prisoner, who was listening intently. While staring at Guiteau, Corkhill asked Blaine how many times he had seen the prisoner prior to the shooting. Blaine's answer shocked everyone except the prosecutor. According to the Secretary of State, Guiteau had visited the State Department at least twenty-five times. On each visit, Guiteau had pleaded for a foreign assignment, but he had never received the slightest encouragement from anyone. Finally, after months of harassment, Blaine lost his temper and told him "never to speak to me again on the Paris Consulship as long as you live."

After Blaine testified, the prosecution called a number of "eye witnesses," individuals who had actually been in the ladies' waiting room at the time of the shooting. The list included the Minister of Venezuela, who had been instructed to appear and testify by his own government, Mrs. Sarah B. White, who was in charge of the ladies' waiting room, Mr. Robert A. Parke, the ticket agent who had grabbed Guiteau, Judson W. Wheeler, a passenger from Virginia, George W. Adams, the publisher of the *Washington Evening Star*, and Jacob P. Smith, the depot janitor.

By and large, the witnesses corroborated Blaine's description of the events that had taken place in the waiting room, and nothing new was learned from their testimony. To everyone's surprise, the day ended without another outburst from the prisoner.

The next two days were not as tranquil.

On Friday, November 18, Guiteau got into a heated argument with George Scoville, then complained to the Court about his beleaguered brother-in-law. "He is no lawyer and no politician," Guiteau declared. "I want first-class talent in this business, and I am going to have it or there's going to be trouble."

Scoville, pushed to the limit of his patience, told the Court that he was disgusted with the prisoner. He was sick and tired of his client's abuse, and distressed that he had to spend an hour or two at the jail every day to prevent the prisoner giving out communications.

For some reason, Judge Cox allowed Guiteau to continue speaking out of order, which he did, telling his perplexed attorney that he had no confidence in his ability to try or win the case. He also told Scoville that he intended to hire two or three of the best lawyers in America to manage his case.

Finally, after berating his own counsel, Guiteau was reminded by the judge that "on several occasions in the courts in the United States the prisoner has been, on account of disorderly conduct, removed from court and the case continued in his absence."

Guiteau got the message and sat down, but the newspaper reporters that were present were appalled by his antics, and before long their editorial pages began to chastise the court for being too lenient. Some referred to the trial as a travesty of justice, while others, such as the *New York Daily Tribune*, called the trial "a vulgar peep-show in a beer garden, which under the guise of a State trial has brought reproach upon American criminal practice . . . A blistering disgrace to the country."

Things went from bad to worse the following day. Shortly after John O'Meara gave a detailed account of Guiteau's gun purchase, the prisoner became agitated and demanded new counsel. While the request was being considered, Guiteau made a very odd—yet prophetic—pronouncement: "I understand that there are one or two disreputable persons hanging around this court-room intending to do me harm. The Chief of Police had very kindly furnished me with an escort, and I have a body-guard now. I want to notify all disreputable persons that if they attempt to injure me they will probably be shot dead by my body-guard." After a moment of nervous laughter, he added, "I have no fears as to my personal safety. There has been considerable loose talk on this subject for a week, and I wish to let the public understand it."

The display of bravado was noted by the court, but it did not deter one of those "disreputable persons" from trying to kill the prisoner. As Guiteau was being taken back to jail, a drunken man, mounted on a sorrel horse, rode up to the police van and shot at him. The ball passed through an upper panel and tore a hole in the left sleeve of Guiteau's coat, but miraculously he was only grazed. Police officer Edelin, riding "shotgun," turned and fired at the drunken man, but missed. The would-be avenger, an accomplished rider, dug his heels into he side of his horse and dashed down First Street. The van gave chase, but was forced to stop when it reached the tracks of the Baltimore & Ohio Railroad.

Officer Edelin made sure the prisoner had not been injured, and the van sped off to the district jail. Inside his cell, Guiteau was examined by two physicians, who noted that he was shaking like a leaf. The warden doubled the guard, then promised his prisoner that no unknown visitors would be allowed to enter the jail.

The man who fired at Guiteau had been seen outside the courthouse the day before. In fact, he had approached one of the guards and asked to see the prisoner. The guard inquired if he had a gun, which he did, then refused the request. The man was later described as being slightly over five feet tall, with a dark complexion. He was wearing a well-worn suite and a black cap.

A reporter visiting Guiteau in jail that afternoon found him washing his wound, but still as cocky as ever. "I wish you to say in your paper," the assassin joked, "that the Lord is opposed to my being shot."

Meanwhile, an alarm was sent out from Police Headquarters instructing officers to scour the countryside and apprehend any "suspicious characters." Before long, a man fitting the description of the assailant was spotted near the Soldier's Home. He was ordered to stop and dismount, but instead of complying, he shouted a profanity and rode off into the woods. The police gave chase and a running gun battle ensued. Nobody was hit during the exchange of gunfire, and the pursuit ended in the front yard of a farm house, when William Jones, still in his cups, was arrested and dragged back to the Second Precinct Station.

Then things really got weird.

Soon, it was reported that Mr. Jones was a well-known "crank," a polite term for someone who was somewhere between eccentric and just plain crazy. Jones was 29 years old and the owner of a fine farm on Bates Road, about three miles north of the city. Among other peculiarities, Jones was fond of impersonating police officers, and he took great delight in 'arresting" and "questioning" unsuspecting citizens. He had been pulling pranks for the past two years, but those who knew him best said he was more half-witted than crazy.

Whatever the case, he was smart enough to demand legal counsel and then deny committing the crime. "It wasn't I that shot at him," he told a visitor. "I want to see them prove it."

The assailant's confidence was well placed. Later that evening, Officer Edelin was summoned to identify the shooter, and incredibly, he announced that the police had apprehended the wrong person. "Gentlemen," he said firmly, "this is not the man; I should know the man I fired at yesterday among a million. I not only fail to identify this man Jones as the man, but I could swear that he is not the man."

The top brass were caught off guard, but they nonetheless allowed Officer Edelin to point out the discrepancies between the man he had fired at and the man that was in their custody. "Jones has a light complexion, with a hardly perceptible mustache, whereas the man who fired at Guiteau was a dark, swarthy man apparently about 45 years old, with a very heavy, stumpy black mustache and a keen black eye. Besides, the latter was cool and sober, and the manner in which he planned and executed his work—even though he failed—was that of a clear-headed, determined man rather than of a half-witted crank."

There was also the problem of the gunmen's horse—he rode a sorrel animal with white fore legs. The horse that Jones rode was almost black, and as Edelin pointed out, "It has not a white fleck upon it."

These unexpected complications caused a great stir at Police Headquarters, and the situation became even more bizarre when Perry Carson, who was on duty at the rear of the police van, positively identified Jones as the horsemen who followed the van as it left the courthouse and traveled through the Capitol grounds. Carson had heard two shots, but from his position at the rear, he could not be certain who had fired them.

Despite the lack of evidence and contradictory statements by those present, Jones was arraigned before a judge the following morning, and since he was unable to post a $5,000 bail, he was taken to jail.

Curiously, the case against him was indefinitely postponed.

CHAPTER THIRTY-SEVEN

When the trial resumed on Monday, Guiteau was brought to the courthouse under heavy guard. There was a large group of spectators waiting for him, including many well dressed women who had brought opera-glasses, hoping to catch a glimpse of the infamous assassin who had cheated death on two separate occasions. They were thrilled when Guiteau was given pen and ink and allowed to sell his autograph for one dollar, or if one was so inclined, they could buy a dozen for nine dollars.

Inside the courtroom, the tone was more subdued, and trouble was brewing for the defense team. On Sunday, Scoville had been interviewed by the *Washington Post*, in which he'd criticized Leigh Robinson's attempt to use the malpractice defense. Robinson was furious, and he told Judge Cox that "I have to say that I am not accustomed to learn from an associate counsel his objection to my examination of a witness for the first time from the paper of the following day. It is unnecessary to say that I can have no further association of any kind with such a counsel."

To be sure, the doctors did not cause Garfield's death, but in all likelihood, they did contribute to his demise. Unwittingly, they had administered anesthetics that had eased his pain, but prolonged the risk of infection. The development of such anesthetics in the 19th century allowed physicians to perform longer and more difficult procedures that increased medical knowledge, but also increased the likelihood of death by infection. Many patients were exposed to unsanitary wards, or in Garfield's case, to a recovery room that was exposed to swamp miasma. A lengthy recuperation also meant exposure to a host of diseases, such as gangrene, erysipelas, and blood poisoning.

Garfield's doctors were evenly divided about the relatively new concept of germ infection, which had been theorized in 1864 by Dr. J. Spencer Wells. After studying the work of Louis Pasteur, who discovered that fermentation was promoted by bacteria, Wells came to the conclusion that infection might result from "the presence in the atmosphere of organic germs."

One year later, Dr. Joseph Lister, the son of a well-known physicist, realized that germs caused putrefication in wounds, in the same way they produced mold in organic matter. At the time, almost half of the patients undergoing major surgery died from infection. In the 1870s, Lister was the first to treat wounds with dressings soaked in carbolic acid (a coal-tar derivative), and he was also among the first to suggest that surgeons wash their hands and sterilize their instruments before operating. Incredibly, most surgeons did not wear gowns or gloves, and very few covered their hands, noses, or mouths.

Many of Lister's colleagues scoffed at his "new fangled ideas" regarding infection. One of these skeptics was Dr. David Hayes Agnew, the Philadelphia surgeon who happened to be the chief consultant on

Garfield's wound. Agnew praised some of Lister's works, but he also wrote that "the wound should be examined by fingers or probe."

Dr. Lister would later be described as one of the greatest men of the nineteenth century. (Listerine, the antiseptic mouthwash, would be named in his honor.)

Dr. D. Hayes Agnew would be immortalized by an 1889 Thomas Eakin painting called the "Agnew Clinic."

And poor Charles Guiteau would now be defended solely by his brother-in-law—a man who had handled only two criminal cases in his three decades of practice.

Robinson had timed his request perfectly, fully aware that Judge Cox was still smarting from criticism by the press. Some reporters felt that he was too lenient with Guiteau, others thought he needed to exert more control over the proceedings. One paper wrote that "the prisoner has been suffered by a judge whose backbone seems to be made of tissue paper."

Now that judge had an opportunity to make a major decision.

A decision that would make it harder for the assassin to escape the hangman.

Judge Cox allowed Robinson to withdraw, and later that afternoon, the prosecution called three medical experts to the stand, hoping to quash the idea that the President's death had anything to do with his treatment. Surgeon-General Barnes, Surgeon J.J. Woodward, and Assistant Surgeon D.S. Lamb testified that the wound was mortal and was the cause of death.

To underscore the point, Corkhill produced the bullet that had been fired into the President's back—and removed during the post-mortem examination held at Elberon, New Jersey, on the afternoon of September 20, 1881.

This pistol ball was indented and partly flattened on one side, indicating that it had penetrated deeply and caused great damage. Corkhill encouraged the jury to examine the bullet, then rested his case, having called a total of thirty-two witnesses.

Immediately after the prosecution rested its case, Guiteau was permitted to speak on his own behalf, and true to form, he reacted in a strange way. He refused to stand, then offered a long, rambling statement:

I was not aware that I was expected to speak this morning. I do not care to say anything more than was published in my address last Monday afternoon in the *Evening Star*. That paper was addressed to your Honor and the public, and I presume that most of the jurymen have heard it. I have no set speech to make. So long as I appear, in part, as my own counsel, the best way is for me to make corrections as the case proceeds, just as I have done during the last three or four days. I mean no discourtesy to anybody in the case. I only want to get at the facts.

Scoville began his defense by criticizing the number of witnesses called by the prosecution, then reminding the jury that the simple questions of the case were whether the defendant had committed the act—which he did not deny—and whether he was, at the time, sane or insane. The latter question would be decided after the jury heard expert testimony, but just for good measure, the jury was reminded that the government experts would be paid $100 to $200 a day. On the other hand, the defense experts would not be paid a single penny.

Over the objections of his client, Scoville made it clear that insanity would be the chief plea of the defense. Consequently, he listed the different kinds of mental illness and touched upon their various manifestations. He then presented a fascinating portrait of the Guiteau family, reminding the jury of the fact that the defendant had one uncle, two aunts, and two first cousins who were diagnosed as insane. Scoville's intent was clear—the possibility of a hereditary illness had to be considered.

Scoville finished his opening address on November 23, but he was not entirely pleased by the way the case was proceeding. His presentation had been marred by constant interruptions by his own client, applause from the women in the gallery, a judicial threat to clear the courtroom, and a stern warning that the prisoner would be gagged if he continued to interrupt the proceedings.

On top of everything else, the case was about to be postponed for a day of national Thanksgiving.

The defense fared better after the holiday recess, when Mrs. Frances Scoville (Guiteau's sister) took the stand and reiterated her belief that her brother was insane. She told the court that their mother, Jane Howe Guiteau, became very sick after giving birth to Charles. In the weeks and months that followed, Mrs. Guiteau began to act strangely, and after shaving her head with a razor, she barely spoke to anyone. Incredibly, she had two more children, but one died when he was two years old, and the other when she was twenty months of age. Mrs. Guiteau never recovered from her illness, and eventually she was committed to an insane asylum, where she died when Charles was seven years old.

The most riveting part of her testimony concerned the time that Charles had visited her in Wisconsin in 1875. At this stage of his life,

Guiteau was divorced, disheartened, and disheveled. He was also prone to violent outbursts. Without making eye contact with her brother, she described how he had raised an axe to her, and stated that he looked like a wild animal.

Apparently amused by this, Guiteau laughed.

The next witness was John W. Guiteau of Boston, the defendant's older brother. Without much urging, he told the jury that he was absolutely convinced that Charles was insane. To bolster his claim, he gave an account of a conversation he had with his brother in jail during which Charles stated that he had been inspired by God to shoot the President. Before their talk, John thought that Charles might have been inspired by the Devil, not by God, but afterwards, he concluded that Charles was just insane.

A few more witnesses were called by the defense, and then Guiteau was sworn in and asked to identify about twenty letters that he had written to his father, sister, and brother, between 1857 and 1868. Immediately afterwards, at 3:00 p.m., the court adjourned.

On Tuesday morning, November 29, Guiteau was called to the stand again, and for the next three days he was encouraged to elaborate on the details of his character and career. He did so freely, telling the court about his experience at the Oneida Community, his political aspirations, and his view of Divine Inspiration. He also discussed, in surprising detail, the murder of James A. Garfield. Acknowledging that he had fired the fatal bullet, he went on to explain how he got the idea of murdering the President, the political necessity of the act, his preparation for the deed, its execution and his state of mind afterwards.

The spectators listened in silence as Guiteau casually discussed the crime—and then had the audacity to admit that he still believed that he would some day be President of the United States.

When asked to explain his view of Divine Inspiration, he said, "Inspiration, as I understand it, is where a man's mind is taken position of by—by—by a superior power, and where he acts outside of his own natural—outside of himself."

Guiteau's inspiration had come to him on the evening of May 16, 1881, the evening that New York Senators Platt and Conkling announced that they were resigning from the Senate over a patronage dispute with the White House. When Guiteau heard the news, he was greatly depressed in mind and spirit over the political situation and its consequences for the Republican Party. Before he went to sleep, an "impression" came over him—the thought that all would be well if Garfield was removed from office. The idea, at first, was simply horrifying, but the more he thought about it the more it made sense.

Perfect sense.

A major disruption in the Republican Party would allow the Democrats to take control of the government, and by bankrupting the Treasury, they could start another war—a war they just might win.

Hell, everybody knew that the Democratic Party was filled with unrepentant rebels. If they took control, the South could rise again.

A patriot like Guiteau would never let that happen.

After a short recess, Guiteau returned to the stand, and still under oath, he was asked about Divine intervention. Did he really believe that he was protected by special providence?

"Most emphatically," he replied. When asked to elaborate, he recounted several near-death experiences, starting with the time he jumped from a speeding train in Newark, New Jersey. Not too long after that incident, he was a passenger aboard the ill-fated *Stonington*, the steamboat that collided with the *Narragansett* in Long Island Sound. Thirty to seventy passengers died that night, but Guiteau escaped without a scratch.

The same could be said for his time in jail. Since his arrest, there had been two serious attempts on his life, and a third incident that was being portrayed as a "misunderstanding." The defendant was convinced that Providence had protected him from the likes of Sergeant Mason and William Jones, and he stunned the courtroom by predicting that one day, instead of saying "Guiteau the assassin," the public would say "Guiteau, the patriot."

CHAPTER THIRTY-EIGHT

The cross-examination of Guiteau was handled by John K. Porter, a prominent New York trial judge and lawyer, once described in glowing detail by the *Albany Law Journal*: "In our opinion, Mr. Porter comes nearer to being a genius than any other man at our bar. If we were to point out his most prominent and potent characteristic, we should say it is his dramatic power."

Judge Porter was no stranger to high profile cases or controversial defendants. In 1861, he successfully defended Horace Greeley, the publisher of the *New York Tribune*, in a libel suit brought by Congressman De Witt C. Littlejohn.

In 1874, he became embroiled in the Tilton v. Beecher lawsuit, the notorious scandal that shook the very foundation of the Plymouth Church. In that case, a man named Theodore Tilton accused famed American preacher and orator Reverend Henry Ward Beecher of committing adultery with Tilton's wife, Elizabeth. Porter was an active member of Beecher's defense team, and due to his brilliant oration, he managed to win an acquittal from the jury. His honor would later describe the trial (rather immodestly) as "unquestionably the greatest lawsuit of the Nineteenth Century."

Now, at age sixty-two, Porter was involved in a criminal case quite unlike any other that had come before, and the pressure to obtain a conviction was enormous. In order to succeed, Porter would have to convince the jury that Guiteau was sane, and based upon his past—and his courtroom antics—that would not be an easy task. If the truth be told, there was nothing easy about this particular trial. Even the location was a problem. Francis L. Wellman wrote that the courtroom was filled with the "scum of Washington," and that on account of the crowds, "the doors of the court were kept shut, and many of the expert physicians became ill in consequence of the excessively foul air. One doctor died from the effects of the lung infection."

Nevertheless, Porter rose to the occasion, conducting a cross-examination that is still considered one of the great masterpieces of forensic skill:

MR. PORTER. "Are you a man of truth?"

GUITEAU. "Most decidedly, Judge, I am in dead earnest in anything I do."

MR. PORTER. "I think you were converted at the age of seventeen, or thereabout?"

GUITEAU. "Yes, sir."

MR. PORTER. "From that time on you have been a man of truth, have you not?"

GUITEAU. "Yes, sir."

MR. PORTER. "And, as you believe, a Christian man?"

GUITEAU. "I hope so, Judge."

MR. PORTER. “You have hated all shams?”
GUITEAU. “Most decidedly.”
MR. PORTER. “And you do now?”
GUITEAU. “I do.”
MR. PORTER. “You have had no bad habits?”
GUITEAU. “I think not.”
MR. PORTER. “Did you pass through the ordeal of the Oneida Community and maintain your virtue?”
GUITEAU. “Well, not absolutely.”
MR. PORTER. “I thought you said yesterday that you did?”
GUITEAU. “I said, or intended to say that I had been mostly a strictly virtuous man . . . . As a matter of fact, I had to do with three distinct women. But there is no pleasure in that kind of business there. Aside from that, I was strictly virtuous.”

After Guiteau contradicts himself, he is questioned about his business as a lawyer in Chicago and New York, and the jury learns that his practice was limited to collection work. He also admits owing office rent and boardinghouse bills, which makes him a sham artist.

MR. PORTER. “Did you say, as Mr. John R. Scott swears, on leaving the depot on the day of the murder of the President, ‘General Arthur is now the President of the United States’?”
GUITEAU. “I decline to say whether I did or not.”
MR. PORTER. “You thought so, did you not? You are a man of truth?”
GUITEAU. “I think I made a statement to that effect.”
MR. PORTER. “You thought you had killed President Garfield?”
GUITEAU. “I thought the Deity and I had done it, sir.”

MR. PORTER. "Who bought the pistol, the Deity or you?"

GUITEAU. (excitedly). "I say the Deity inspired the act, and the Deity will take care of it."

MR. PORTER. "Who bought the pistol, the Deity or you?"

GUITEAU. "The Deity furnished the money by which I bought it, as the agent of the Deity."

MR. PORTER. "I thought it was somebody else who furnished the money?"

GUITEAU. "I say the Deity furnished the money."

By implicating the Deity, Guiteau had exposed himself to ridicule, and he had also alienated most of the jury, which was composed of "Christian men." In the following segment, he recklessly plunges ahead, sticking to the inspiration story.

MR. PORTER. "Were you inspired to remove the President by murder?"

GUITEAU. "I was inspired to execute the divine will."

MR. PORTER. "By murder?"

GUITEAU. "Yes, sir, so-called murder."

MR. PORTER. "You intended to do it?"

GUITEAU. "I intended to execute the divine will, sir."

MR. PORTER. "You did not succeed?"

GUITEAU. "I think the doctors did the work."

MR. PORTER. "The Deity tried, and you tried, and both failed, but the doctors succeeded?"

GUITEAU. "The Deity confirmed my act by letting the President down as gently as He did."

In retrospect, Porter's reference to the doctors seems risky. If the defense had been willing to use the "malpractice defense," they could have introduced the results of the President's autopsy, which clearly showed that the White House physicians had no idea where the bullet was located. As James C. Clark noted, "In the early weeks of their treatment of the president, the doctors continually poked and probed the wound in an effort to determine the track and location of the bullet. They decided it had traveled downward and to the right after entering the back, hitting the liver, and stopping to the right of the groin about five inches above the navel."

The autopsy later showed that the ball had fractured the right eleventh rib, then passed through the spinal column in front of the spinal canal, fracturing the body of the first lumbar vertebra. Contrary to earlier opinion, the ball had lodged below the pancreas, about two and a half inches left of the spine. The immediate cause of death was secondary hemorrhage—over a pint of blood was found in the President's abdominal cavity.

MR. PORTER. "Do you think that it was letting him down gently to allow him to suffer with torture, over which you professed to feel so much solicitude, during those long months?"

GUITEAU. "The whole matter was in the hands of the Deity. I do not wish to discuss it any further."

MR. PORTER. "Did you believe it was the will of God that you should murder him?"

GUITEAU. "I believe that it was the will of God that he should be removed, and that I was the appointed agent to do it."

MR. PORTER. "Did He give you the commission in writing?"

GUITEAU. "No, sir."

MR. PORTER. "Did He give it in an audible tone of voice?"

GUITEAU. "He gave it to me by his pressure upon me."

MR. PORTER. "Did He give it to you in a vision of the night?"

GUITEAU. "I don't get my inspirations in that way."

MR. PORTER. "Did you contemplate the President's removal otherwise than by murder?"

GUITEAU. "No, sir, I do not like the word murder. I don't like that word. If I had shot the President of the United States on my own personal account, no punishment would be too severe or too quick for me; but acting as the agent of the Deity puts an entirely different construction upon the act, and that is the thing that I want to put into this court and the jury and the opposing counsel. I say this was an absolute necessity in view of the political situation, for the good of the American people, and to save the nation from another war. That is the view I want you to entertain, and not settle down on a cold-blooded idea of murder."

Guiteau probably did not realize that Porter was making light of his "inspiration." Nor did he seem to realize how foolish he sounded by asking the judge and jury not to view his act as murder. In the following segment, Porter continues to dismantle the defendant's twisted logic.

MR. PORTER. "You mentioned the other day that you never struck a man in your life. Was that true?"

GUITEAU. "I do not recall ever striking a man, sir. I have always been a peace man, naturally very cowardly, and always kept away from any physical danger."

MR. PORTER. "But morally brave and determined?"

GUITEAU. "I presume so, especially when I am sure the Deity is back of me."

MR. PORTER. "When did you become sure of that?"

GUITEAU. "I became sure of it about the first of June as far as this case is concerned."

MR. PORTER. "Before that you did not think He was back of you? Who did you think was back of you with a suggestion of murder?"

GUITEAU. "It was the Deity, sir, that made the original suggestion."

MR. PORTER. "I thought you said that the Deity did not make the suggestion until the first of June?"

GUITEAU. "I say that the Deity did make the suggestion about the middle of May, and that I was weighing the proposition for the two weeks succeeding. I was positive it was the will of the Deity about the first of June."

MR. PORTER. "Whose will do you think it was before that?"

GUITEAU. "It was the Deity's will. No doubt about that."

MR. PORTER. "But you were in doubt as to its being His will?"

GUITEAU. "I was not in any doubt."

MR. PORTER. "Not even the first two weeks?"

GUITEAU. "There was no doubt as to the inception of the act from the Deity; as to the feasibility of the act, I was in doubt."

MR. PORTER. "You differed in opinion, then, from the Deity?"

GUITEAU. "No, sir, I was testing the feasibility of the act, whether it would be feasible."

MR. PORTER. "Did you suppose that the Supreme Ruler of the Universe would order you to do a thing which was not feasible?"

At this juncture, Guiteau was clearly flustered, but Porter kept up the pressure. The judge was determined to show that the defendant had a proclivity toward violence. First, he asked Guiteau if he had struck his father in the back during a heated argument. Guiteau said that he had no recollection of such an incident. Then Porter asked him if he had threatened his sister with an axe.

MR. PORTER. "Your sister swears that in 1876, when you were thirty-five years old, that at her place, while you were an inmate of her family, you raised an axe against her life. Is that true?"

GUITEAU. "I don't know anything about it, sir."

MR. PORTER. "You heard your lawyer, in his opening, allude to that evidence, and you shouted out at the time that it was false?"

GUITEAU. "That is what I did say, but you need not look so fierce on me. I do not care a snap for your fierce look. Just cool right down. I am not afraid of you, just understand that. Go a little slow. Make your statements in a quiet, genial way."

MR. PORTER. "Well, it comes to this then, you thought God needed your assistance in order to kill President Garfield?"

GUITEAU. "I decline to discuss this matter with you any further."

Rattled and angry, Guiteau had been caught in another bold lie, and now he was beginning to feel trapped. Matching wits with a seasoned prosecutor was proving to be more difficult than first imagined, but he was not about to surrender any ground.

MR. PORTER. "When you sacrificed that one life, [Garfield] it was by shooting him with the bull-dog pistol you bought?"

GUITEAU. "Yes, sir, it was. That should have been my inspiration. Those are the words that ought to go in there, meaning the Deity and me, and then you would have got the full and accurate statement. I did not do this work on my own account, and you cannot persuade this court and the American people ever to believe I did. The Deity inspired the act. He has taken care of it so far, and He will take care of it."

MR. PORTER. "Did the American people kill General Garfield?"

GUITEAU. "I decline to talk to you on that subject, sir. You are a very mean man and a very dishonest man to try to make my letters say what they do not say. That is my opinion of you, Judge Porter. I knew something about you when you were in New York. I have seen you shake your bony fingers at the jury and the court, and I repudiate your whole theory on this business."

MR. PORTER. "Did it occur to you that there was a commandment, 'Thou shalt not kill'?"

GUITEAU. "It did. The divine authority overcame the written law."

MR. PORTER. "Is there any higher divine authority than the authority that spoke in the commandments?"

Still fuming, Guiteau looked away and refused to answer the question.

* * *

MR. PORTER. "Why did you think you would go to jail for obeying a command of God?"

GUITEAU. "I wanted to go there for protection. I did not want a lot of wild men going to jail there. I would have been shot and hung a hundred times if it had not been for those troops."

MR. PORTER. "Would there have been any wrong in that?"

GUITEAU. "I won't have any more discussion with you on this sacred subject. You are making light of a very sacred subject and I won't talk to you."

MR. PORTER. "Did you think to shoot General Garfield without trial—"

GUITEAU. (interrupting.) "I decline to discuss the matter with you, sir."

MR. PORTER. "Had Garfield ever been tried?"

GUITEAU. "I decline to discuss the matter with you, sir."

MR. PORTER. "Did God tell you he had to be murdered?"

GUITEAU. "He told me he had to be removed, sir."

MR. PORTER. "Did he tell you General Garfield had to be killed without trial?"

GUITEAU. "He told me he had to be removed, sir."

MR. PORTER. "When did He tell you so?"

GUITEAU. "I decline to discuss the matter with you."

MR. PORTER. "Would it incriminate you if you were to answer the jury that question?"

GUITEAU. "I don't know whether it would or not."

After demonstrating that Guiteau understood the difference between right and wrong by making plans to protect himself, Porter reminded the court that the prisoner had appointed himself judge, jury, and executioner.

And then Porter applied the coup de grace.

MR. PORTER. "You shot him [Garfield] in the back?"

GUITEAU. "I did not fire at any particular place."

MR. PORTER "Did you not fire for the hollow of his back?"

GUITEAU. "My intention was to shoot him in the back"

MR. PORTER. "Did you think that if he got two balls in his back it would remove him?"

GUITEAU. "I thought so."

MR. PORTER. "And you intended to put them there?"

GUITEAU. "I did."

MR. PORTER. (in a solemn manner.) "And from that hour to this you have never felt regret or remorse?"

GUITEAU. "I regret giving pain or trouble to any one, but I have no doubt as to the necessity of the act or the divinity of the act."

MR. PORTER. "You have never hinted at any remorse?"

GUITEAU. "My mind is a perfect blank on that subject."

MR. PORTER. "Do you feel any more remorse about rendering his wife a widow and her children fatherless than about breaking the leg of that puppy dog?"**

GUITEAU. "I have no conception of it as murder or killing."

MR. PORTER. "And you feel no remorse?"

GUITEAU. "Of course I feel remorse so far as my personal feelings are concerned; I feel remorse as much as any man and regret the necessity of the act, but . . ."

MR. PORTER. "The cross-examination is closed."

** A reference to one of Guiteau's acts during his teenage years.

CHAPTER THIRTY-NINE

The Gunfight at the O.K. Corral occurred on October 26, 1881, about one month after Chester A. Arthur took the oath of office and became the 21st President of the United States. In a sense, the trouble out West was indicative of the trouble back East, and the foul mood of the nation. Arthur did not enter the White House with any sense of joy or triumph, but not because he did not want the job. His gloom was caused by the recent death of his wife, and of course, the assassination of James Garfield. Both events had shaken him to the core, but they would also prove that the new President possessed resiliency and strength in the face of tragedy. Friends and foes knew that Arthur was a man of impeccable manners and charming conversation, and now they were learning that he also had a backbone.

Like those who came before him, there were good signs and bad signs swirling around his ascension to the highest office in the land. On the positive side, he was intelligent, polite, and a good administrator. His negatives included no national experience, no public confidence, and a closeness to the New York Stalwarts and the despised Roscoe Conkling.

In the beginning of his term, public sympathy was abundant, which was also a positive sign. But he had inherited a volatile Secretary of State, and thanks to James G. Blaine, the goodwill would rapidly expire. Much to his credit—and to the dismay of some supporters—Arthur became his own man and surprised the Washington establishment by refusing to engage in partisan bickering. Remaining above the fray was a smart move, especially since he had slim Republican majorities in both houses. The strategy allowed him to focus on long-held concerns, and during his brief term, he made some interesting, and thoughtful, suggestions.

Among his most important efforts were suggesting a building for the Library of Congress, urging repeal of all internal taxation (except for excise duties on tobacco and liquor), and a discussion of a line item veto. Later in his term, his efforts grew bolder, and he took on civil service reform, surplus and the tariff, foreign affairs and immigration, Naval reform, and civil rights.

He also found time for frivolous pursuits. Historian Justus D. Doenecke wrote: "If the man was haunted by hidden tragedies as he entered the Presidency, he still possessed a magnificent sense of style. Few Presidents have been as concerned with the ceremonial and the symbolic."

During and after Gutieau's trial, Arthur kept himself busy by making substantial changes to the Executive Mansion. As Doenecke noted, "He [Arthur] renovated the White House on a grand scale, supervising the project himself. Twenty-four wagonloads of furniture and clothing were auctioned off, including a pair of Abraham Lincoln's trousers."

Unlike his predecessor, Arthur was not one to burn the candle at both ends. In contrast to Garfield, who was a tireless administrator, Arthur arrived in his office about ten o'clock in the morning, received Congressmen until noon, ate a hearty lunch, and entertained visitors by appointment until four or five o'clock in the afternoon. From five to seven-thirty, he did whatever he pleased, which often included reading, resting, or riding his horse around the Capitol grounds. Sunday and Monday he reserved for himself, and since Arthur was a loner, he seldom had company on those two days. Twice a week, at noon, he met with his cabinet, and three times a week, for one hour, he greeted the public.

While Arthur did not inherit his predecessor's work ethic, he did inherit many of the same problems that Garfield faced, including the major concerns of the day: Mormonism, Chinese immigration, and the treatment of the Indians.

In Garfield's Inauguration Speech of March 4, 1881, he referred to Mormon polygamy as a "criminal practice," and then added that "the Mormon church not only offends the moral sense of mankind by sanctioning polygamy, but prevents the administration of justice through the ordinary instrumentalities of the law."

Garfield was referring to the fact that Utah juries were refusing to indict or try members of the Mormon Church who were openly practicing polygamy. Their reluctance to prosecute was understandable in light of the state populace. In Utah, in 1882, Mormons outnumbered non-Mormons eight to one.

In Arthur's first annual speech, he went even further than Garfield, implying that Mormonism destroyed family relations and endangered the existing social order of the nation. In fact, he referred to polygamy as an "odious crime" and suggested that the wives of bigamists should be allowed to testify against their husbands in a court of law. He also proposed that all Mormon marriages be certified by the Utah Supreme Court.

It should be noted that Congress had already ruled that plural marriage was illegal, and in 1879, the United States Supreme Court rendered a decision agreeing with the ruling. In its decision, the court held that religious duty was not a defense to a criminal indictment. Nonetheless, Arthur continued to rail against the "threat" of Mormonism, which would eventually lead to the passage of the Edmunds Act in the winter of 1882. The act would make plural marriage a crime, and furthermore, it would disqualify polygamists from jury duty, prohibit them from holding elective office, and bar them from voting in the state of Utah.

Arthur's "Chinese problem" centered on unlimited immigration—the controversial subject that had nearly cost Garfield the Presidency. During the California gold rush, large numbers of Chinese laborers came to the United States, welcomed with open arms by the railroad industry and others who were willing to exploit them. By the time Arthur took office, there were roughly 300,000 Chinese in the country. Most of them lived in California, mainly in San Francisco. Once the gold fields ran dry and the railroads were completed nobody needed cheap labor, so the Chinese turned to other trades, such as boot, shoe, and broom manufacturing. Their success was met with open hostility, exacerbated by their foreign customs, language difficulty, and "anti-Christian" rituals.

Early in 1882, a bill would be introduced that would exclude Chinese laborers from entering the country for the next twenty years, and would deny citizenship to Chinese residents. The bill would be supported by the labor movement, western and southern politicians, and much of the general public. Arthur would veto the bill and call it "undemocratic and hostile to the spirit of the institutions." The Chinese, he would argue, had made a significant contribution to the American economy. In fact, he argued, the transcontinental railroad could not have been built without their labor. Furthermore, he warned that exclusionist policies "might have a direct tendency to repel Oriental nations from us to drive their trade and commerce into more friendly hands."

Faced with overwhelming opposition, Arthur would eventually be forced to sign the Chinese Exclusion Act, but not before extracting some major changes from its sponsors. He would not fare much better with the "Indian problem," but again, it would not be for lack of trying. Unlike his predecessor, Arthur was not contemptuous of the Native American. Garfield had been openly hostile to the western tribes, claiming in 1868 that "The race of red men would be remembered only as a strange, weird, dream-like specter, which had once passed before the eyes of men, but had departed forever." He went on to suggest that they be allowed to become extinct "as quietly and humanely as possible."

Arthur had a much different view. He was determined to introduce the Indian population to "the customs and pursuits of civilized life." Once the Indians were exposed to these customs and pursuits, they would gradually be absorbed into the mass of American citizenry. Believing this to be true, he would urge the extension of federal law to cover Indian reservations. "Their hunting days are over," he would declare. "Give them the assurance of permanent title to the soil and they will gladly till it."

With the press and the public focused on Guiteau's trial, Arthur was able to achieve many of his goals and to become, in the words of one historian, "one of the nation's greatest political surprises." But neither the press nor the public knew that the new President had been diagnosed with Bright's Disease, a fatal kidney ailment.

Chester A. Arthur and Charles Guiteau were now living on borrowed time, but only one of them realized that the end was near—the sane one.

CHAPTER FORTY

The second phase of Guiteau's trail began on December 5, and as many expected, it quickly became a contest between expert witnesses in the field of psychiatry. Since the question of jurisdiction has been resolved, and the malpractice defense abandoned, the only issue left to be determined was whether the defendant was sane or insane. If Scoville could convince the jury that his client was a lunatic, they might send him to an asylum instead of the gallows, but it would not be easy. Public sentiment demanded justice, and for most, that meant death by hanging.

The first defense witness was Dr. James G. Kiernan, a twenty-nine-year-old neurologist from Chicago. According to Charles E. Rosenberg, the author of *The Trial of the Assassin Guiteau*, "Kiernan was still a staunch, indeed embittered, opponent of the psychiatric establishment." In an editorial in the *Chicago Medical Review*, he had written "That long residence in an insane asylum has a deteriorating effect on a mediocre mind. That such effect is exerted is shown by the occurrence of insanity by superintendents."

Kiernan's bitterness stemmed from the fact that he had been dismissed from the Ward's Island Asylum in 1878, not for doing something wrong, but for refusing to sign a death certificate stating that Nathan Odenwald, a patient, had died of some innocuous infection when, in reality, he had been beaten to death by two hospital orderlies. After his dismissal, both orderlies were found guilty at an unpublicized inquest.

When Kiernan took the stand, Scoville chose to elicit his opinion about the connection between heredity and insanity. He did so by asking a long, hypothetical question, reminding the doctor—and the jury—that the defendant had been sent to an insane asylum when he was thirty-five; that many persons observing his conduct believed him to be insane; that *he* believed that he had been inspired by God to remove the President; that immediately after the shooting he appeared calm, as if relieved by the performance of a great duty. Considering these facts, did Dr. Kiernan think that Charles Guiteau was sane or insane at the time of shooting President Garfield?

"Assuming these propositions to be true," Kiernan replied, "I should say that the prisoner was insane."

After a short recess, the defense team presented a long line of mental health experts, all of them disciples of the school of moral insanity, which referred to a type of mental disorder consisting of abnormal emotions and behaviors in the apparent absence of intellectual impairments, delusions, and hallucinations. The term "moral insanity" was coined by Dr. James Cowles Prichard in 1835, and he defined the malady as "madness consisting in a morbid perversion of feelings, affections, and active powers, without any illusion or erroneous conviction impressed upon the understanding; it sometimes co-exists with an apparently unimpaired state of the intellectual faculties."

Kiernan's testimony was supported by Dr. Charles H. Nicholls, Superintendent of the Bloomingdale Asylum for the Insane, Dr. William W. Golding, Superintendent of the Government Hospital for the Insane, Dr. James H. McBride, of the Insane Asylum of Milwaukee, Dr. Walter Channing, who had been connected with the Asylum for Insane Criminals at Auburn, New York, and Dr. Theodore W. Fisher, who had studied mental diseases for over twenty years at the Boston Lunatic Asylum.

As expected, all of the defense witnesses testified that Guiteau was unquestionably insane.

The prosecution began its rebuttal by calling General William T. Sherman to the stand, and as planned, the general told the court that he had investigated the shooting and had come to the conclusion that it was the act of one man, and one man alone. In an incredible display of hubris, Guiteau thanked the general for sending troops to the jail to protect him.

The District Attorney continued his rebuttal by presenting a number of witnesses from Freeport, Illinois, all of them old acquaintances of the defendant, each convinced that he was sane. Horace Tarbox, a capitalist, testified to the sanity of the Guiteau family and then told the court that Luther Guiteau, Charles' father, was the third smartest man in the county. He mentioned the names of the men who were smarter, prompting an outburst from the prisoner. Smiling, Guiteau told the court that both men were dead, which made his father the smartest man in Stephenson County!

On Monday, December 12, the defense called their most important witness to the stand, Dr. E.C. Spitzka, of New York City. Spitzka was a noted alienist, neurologist, and anatomist. He was also a practicing surgeon at Mount Sinai Hospital. Under oath, the eminent physician stated that he had spent six years studying nervous and mental diseases, and had been called as an expert witness in at least twenty-five previous cases.

Dr. Spitzka had examined Guiteau the previous day, and had pronounced him to be unquestionably insane. While on the stand, he testified that he had "no doubt" that the prisoner was both insane and a "moral monstrosity."

Under a sharp and often sarcastic cross-examination, the prosecution attempted not only to discredit the witness, but also to challenge his education and expertise. Walter Davidge got the witness to admit that he had never been in charge of an insane asylum, nor had he ever been a professor in a medical school. Irritated by this line of questioning, Spirtzka shot back that he had taught at Columbia Veterinary College. The admission provoked the following exchange:

DAVIDGE: What sort of college is that?

SPITZKA: A college where physicians are instructed in the art of treating the lower animals.

DAVIDGE: Horses, mainly, I suppose?

SPITZKA: Yes; the branch which I treat is the branch pursued by such men as Thomas Huxley, Baron Huguet, and other of our eminent scientists. I have no reason to be ashamed of it.

DAVIDGE: All these doctors, and the doctors belonging to this college are called "horse doctors," are they not?

SPITZKA: I never have treated any lower animal except the ass, and that animal had two legs.

DAVIDGE: But you are a veterinary surgeon, are you not?

SPITZKA: In the sense that I treat asses who ask me stupid questions I am.

Shortly after this exchange, George Corkhill, the District Attorney, questioned Spitzka about his preconceived opinion regarding the mental condition of the prisoner. The New York neurologist had written several articles, flatly declaring that Guiteau was insane, and stating that it would be a terrible tragedy if the case ever came before a jury. Rosenberg cites the following example, which appeared in the October 29th issue of the *New York Medical Record*:

> There is not a scintilla of doubt in my mind, that if Guiteau with his hereditary history, his insane manner, his insane documents and his insane actions were to be committed to any asylum in the land, he would be unhesitatingly admitted as a proper subject for sequestration . . . A thorough study will convince an impartial and competent jury of medical examiners, before whom such a case should be laid, that Guiteau is not only now insane, but that he was never anything else, that his crime was the offspring of insanity, and that in every act he will betray the characteristic features of querulent monomania.

Trying to present Spitzka as an arrogant know-it-all, Corkhill reminded the jury that the young doctor also held some strong views about religion. "Do you believe in God," Corkhill asked. Spitzka remained calm, despite the calculated attempt to badger him, he replied, "I refuse on principle to answer such a question; it seems to me impertinent in a country that guarantees civil and religious liberty."

Spitzka's reply, though honest, did not sit well with the jury. In a day and age when religious adherence was paramount, citizens were expected to be unequivocal in their belief and support of the Almighty. Following this exchange, the prosecution presented a battery of "insane experts," each testifying that Guiteau was sane. The succession began with Dr. Allen Hamilton, a prominent New York alienist, who testified that Guiteau was sane, though eccentric, and that he was able to distinguish the difference between right and wrong. Hamilton spent three weeks in the courtroom, and he did not enjoy the experience. In his book, *Recollections of an Alienist*, he described the setting in stark detail:

> The trial lasted seventy-two days, and I spent three weeks in the foul court room, breathing the worst of bad air emanating from the diseased lungs of scores of dirty negroes and the unwashed bodies of filthy loungers whose damp clothes fairly reeked with all sorts of stinks. The windows were usually closed, and the place was heated to an insufferable degree.

Hamilton was followed by a steady stream of physicians, including Dr. Samuel Worcester, Superintendent of the Massachusetts Homeopathic Asylum, Dr. Abram Shew of the Connecticut Hospital for the Insane, Dr. Jamin Strong, Superintendent of the Cleveland Asylum for the Insane, S.H. Talcott, Superintendent of the State Homeopathic Asylum for the Insane at Middletown, New York, and a half-dozen others who the prosecution presented as expert witnesses.

After the Christmas recess, the government presented its star witness, Dr. John Gray, the Superintendent of the Utica Asylum and the longtime editor of the *American Journal of Insanity.* Gray testified that Guiteau "understood the nature and consequences of his act, appeared to reason coherently, and hence, following the generally accepted rule of law, was guilty." He went on to underscore the main contention of the prosecution's expert witnesses; insanity could not be inherited, only the tendency or predisposition to it. Insanity, they unanimously agreed, was a disease, the disease a result of processes taking place over the course of a lifetime. Consequently, insanity could not be hereditary.

The government had cleverly saved Gray to conclude and summarize their case, and in many ways, he was the perfect choice. As Charles E. Rosenberg noted, "Gray was a man of national reputation and experience, a dignified, indeed magisterial, witness. The mere recital of his credentials was overwhelming, emphasized as it was by the Utica physician's grave and didactic manner."

Even so, at the conclusion of Gray's testimony, the question remained, unresolved in the minds of many: Was Charles Guiteau insane?

Twenty-four medical specialists had been called to testify at the trial, and eight of them were respected enough to be listed in the *Dictionary of American Biography* due to their accomplishments in the field of psychiatry. Four of these gentlemen had testified for the defense and four for the prosecution. Which group would the jury believe? Would the jury even care if the defendant was insane? Insane or not, Americans were of one mind, demanding that justice come down on the man who had murdered their leader. Writing in 1881, after the assassination but before the criminal trial, William Ralston Balch summed up the general feeling of the populace:

> All this time possibly the reader has asked what of the assassin? I have purposely reserved any notice of this miscreant as long as convenient, for I do not deem him deserving of any more notice than is rendered absolutely necessary to comprehend the full story.

The only thing standing between Guiteau and the hangman were the closing arguments of the defense and the prosecution, and as the public would soon learn, even the closing arguments would prove historically significant.

CHAPTER FORTY-ONE

George Scoville was determined to give a long and detailed summation, knowing that his brother-in-law's life was on the line, and that this would be his last chance to sway the jury. He did not, by any measure, squander the opportunity. In fact, he gave one of the longest closing arguments ever delivered in the District's criminal courts, taking a full five days to present his final remarks.

Scoville complained bitterly about the prosecution's tactics, which in his mind, included distorted evidence, rehearsed witnesses, and a general contempt for due process of law. He bluntly characterized the government's behavior as a conspiracy to hang Guiteau—a man they all knew was insane. During his five-day oration, Scoville was interrupted 147 times by government counsel, but he forged ahead, determined to prove that his client was not responsible for his repulsive actions.

Most observers, including many in the press, admired his pluck, but not everyone appreciated his courtroom demeanor. Dr. Hamilton, the New York alienist who complained about the four-smelling air in the courtroom, also wrote a few choice words about Scoville:

> Scoville was a type of the abusive provincial lawyer, but was much in earnest, and despite his constant violation of the ethics of his profession and exhibitions of bad taste, fought valiantly for his unfortunate relative, who gave him a great deal of trouble. Like all men more or less ignorant of psychiatry, he confidently asked questions of opposing experts that got him into trouble.

On Friday, January 20, Scoville confined his criticism to the testimony of the prosecution's experts. He began with Dr. Hamilton, and then turned to Dr. Gray, whom he characterized as the big gun who was supposed to sway the jury with his overwhelming declarations.

"Gray is a big gun with a big mouth," Guiteau shouted. "I will mark him."

The outburst was met by boos and hisses, and the crowd became even angrier when Judge Cox announced that Guiteau would be permitted to address the jury the following day. Apparently, the judge had met with some of his colleagues on the bench, and they had advised him to allow Guiteau to address the court.

When the trial resumed on Saturday, Guiteau was led to the witness stand, where he sat down and calmly addressed the jury. "I am going to sit down because I can talk better. I am not afraid of any one shooting me. Shooting is on the decrease." The prisoner adjusted his glasses and proceeded to read a speech he had written in jail. In essence, he declared that he should not be held responsible for the death of President Garfield, as he was acting under orders from God. He concluded the bizarre performance by threatening all those who would seek to do him harm:

> Put my body in the ground if you will; that is all you can do; but thereafter comes a day of reckoning. The mills of the gods grind slow, but they grind sure, and they will grind to atoms every man that injures me. As sure as a hair of my head is injured, this nation will go down in the dust, and don't you forget it.

Monday morning, January 23, marked the eleventh week of the trial, and the day that Judge John K. Porter began the government's closing argument. Speaking directly to the jury, and in a sense to the entire nation, Porter delivered a persuasive and powerful condemnation of the prisoner, describing him as a cold-blooded assassin. A man without a conscience or a soul.

Porter continued the verbal assault on Tuesday morning, and despite repeated interruptions from Guiteau, he managed to deliver one of the most memorable summations in American history. The effectiveness of his presentation can be seen in the answer he gave to the question, *Who killed President Garfield*?

> The prisoner tells you, with his characteristic impudence and effrontery, that the responsibility is upon *Secretary Blaine* . . . But who else is responsible? As the prisoner would have you believe, *John H. Noyes* . . . Who else killed Garfield? *The prisoner's father.* Who else killed Garfield? Why, *the mother of the prisoner.* Who else?

Once again, Judge Porter answered his own question, naming every person or group that Guiteau had blamed for his wretched existence . . . *Uncle Abraham, Francis Guiteau, Cousin Abby Maynard, the Oneida Community, the Chicago Convention, the electors of the United States, the Press*, and of course, *the Lord.*

Finally, Porter reminded the jury that he had not asked an abstract question. "It is the direct question whether *this* man [Guiteau] killed him; whether if he did, he was sane or insane; whether, if sane, he was so to such a degree that he did not know legal and moral right from wrong in respect of this act."

In closing, he asked the jury to be prompt with their verdict, and expressed his hope that the verdict would "represent the dignity and majesty of the law."

Porter got his wish. After Judge Cox charged the jury, they retreated to an anteroom, and thirty minutes later they reached a verdict. The twelve male members of the jury returned in a solemn procession, their mood in concert with that of the dark and gloomy courtroom. The District Court did not contain gas fixtures, so now, at 5:35 p.m., the room was lit by candles. The candlelight cast an eerie pall on the proceedings, and when Guiteau was brought back, he seemed nervous, troubled by the dim light and countless shadows.

Judge Cox returned to the bench, and the clerk asked the jury foreman whether the jury had agreed upon a verdict.

The foreman replied, "Guilty as indicated."

There was a loud outburst of cheering, which the bailiffs promptly discouraged. Once order was restored, Scoville demanded a poll of the jury, which Cox granted. One by one, the members were called by name, and each responded, "Guilty."

Guiteau was furious, and as he had done throughout the trial, he interrupted the proceeding by shouting at the jury. "My blood will be upon the heads of that jury; don't you forget it." The judge told him to be quiet, but Guiteau added, "God will avenge this outrage!"

Judge Cox thanked the jury for sitting through a very long and tedious trial, and then he dismissed them.

Scoville promptly appealed for a new trial, and on February 4, 1882, Judge Cox, having considered all the matters that had been presented, felt compelled to overrule the motion for a new trial. Once again, Guiteau was livid, but this time his venom was aimed at poor George Scoville. "I have been doing well, but your theory is wrong. Your theory is too small."

Scoville begged his client to keep quiet, but Guiteau was determined to have his say. Judge Cox, desiring to be fair, did not intercede, so the defendant continued his attack:

> You convicted me with your jackass theories and consummate nonsense . . . You convicted me by your wild theory and consummate asinine character all through . . . Your intentions were good, but you are deficient in brains and theory. Let me alone and I will pull out of this. You got me into this trouble.

Mercifully, the District Attorney interrupted, asking the court to pass sentence in accordance with the verdict. Judge Cox told the prisoner to stand up, and then, in part, he reminded Guiteau that he had had as fair and impartial a jury as ever assembled in a court of justice. He had also "been defended by counsel with a zeal and devotion that merit the highest encomium." The prisoner seemed unimpressed, but the judge went on, "I certainly have done my best to secure a fair presentation of the defense."

Judge Cox paused momentarily, and then he announced that it was necessary for him to pronounce the sentence of the law that Guiteau be taken to the common jail of the District, from whence he came, and there be kept in confinement, and on Friday, the 30th of June, 1882, be taken to the place prepared for the execution, within the walls of said jail, and there, between the hours of 12 noon and 2:00 p.m., be hanged by the neck until he was dead. He paused again, then added, "And may the Lord have mercy on your soul."

"And may God have mercy on your soul!" Guiteau cried out. "I had rather stand where I am than where that jury does or than where your Honor does. I am not afraid to die."

Although Scoville took exception to the harsh sentence, the District Attorney, and many of the onlookers, seemed pleased. Judge Cox adjourned the court, and as Guiteau was being dragged off to jail, he began to struggle wildly. His last words to the court were typically defiant. "I will have a flight to glory, and I am not afraid to go . . . I know how I stand on this business, and so does the Lord, and he will pull me through with the help of two or three good lawyers, and all the devils in hell can't hurt me!

CHAPTER FORTY-TWO

The conviction of America's most despised criminal ended the first high-profile murder trial in which the insanity defense was considered, but it did not curtail the public's morbid fascination with Charles Guiteau. Sensational stories appeared in many of the nation's leading newspapers, including *The New York Times*, which published a series of articles after the trial was over.

On February 1, the *Times* reported that Guiteau's relatives had agreed to sell his corpse to J.H. Ridgway, a Philadelphia manufacturer of refrigerators and refrigerated railway cars. Supposedly, Ridgway wanted to exhibit the assassin's body, and in return for the exclusive right to tour the nation, he would assume all expenses and split the profits with Guiteau's brother and sister.

On February 18, the newspaper reported that Francis Scoville, the condemned man's sister, had sent a letter to Lucretia Garfield, begging the widow to intercede on her brother's behalf. Apparently, Mrs. Scoville wanted Mrs. Garfield to ask President Arthur to spare the life of Charles Guiteau, a man many believed was unquestionably insane. Mrs. Garfield expressed her feeling through one of her husband's lifelong friends, who released the following statement:

> Toward the slayer of her husband she cherishes no malice: He must answer above to his God and the American people. For the sister and all members of his family she feels only profound pity. Further than this, she asks to be left alone with her sorrow, and to be spared being dragged into useless and torturing publicity.

In late June, Francis Scoville and her daughter would travel to Cleveland to beg Mrs. Garfield to reconsider her decision. Mrs. Garfield would not be at home when they arrived, so they would wait in the library until she and her daughter, Mollie, returned. The widow would refuse to see them, and Mollie would later record her own feelings in her personal diary: "Whenever I think of any of those people my blood boils up in my veins and I feel as if I could tear them all to pieces."

Francis Scoville's desperate act might have been a reaction to a story that had appeared in the *Times* in late April. Her husband, George Scoville, had finally had enough of Charles Guiteau, and on April 24, he withdrew from the case. On May 9, the case was appealed to the Supreme Court of the District of Columbia, which unanimously refused to order a new trial. A motion for a new hearing was turned down on June 5, and a final appeal to the United State Supreme Court was rejected on June 19, 1882.

On June 28, *The New York Times* announced that the assassin's end was near, the gallows prepared, and President Arthur unwilling to hear any appeals. "Another night watch will be the last that Warden Crocker will need to set upon the assassin of President Garfield, and then the wretched criminal will be beyond the power of mischief and consigned to such judgement as may hereafter await him."

With death staring him in the face, Guiteau continued to act as he had since his first day of incarceration, showing no feeling, betraying no nervousness, and still clinging to the hope that he would receive a presidential pardon. Even though he was scheduled to die in 12 hours, he ordered a huge lunch, and was served a four-egg omelet, a pound of beefsteak, fried potatoes, six slices of toast, and coffee. He ordered the exact same meal for supper—plus a basket of raspberries and a pint of milk.

Guiteau had survived two murder attempts during his trial, and on the last full day of his life, he was involved in a final ploy to cheat the hangman. After supper, his brother and sister came to visit him, and they were kind enough to bring a large bouquet of flowers. The warden allowed them to stay for almost an hour, but after they left he noticed a white powder on some of the petals. The bouquet was immediately removed from the cell and later examined by an independent laboratory, which determined that it contained over five grains of white arsenic—more than enough to kill anyone who ingested the poison.

George Corkhill, the District Attorney who had led the prosecution team, promised a swift and thorough investigation, but neither Francis Scoville nor John W. Guiteau was ever charged with a crime, and the matter was soon forgotten.

On the morning of June 30, execution day, Guiteau had his boots blackened and then calmly listened as the warden read the death warrant to him. The warrant, delivered to the Clerk of the Criminal Court after the hanging, read as follows:

> I, John S. Crocker, Warden of the jail of the District of Columbia, do hereby certify that by virtue of the within writ I did proceed to carry into execution the sentence of the court as within directed, and did cause the within named Charles J. Guiteau to be hanged by the neck until he was dead, between the hours of 12 A.M. and 2 P.M. of the said 30th day of June, A.D. 1882, within the walls of the jail of the said District of Columbia as therein commanded.

Guiteau had spent a restless night, tossing and turning in his cell, but after the warrant was read to him, he seemed unusually calm. "My heart is tender," he told the prison chaplain. "I don't think I can go through this ordeal without weeping, not because of any great weakness, for the principle in me is strong, but because I am nearer the other world. I hold to the idea that God inspired me."

When the hour of execution arrived, Guiteau had his arms tied behind his back, and then he was led out of his cell by an armed guard. They marched the condemned man into a narrow courtyard, roughly 30 feet in width, surrounded by the thick outer walls of the jail. Not surprisingly, the event had drawn a large crowd of newspaper writers and curiosity seekers.

Much to the warden's dismay, the prisoner tripped on the first step of the scaffold and stubbed his toe. After a moment, the death march continued, and when they reached the top of the scaffold, Guiteau was permitted to recite a "prayer" that he had written for the occasion:

The American press has a large bill to settle with Thee, righteous Father, for their vindictiveness in this matter. Nothing but blood will satisfy them, and now my blood be on them and this nation and its officials. Arthur the President is a coward and an ingrate. His ingratitude to the man that made him and saved his party and land from overthrow has no parallel in history. But Thou, righteous Father, will judge him. Father, Thou knowest me, but the world hath not known me, and now I go to Thee and the Savior without the slightest ill will toward a human being. Farewell, ye men of earth.

In a final display of characteristic hubris, he entertained the crowd by reading a few versus of poetry he'd written himself. "If set to music they may be rendered very effective," he explained, and then proceeded in a high-pitched childlike voice:

I am going to the Lordy; I am so glad,
I am going to the Lordy; I am so glad,
I am going to the Lordy,
Glory hallelujah! Glory hallelujah!
I am going to the Lordy!

I love the Lordy with all my soul,
Glory Hallelujah!
And that is the reason I am going to the Lord,
Glory hallelujah! Glory hallelujah!
I am going to the Lord.

I saved my party and my land,
Glory hallelujah!
But they have murdered me for it,
And that is the reason I am going to the Lordy,
Glory hallelujah! Glory hallelujah!
I am going to the Lordy!

I wonder what I will see when I get to the Lordy,
I expect to see most glorious things,
Beyond all earthly conception,
When I am with the Lordy!
Glory hallelujah! Glory hallelujah!
I am with the Lord.

When Guiteau had finished, the hangman placed a black hood over his face, and a moment later, the trapdoor dropped under his feet, the rope snapping his neck and killing him instantly. Guiteau's body was never returned to his family. Francis Scoville "was without means," and could not afford a private burial. John W. Guiteau was unwilling to assume the risk of taking charge of the body, believing that he would be powerless to prevent body snatchers from stealing the corpse. After an autopsy that discovered nothing more abnormal than an enlarged spleen, the body of Charles Guiteau was interred, without ceremony, in the northeast corner of the jail.

Almost immediately, there were rumors that the guards intended to dig up the body and sell it to the highest bidder. Fearing scandal, the warden had the body exhumed, and then it was sent to the National Museum of Health and Medicine, where the skin was bleached off, and the skeleton, spleen, and brain preserved and placed in storage.

The public thought they had finally heard the last of Charles Guiteau, but they were wrong. Shortly after his death, a new industry sprang up, supported by America's growing fascination with violent criminals. Novelties of the Guiteau order were shown in the shops of Washington, D.C. and sold by vendors on the streets near the White House. A decent trade was also done through the mail. Throughout the nation there was a steady demand for items related to the trial, the most popular being facsimile bullets and photographs of the assassin. One enterprising merchant was selling pieces of the rope by which Guiteau was hanged. The catalog description boasted that "these are, perhaps, an inch long and fancifully bound on the ends with official red tape."

The grisly souvenirs were being sold for 25 cents apiece, and the buyer also received a certificate of authenticity signed by a jail official.

The most interesting, and perhaps, revealing, "relic of the hanging," was a small square of roofing tile from the National Museum of Health and Medicine. The seller guaranteed—in writing—that this was the actual roofing material upon which the bones of Charles Guiteau were bleached in the summer sun, under the watchful eye of a government official.

Each square was inscribed with the words, "Charles Guiteau, lawyer, politician, and theologian."

In the words of *The New York Times*, these made a "charming memento," were a solid investment, and accordingly, should be in the hands of every true American.

THE END.

ENDNOTES

Chapter 1

1. "It seems to me as foolish as it does to you . . ." *New York Times*, July 3, 1881.

2. Years later, both sons would describe . . . Brown, *The Life and Public Services of James A. Garfield, Twentieth President of the United States*, p. 215.

3. If all went well, they would be back . . . Ogilvie, *History of the Attempted Assassination of James A. Garfield*, pp. 29-30.

4. "They would have the President surrounded by a bodyguard . . ." Balch, *The Life of James Abram Garfield, Late President of the United States*, pp. 677-678.

5. The officer, a man named Patrick Kearney . . . Hayes and Hayes, *A Complete History of the Life and Trial of Charles Julius Guiteau, Assassin of President Garfield*, p. 195.

6. "My God! What is this?" Taylor, *Garfield of Ohio. The Available Man*, p. 264.

7. The second bullet hit Garfield square in the back . . . McCabe, *Our Martyred President*, p. 691.

8. "I remember I stopped just outside . . ." Hayes and Hayes, *A Complete History of the Life and Trial of Charles Julius Guiteau, Assassin of President Garfield*, p. 183.

9. "There were two shots fired . . ." Ibid., p. 195.

10. "Keep quiet, my friend . . ." Ibid., p. 55.

11. "How many hours of sorrow I have passed . . ." Peskin, *Garfield*, p. 597.

12. "In my right leg and foot . . ." Ogilvie, *History of the Attempted Assassination of James A. Garfield*, p. 39.

13. "When I placed my finger in the wound . . ." Ibid., p. 39.

14. "I thank you, Doctor . . ." Ibid.

15. "I did it . . . I will go to jail for it . . ." Hayes and Hayes, *A Complete History of the Life and Trial of Charles Julius Guiteau, Assassin of President Garfield*, p. 197.

16. "I have nothing to say . . ." Ibid., p. 198.

17. "Not a living soul . . ." Ogilvie, *History of the Attempted Assassination of James A. Garfield*, p. 59.

18. "I wanted to see what kind of quarters . . ." Ibid.

Chapter 2

19. "I had noticed this man . . ." Ogilvie, *History of the Attempted Assassination of James A. Garfield*, p. 36.

20. "When the President and Secretary Blaine entered . . ." Ibid.

21. "Rockwell, I want you to send a message . . ." Brown, E.E. *The Life and Public Services of James A. Garfield, Twentieth President of the United States,* p. 217.

22. Ironically, Clara Barton, the founder of the American Red Cross . . ." Taylor, *Garfield of Ohio. The Available Man.*, p. 264.

23. Those cabinet members who were not at the depot . . . Ridpath, *The Life and Work of James A. Garfield, Twentieth President of the United States*, p. 520.

24. They agreed to search for the ball . . . Brown, E.E. *The Life and Public Services of James A. Garfield, Twentieth President of the United States,* p. 219.

25. "Perhaps he thought it would be a glorious thing . . ." Balch, *The Life of James Abram Garfield, Late President of the United States*, p. 599.

26. "God's will be done . . ." Brown, E.E. *The Life and Public Services of James A. Garfield, Twentieth President of the United States,* p. 220.

27. Naturally, this sent shock waves . . . Ogilvie, *History of the Attempted Assassination of James A. Garfield*, p. 40

28. "It is impossible that he could have shot himself . . ." Thayer, *From Log Cabin to the White House: Life of James A. Garfield*, p. 400.

29. "Mrs. Garfield, Elberon, Long Branch . . ." Balch, *The Life of James Abram Garfield, Late President of the United States*, p. 595.

30. "I need to pack . . ." Ogilvie, *History of the Attempted Assassination of James A. Garfield*, pp. 42-43

31. "Executive Mansion, Washington, D.C., July 2 . . ." Balch, *The Life of James Abram Garfield, Late President of the United States*, p. 600.

32. The train left at 12:30 . . . Thayer, *From Log Cabin to the White House: Life of James A. Garfield*, p. 400.

33. "The President has returned to his normal condition . . ." Ridpath, *The Life and Work of James A. Garfield, Twentieth President of the United States*, p. 520.

34. The reaction from the shot . . . Ibid., p. 521.

35. "No official bulleting has been furnished . . ." Ibid.

36. Arthur was advised to prepare himself . . . McCabe, *Our Martyred President. The Life and Public Services of Gen. James A. Garfield*, p. 544.

37. "Well, my dear . . . you are not going to die . . ." Balch, *The Life of James Abram Garfield, Late President of the United States*, pp. 610-611.

38. "Go back and tell him that I am undressing . . ." Ibid.

39. "The President's condition is greatly improved . . ." Ridpath, *The Life and Work of James A. Garfield, Twentieth President of the United States*, p. 523.

Chapter 3

40. "The law of heredity has long been suspected . . ." Ridpath, *The Life and Work of James A. Garfield, Twentieth President of the United States*, p. 13.

41. He appears to have been a farmer . . . Conwell, *The Life, Speeches, and Public Services of James A. Garfield, Twentieth President of the United States,* p. 27.

42. "A Latin motto, *In Cruce Vinco* . . ." Ridpath, *The Life and Work of James A. Garfield, Twentieth President of the United States.* p. 15.

43. "Lexington, April 23, 1775 . . ." Ibid., pp. 16-17.

44. Supposedly, Solomon hoisted the stone . . . . Ibid., p. 17.

45. When Thomas Garfield died of smallpox . . . Conwell, *The Life, Speeches, and Public Services of James A. Garfield, Twentieth President of the United States,* p. 33.

46. Eliza was Hosea Ballou's grand-niece . . . McCabe, *Our Martyred President. The Life and Public Services of Gen. James A. Garfield*, p. 18.

47. Incredibly, there was not a single bridge . . . Thayer, *From Log Cabin to the White House: Life of James A. Garfield*, p. 26.

48. By the time they rolled into . . . Bundy, *The Life of Gen. James A. Garfield,* p. 6.

49. The first inhabitants of the region . . . Glazier, *Peculiarities of American Cities*, p. 145

50. In its entirety, the Reserve . . . Ibid., p. 141.

51. To make matters worse . . . Gammon, *The Canal Boy Who Became President*, p. 1.

52. The neighbor applied a blister . . . Thayer, *From Log Cabin to the White House: Life of James A. Garfield*, p. 33.

53. "I have planted four saplings . . ." Balch, *The Life of James Abram Garfield, Late President of the United States* p. 22.

54. The children would often lie awake . . . Gammon, *The Canal Boy Who Became President*, p. 6.

55. What he didn't realize was that . . . Thayer, *From Log Cabin to the White House: Life of James A. Garfield*, p. 50.

56. Although he did not know it at the time . . . Ibid., p. 49.

57. "Who knows . . . . Garfield may even . . ." Ridpath, *The Life and Work of James A. Garfield, Twentieth President of the United State.* p. 52.

Chapter 4

58. The result of this construction . . . Glazier, *Peculiarities of American Cities*, p. 147.

59. Unlike Presbyterians, the Disciples . . . Thayer, *From Log Cabin to the White House: Life of James A. Garfield*, p. 45.

60. At mid-century, they had about . . . Balch, *The Life of James Abram Garfield, Late President of the United States*, p. 66.

61. Just beyond the flatland . . . Glazier, *Peculiarities of American Cities*, p. 148.

62. The trees were a great source . . . Ibid., p. 149.

63. "We have met the enemy and they are ours . . ." Garraty, *The American Nation to 1877. A History of the United States*, pp. 197-198.

64. It would also be the most expensive sculpture . . . Glazier, *Peculiarities of American Cities*, p. 150.

65. The drivers, who were usually young . . . Brown, E.E. *The Life and Public Services of James A. Garfield, Twentieth President of the United States*, p. 32

66. From that moment on . . . Brisbin, *The Early Life and Public Career of James A. Garfield*, p. 52.

67. Garfield worked as a mule driver . . . Ibid., p. 55.

68. When he crawled to the bow . . . Ibid., p. 56.

69. The cake was used as a purgative . . . Balch, *The Life of James Abram Garfield, Late President of the United States*, p. 57.

70. Over the next twelve months . . . Garraty, *The American Nation to 1877. A History of the United States*, pp. 324-325.

71. In those days, the Geauga Seminary . . . Thayer, *From Log Cabin to the White House: Life of James A. Garfield*, p. 237.

72. The Geauga yearbook described her as . . . Ibid., p. 282.

73. She was of medium stature . . . Gammon, *The Canal Boy Who Became President*, p. 70.

Chapter 5

74. Charles Guiteau was born here . . . Hayes and Hayes, *A Complete History of the Life and Trial of Charles Julius Guiteau, Assassin of President Garfield*, p. 23.

75. The line was destined to have . . . Wikipedia contributors. "Freeport, Illinois." *Wikipedia, The Free Encyclopedia*, Web. 23, February, 2013.

76. The latter invention would become . . . Ibid.

77. Sadly, neither of her last two children . . . Hayes and Hayes, *A Complete History of the Life and Trial of Charles Julius Guiteau, Assassin of President Garfield*, p. 249.

78. According to family record . . . Rosenberg, *The Trial of the Assassin Guiteau*, p. 95.

79. It was this belief that led . . . Hayes and Hayes, *A Complete History of the Life and Trial of Charles Julius Guiteau, Assassin of President Garfield,* p. 242.

80. From that moment on, no doctors . . . Ibid.

81. Under her influence, Charles became . . . Ibid., p. 23

82. "Franky" was six years older than Charles . . ." Rosenberg, *The Trial of the Assassin Guiteau*, p. 15.

83. The *Tribune* has described Iowa . . . Hayes and Hayes, *A Complete History of the Life and Trial of Charles Julius Guiteau, Assassin of President Garfield,* p. 23.

84. Moreover, his sexual appetites . . . Ibid., p. 117.

85. In the case of prolonged addiction . . . Ibid.

86. Masturbation is a very degrading . . . Stout, *Our Family Physician*, pp. 288-289.

87. "All kinds of stimulating and heating . . ." *Carrie McLaren, Kellogg, Graham and the Crusade for Moral Fiber,* www.stayfreemagazine.org, 1/14/2007.

88. The Morsel, originally designed to moderate . . . Ibid.

89. The finished product was rather tasty . . . James T. Ehler, www.foodreference.com, 1/14/2007.

90. Dr. Kellogg's view of self-stimulation . . . *Carrie McLaren, Kellogg, Graham and the Crusade for Moral Fiber*, www.stayfreemagazine.org, 1/14/2007.

91. "Dear sister . . . I think I should live . . ." Rosenberg, *The Trial of the Assassin Guiteau*, p. 16.

92. "I want . . . to go to school two or three years . . ." Ibid., p. 17.

93. When the major died, he left his favorite . . . Ibid.

94. The most famous—or infamous—rule . . . "The Oneida Community," Randall Hillebrand, www.nyhistory.com, pp. 3-4.

95. Noyes called this practice "Complex marriage" . . . Ibid., p. 4.

96. If an older female was involved . . . Ibid.

97. Only Noyes was immune from Mutual Criticism . . . Ibid.

98. "I have been looking quite anxiously . . ." Letter to Charles Olds. Ann Arbor, Michigan. March 4, 1860.

99. "My confidence in you is continuously increasing . . ." Rosenberg, *The Trial of the Assassin Guiteau*, p. 18.

100. "I cannot but in this connection confess my gratitude . . ." Letter to Charles Olds. Ann Arbor, Michigan. June 10, 1860.

Chapter 6

101. The observant Frenchman, Alexis de Tocqueville . . . Garraty, *The American Nation to 1877. A History of the United States*, p. 286.

102. "Nothing must interfere with the fulfillment . . ." Ibid., p. 313

103. "In the United States a man builds . . ." Ibid., p. 297.

104. In 1850 it was a green field . . . Ridpath, *The Life and Work of James A. Garfield, Twentieth President of the United States*, p. 52.

105. The goals were straightforward . . . Brown, *The Life and Public Services of James A. Garfield, Twentieth President of the United States*, p. 54.

106. "Well, sir, what is your business with us? . . ." Thayer, *From Log Cabin to the White House*, p. 278.

107. The sight of a half-swept floor . . . Gammon, *The Canal Boy Who Became President*, p. 50.

108. When he first entered the Institute . . . Ibid., p. 51.

109. "He was a most entertaining teacher . . ." Thayer, *From Log Cabin to the White House*, p. 322.

110. Even worse, he was convinced . . . Garraty, The American Nation to 1877. *A History of the United States*, p. 382.

111. When word of these events reached Ohio . . . Ibid., p. 377

112. "The lightning of divine wrath . . ." Thayer, *From Log Cabin to the White House*, p. 302.

113. "Both thy bondmen, and thy bondmaids . . ." Leviticus, 25:44.

114. "Secure thy toil, uncursed their peaceful life . . ." Garraty, *The American Nation to 1877. A History of the United States*, p. 375.

115. Between 1850 and 1855 . . . Ibid., p. 353.

116. They were even more enamored by Thoreau . . . Ibid., p. 354

117. "There are three reasons why I have decided . . ." Bundy, *The Life of Gen. James A. Garfield*, p. 31.

118. "If I live . . . I shall pay you . . ." Thayer, *From Log Cabin to the White House*, p. 327.

Chapter 7

119. One day, he would make a point of climbing . . . Balch, *The Life of James Abram Garfield, Late President of the United States*, p. 76.

120. Ohio was pretty, but there was nothing . . . Conwell, *The Life, Speeches, and Public Services of James A. Garfield, Twentieth President of the United States*, p. 103.

121. The Colonel's will, written shortly before his death . . . Sylvia Kennick Brown, Williams College timeline, Williams College Archives, special collections.

122. The game would create quite a stir . . . Ibid.

123. "My name is Garfield, from Ohio . . ." Thayer, *From Log Cabin to the White House*, p. 328.

124. He would remember him as . . . Gammon, *The Canal Boy Who Became President*, pp. 57-58.

125. "He was not sent to college . . ." Lossing, *A Biography of James A. Garfield, Late President of the United States*, p. 90.

126. Garfield, as a student, was one who would . . . Gammon, *The Canal Boy Who Became President*, p. 59.

127. "The college life of Garfield was so rounded . . ." Ibid., pp. 59-60.

128. "Old autumn, thou art here! . . ." Ibid., p. 62.

129. "Bottles to right of them . . ." Lossing, *A Biography of James A. Garfield, Late President of the United States*, p. 91.

130. For every village, state and nation . . . Brisbin, *The Early Life and Public Career of James A. Garfield*, p. 84.

131. He also had the best campaign slogan . . . Garraty, *The American Nation to 1877. A History of the United States*, p. 388.

132. "There is no other side . . ." Ibid., p. 387.

133. The opposition called him a "filthy reptile" . . . Ibid.

134. "That damn fool will get himself killed . . ." Ibid.

135. Overnight, the caning incident became . . . Ibid.

136. In the south, it was seen as cold-blooded murder . . . Ibid., p. 386

137. "You are not Satan, and I am not . . ." Balch, *The Life of James Abram Garfield, Late President of the United States*, p. 86.

138. That June, forty-two students graduated . . . Ibid., p. 87.

Chapter 8

139. "The present dress of women . . ." Bible Communism: A Compilation From the Annual Reports and Other Publications of the Oneida Association and its Branches, p. 62.

140. By wearing their hair in this fashion . . . *Old Mansion House Memories By One Brought Up In it.* Harriet M. Worden, p. 11.

141. "So, though they have taken away . . ." Confessions of John H. Noyes Part I: Confession of religious experience: Including A History of Modern Perfectionism. John Humphrey Noyes., p. 95.

142. "When weariness overcame me in these excursions . . ." Ibid.

143. Noyes referred to his disorder . . . Ibid.

144. Never one to question a vision . . . Ibid., p. 96.

145. "A persuasion fell upon me . . ." Ibid., p. 96.

146. "I was no longer tormented . . ." Ibid.

147. "To John H. Noyes as such we submit . . ." History of the Oneida Community. Oneida Community Books, Pamphlets, and Serials: 1834-1972. Constance Noyes Robertson. p. 97.

148. "There is some romance in beginning . . ." Ibid., pp. 97-98.

149. "On the admission of any member . . ." First Annual Report of the Oneida Association: Exhibiting Its History, Principles, and Transactions to January 1, 1849, p. 16.

150. The surrender of worldly goods . . . Ibid., p. 14.

151. "We have been stirred by the great pulse of patriotism . . ." Life of John Humphrey Noyes, Volumes IV-VI, the O.C. Part II Journals: Circular & References to Periodicals. 1855-1863. May 2, 1861.

152. "Some discussion in our evening meetings . . ." Ibid., August 7, 1862.

153. "I submit myself to the Providence of God . . ." Ibid., August 13, 1962.

154. Little is known about Guiteau's view of slavery . . . Hayes and Hayes, *A Complete History of the Life and Trial of Charles Julius Guiteau, Assassin of President Garfield*, p. 244.

155. Indeed, many things were forbidden . . . History of the Oneida Community. Oneida Community Books, Pamphlets, and Serials: 1834-1972. Constance Noyes Robertson.

156. Supposedly, he wanted to find out . . . Hayes and Hayes, *A Complete History of the Life and Trial of Charles Julius Guiteau, Assassin of President Garfield*, p. 253.

157. "At other times he would be cheerful . . ." Ibid., p. 247.

158. "He was absorbed in himself . . ." Ibid., p. 253.

159. By the time Guiteau arrived . . . The Oneida Community. The First Hundred Years, pp. 22-23.

160. After the investigation, the individual . . . Ibid., pp. 10-11.

161. The criticisms were administered . . . Ibid., p. 20.

162. Early on, he began to complain that Noyes . . ." Hayes and Hayes, *A Complete History of the Life and Trial of Charles Julius Guiteau, Assassin of President Garfield*, p. 25.

163. He despised criticism, describing it as . . . Ibid., p. 125.

164. The committees mixed praise with faultfinding . . . The Oneida Community, The First Hundred Years, p. 20.

165. In light of these views . . . Ibid., p. 21.

Chapter 9

166. "I have attained the height of my ambition . . ." Gammon, *The Canal Boy Who Became President*, p. 66.

167. The teachers were poor, the students were poor, . . . Brisbin, *The Early Life and Public Career of James A. Garfield*, p. 90.

168. His salary was $800 a year . . . Thayer, *From Log Cabin to the White House*, p. 349.

169. "A bow of recognition or a single word . . ." Brisbin, *The Early Life and Public Career of James A. Garfield*, p. 90.

170. One of his favorite classroom tricks . . . Barbara Holland, *Hail To The Chiefs*, p. 144.

171. Under Garfield's supervision, the attendance at Hiram . . . Balch, *The Life of James Abram Garfield, Late President of the United States*, p. 90.

172. No matter how old the pupils were . . . Brisbin, *The Early Life and Public Career of James A. Garfield*, p. 96.

173. The comb of the roof at the court house . . . Thayer, *From Log Cabin to the White House*, p. 358.

174. He had recently caused a stir . . . Conwell, *The Life, Speeches, and Public Services of James A. Garfield, Twentieth President of the United States*, p. 113.

175. Afterwards, Denton faded into obscurity . . . Ibid., p. 116.

176. "I am very much obliged to you . . ." Brisbin, *The Early Life and Public Career of James A. Garfield*, p. 99.

177. Surprisingly, Garfield had no intention . . . Brown, *The Life and Public Services of James A. Garfield, Twentieth President of the United States*, p. 74.

178. In the few law cases he took . . . Ibid., p. 75

179. It was during this historic meeting . . . Garraty, *The American Nation to 1877. A History ofthe United States*, p. 393-395.

180. Two years later, it would enable Lincoln . . . Ibid.

181. Fittingly, this was the first pleasure trip . . . Thayer, *From Log Cabin to the White House*, p. 368.

182. Though literally repulsed by Brown's exploits . . . Garraty, *The American Nation to 1877. A History ofthe United States*, p. 395.

183. He took his seat in January 1860 . . . Balch, *The Life of James Abram Garfield, Late President of the United States*, p. 105.

184. He also produced a controversial report . . . Ibid., pp. 106-107.

185. No senator was more frequently called . . . Thayer, *From Log Cabin to the White House*, p. 371.

186. According to at least one historian . . . Garraty, *The American Nation to 1877. A History of the United States*, p. 388.

187. "How easy it would be for the American people . . ." Lossing, *A Biography of James A. Garfield, Late President of the United States*, p. 126.

188. When Congress proposed a Constitutional Amendment . . . Thayer, *From Log Cabin to the White House*, p. 353.

189. Furthermore, he declared that . . . Ibid.

190. "We, the people of the State of South Carolina . . ." Lossing, *A Biography of James A. Garfield, Late President of the United States*, p. 119.

191. A few brave souls gathered around . . . Ibid., p. 120

Chapter 10

192. Horace Greely, the editor of . . . Garraty, *The American Nation to 1877. A History of the United States*, pp. 401-402.

193. On January 24, 1861, he made a powerful speech . . . Ridpath, *The Life and Work of James A. Garfield, Twentieth President of the United States*, p. 86.

194. "If by coercion it is meant . . ." Bundy, *The Life of Gen. James A. Garfield,* p. 48.

195. "Would you give up the forts . . ." McCabe, *Our Martyred President*, p. 37.

196. "My heart and thoughts are full almost every moment . . ." Bundy, *The Life of Gen. James A. Garfield*, p. 50.

197. "The doom of slavery is drawing near . . ." Ibid., p. 51.

198. It follows, from these views . . . Lossing, *A Biography of James A. Garfield, Late President of the United States*, p. 137.

199. The civil war had finally begun . . . Garraty, *The American Nation to 1877. A History of the United States*, pp. 402.

200. The "loyal states" also had a huge economic advantage . . . Ibid., p. 403.

201. At the time, Ohio's population and wealth . . . McCabe, *Our Martyred President*, p. 39.

202. Remarkably, most Ohioans remained loyal . . . Ibid., p. 40.

203. When Lincoln issued a call for 75,000 men . . . Brisbin, *The Early Life and Public Career of James A. Garfield*, p. 122.

204. "Even a company of "colored men" offered to serve . . ." McCabe, *Our Martyred President*, p. 54.

205. "You do not dare to make war on cotton . . ." Garraty, *The American Nation to 1877. A History of the United States*, p. 403.

206. The mission was a complete success . . . Balch, *The Life of James Abram Garfield, Late President of the United States*, p. 124.

207. "I regard my life as given to the country . . ." Brown, *The Life and Public Services of James A. Garfield, Twentieth President of the United States*, p. 83.

208. Somehow, Garfield managed to submit . . . Ridpath, *The Life and Work of James A. Garfield, Twentieth President of the United States*, p. 95.

209. "Colonel, you will be at so great a distance from me . . ." Brisbin, *The Early Life and Public Career of James A. Garfield*, p. 131.

210. Outnumbered, but determined to fight . . . Brown, *The Life and Public Services of James A. Garfield, Twentieth President of the United States*, p. 91.

211. "God bless you, boys! . . ." Ibid., p. 98

212. "I see now, that favorably as it terminated . . ." Ibid., p. 99

213. "Soldiers of the eighteenth brigade . . ." Ridpath, *The Life and Work of James A. Garfield, Twentieth President of the United States*, p. 106.

214. "General Garfield and his troops . . ." Brown, *The Life and Public Services of James A. Garfield, Twentieth President of the United States*, p.109.

Chapter 11

215. "I will tell you what to do . . ." Hayes and Hayes, *A Complete History of the Life and Trial of Charles Julius Guiteau, Assassin of President Garfield*, p. 245.

216. Then, according to the authorities . . . Peskin, *Garfield*, p. 583.

217. "The abolitionists refused to have anything to do with the war . . ." Life of John Humphrey Noyes. Volumes, IV-VI, The O.C. Part II Journals. George Wallingford Noyes. Vol. IV, 1855-1863. February 13, 1863.

218. A typical week might include . . . Old Mansion House Memories By One Brought Up In it. Harriet M. Worden, p. 13.

219. "Sexual shame was the consequence of the fall . . ." Bible Communism. John Humphrey Noyes, p. 54.

220. "When the will of God is done . . ." History of the Oneida Community. Oneida Community Books, Pamphlets, and Serials: 1834-1972. Constance Noyes Robertson, p. 95.

221. "In the Kingdom of Heaven . . ." Bible Communism. John Humphrey Noyes, pp. 82-91.

222. One can only imagine how Guiteau felt . . . Ogilvie, *History of the Attempted Assassination of James A. Garfield*, p. 122.

223. "It is the glory of man to control . . ." Male Continence: Or Self-Control In Sexual Intercourse. A letter of inquiry answered. John H. Noyes, p. 6.

224. "The useless expenditure of seed . . ." Bible Communism. John Humphrey Noyes, p. 49

225. Before long, he became an object of scorn . . . Rosenberg, *The Trial of the Assassin Guiteau*, p. 19.

226. "He is not as neat in his personal habits . . ." Worden, Old Mansion House Memories By One Brought Up In It, p. 19.

227. "Dear friends: I have delayed writing until now . . ." Letter to Mr. T.L. Pitt. Wallingford, July 12, 1864.

228. "Monday Mr. Bloom and myself . . ." Ibid.

229. "Dear Mr. Hamilton: I have a delicate matter on my heart . . ." Letter to Mr. Hamilton, February 28, 1866.

230. She could hardly have a conversation with him . . . Hayes and Hayes, *A Complete History of the Life and Trial of Charles Julius Guiteau, Assassin of President Garfield*, p. 250.

231. Once a loyal member, he now characterized . . . Ibid., p. 125.

232. "The movement about to be made . . ." Inventory of letters from C.J. Guiteau. Sent to District Attorney Corkhill, from J.H. Noyes. Undated, p. 22.

233. "Do you say that the establishment . . ." Ibid., p. 25.

234. "If a man have big ideas he is usually deemed *insane* . . ." Ibid., p. 29.

Chapter 12

235. Out of a total enlistment of three million . . . Civil War Trust. www.civilwar.org

236. It was odd that a seasoned warrior . . . McFeely, *Grant*, p. 112.

237. Albert Sidney Johnston and Pierre Gustave Toutant Beauregard . . . Ibid.

238. Unwilling to imagine such an audacious assault . . . Ibid.

239. "On the morning of the memorable . . ." Ibid., p. 111.

240. Garfield had whipped Marshall rather easily . . . Garraty, *The American Nation to 1877. A History of the United States*, p. 406.

241. "Look . . . There is Jackson . . ." Ibid.

242. Instinctively, Garfield called up his reserves . . . . McCabe, *Our Martyred President*, p. 86.

243. Sadly, more Americans died at Shiloh . . . McFeely, *Grant*, p. 115.

244. Beauregard had moved his troops farther south . . . McCabe, *Our Martyred President*, p. 87.

245. "The ladies at the tavern . . ." Civilians, Soldiers, and the Sack of Athens, Alabama. Theodore J. Karamanski. www.lib.niu 1997. p. 2.

246. "I see nothing for two hours . . ." Ibid.

247. Later, he would claim that he was just following orders . . . The sack of Athens, Holly Hollman. *The Decatur Daily*, April 11, 2005.

248. "I was at the head of my brigade . . ." Ibid., p. 4.

249. Addressing the court, he said . . . Ibid., p. 5.

250. Referring to Turchin's men . . . Karamanski, *Civilians, Soldiers, and the sack of Athens, Alabama*, p. 3.

251. In a brazen attempt to sway public opinion . . . Hollman, *The Sack of Athens*, p. 5.

252. In closing, she added, "It seems very strange . . ." Karamanski, *Civilians, Soldiers, and the sack of Athens, Alabama*, p. 4.

253. Despite his initial misgivings . . . Hollman, *The Sack of Athens*, p. 5.

254. "[He] allowed his command to disperse . . ." Official records: War of the rebellion, Series 1, pp. 273-277. www.reformed-theology.org

255. He died at the hospital on June 18, 1901 . . . Hollman, The sack of Athens, p. 6.

256. Porter would be charged with insubordination . . . Major General Fitz-John Porter. The American Civil War. www.swcivilwar.com, p.1.

257. "Damn the torpedoes! Full speed ahead!" Admiral David G. Farragut. Damn The Torpedoes! Full speed ahead! www.trinityriverseminars.com, p. 1.

258. When asked about his court-martial . . . Fitz-John Porter. Wikipedia.org, p.2.

Chapter 13

259. "No . . . that was not thc rcason . . ." Gammon, *The Canal Boy Who Became President*, p. 84.

260. He had asked for a West Point man . . . Brisbin, *The Early Life and Public Career of James A. Garfield*, p. 192.

261. When the Civil War broke out . . . Williams S. Rosencrans source page www.aotc.net/Rosencrans, p.1.

262. "I was delighted at the promotion . . ." Ibid., p.2.

263. "I beg in behalf of this army . . ." Ibid.

264. "When Garfield arrived, I must confess . . ." Gammon, *The Canal Boy Who Became President*, p. 85.

265. "With the selection of General Garfield . . ." Ridpath, *The Life and Work of James A. Garfield, Twentieth President of the United States*, pp. 123-124.

266. "I am clearly of opinion that the negro project . . ." Ibid., p. 129.

267. "There will be sixty-five thousand . . ." Ibid., p. 133.

268. "It is understood, sir, by the general officers . . ." Bundy, *The Life of Gen. James A. Garfield*, p. 61.

269. Rosencrans had no way of knowing it . . . Encyclopedia of the American Civil War. Volume I. David S. Heidler and Jeane T. Heidler. pp. 427-431.

270. The bottom portion fought on . . . Cist, *The Army of the Cumberland*, p. 206.

271. "Let me go to the front . . ." Ridpath, *The Life and Work of James A. Garfield, Twentieth President of the United States*, pp. 154-155.

272. "As you will . . ." Ibid., pp. 154-155.

273. A volley of a thousand Minnie-balls . . . Gammon, *The Canal Boy Who Became President*, p. 88-89.

274. From that day on he was known . . . Cist, *The Army of the Cumberland*, p. 227.

275. He had been the youngest man in the Ohio Senate . . . Brown, *The Life and Public Services of James A. Garfield, Twentieth President of the United States*, p. 130.

Chapter 14

276. "Here at last . . ." Inventory of letters from C.J. Guiteau, sent to District Attorney Corkhill, from J.H. Noyes, not dated, p. 23.

277. "The millions inhabiting the earth . . ." Rosenberg, *The Trial of the Assassin Guiteau*, p. 21.

278. In less than a week, Guiteau produced . . . Inventory of letters from C.J. Guiteau, sent to District Attorney Corkhill, from J.H. Noyes, May, 1865, p. 30.

279. "The grand object of the paper . . ." Ibid., not dated, pp.22-29.

280. "Instead of person's spending one hour . . . ." Ibid.

281. Obviously, the *Theocrat* would be . . . . Ibid., p. 31.

282. "I marvel at the community's patience . . ." Letter to Oneida Community, Charles J. Guiteau. July 20, 1865.

283. "But we are in favor of intelligent . . ." Bible Communism. J.H. Noyes, p. 51.

284. "First . . . There must be . . ." Essay on Scientific Propogation. J.H. Noyes, p. 12.

285. "There can be no doubt that by segregating . . ." Ibid., p. 15.

286. Nine of the children . . . Parker, *A Yankee Saint: John Humphrey Noyes and the Oneida Community*, p. 257.

287. "My object in leaving clandestinely . . ." Daily Journal of Oneida Community. Volume 2, No. 106. Friday, November 2, 1886.

288. "In regard to a financial settlement . . ." Ibid.

289. "Perhaps it is useless . . ." Daily Journal of Oneida Community. Volume 2, No. 129, Thursday, November 29, 1866.

290. "I regret that you should . . ." Inventory of letters from C.J. Guiteau, sent to District Attorney Corkhill, from J.H. Noyes, New York, December 5, 1866.

291. "I write to ascertain if you *intend* to pay . . ." Ibid., New York, February 8, 1868.

292. "If you want to spend 10 or 20 years . . ." Ibid., New York, February 19, 1868.

293. "Again, I warn you, if you fall into . . ." Ibid., New York, March, 2, 1868.

294. "Come on! . . . I am ready for a fight . . ." Ibid., New York, March 7, 1868.

295. "When I get the money . . ." Rosenberg, *The Trial of the Assassin Guiteau*, p. 24.

296. The result was that most of the Oneida women . . . Ibid., p. 26.

297. "I have no ill will toward him . . ." Ibid.

298. "A hypocrite, a swindler; cunning and crafty . . ." Wellman, *The Art of Cross-Examination*, p. 359.

Chapter 15

299. "I will take no steps whatever . . ." Peskin, *Garfield*, p. 141.

300. "I would . . . rather be in Congress . . ." Ibid.

301. He had heard-probably from Secretary Stanton . . . Brown, *The Life and Public Services of James A. Garfield, Twentieth President of the United States*, p. 128.

302. The Republican majority in Congress . . . Ridpath, *The Life and Work of James A. Garfield, Twentieth President of the United States*, pp. 165-166.

303. He . . . returned to Congress . . . Balch, *The Life of James Abram Garfield, Late President of the United States*, p. 242.

304. "On one occasion, Salmon P. Chase . . ." Ridpath, *The Life and Work of James A. Garfield, Twentieth President of the United States*, p. 177.

305. "The right of a state . . ." Ibid., p. 188.

306. "Mr. Speaker, we shall never know why slavery . . ." Ibid., p. 190.

307. One of them was killed instantly . . . Brown, *The Life and Public Services of James A. Garfield, Twentieth President of the United States*, p. 138.

308. "Fellow citizens, clouds and darkness . . ." Ibid., p. 139.

309. When asked to repeat his words . . . Lossing, *A Biography of James A. Garfield, Late President of the United States*, p. 357.

310. To him, statistical tables were full of . . . Peskin, *Garfield*, p. 260.

311. This is the age of statistics . . . Ridpath, *The Life and Work of James A. Garfield, Twentieth President of the United States*, p. 214.

312. The defendants were obviously guilty . . . Conwell, *The Life, Speeches, and Public Services of James A. Garfield, Twentieth President of the United States*, p. 245.

313. "Your decision will mark an era . . ." Ridpath, *The Life and Work of James A. Garfield, Twentieth President of the United States*, p. 201.

314. "Like old John Adams . . ." McCullough, *John Adams*, p. 66.

Chapter 16

315. His performance as the wartime governor . . . McFeely, *Grant*, p. 241.

316. The unrepentant all-white delegations . . . Ackerman, *Dark Horse. The Surprise Election and Political Murder of President James A. Garfield*, p. 3.

317. And as Allan Peskin notes . . . Peskin, *Garfield*, p. 255.

318. If silence is ever golden . . . Bundy, *The Life of Gen. James A. Garfield,* p. 161.

319. "It was not one man who killed Lincoln . . ." Thayer, *From Log Cabin to the White House: Life of James A. Garfield*, p. 389.

320. With these statements the President had . . . Peskin, *Garfield*, p. 258.

321. In the end, the Radicals failed . . . Garraty, *The American Nation to 1877. A History of the United States*, p. 435.

322. "I gave eighty days' hard work . . ." Lossing, *A Biography of James A. Garfield, Late President of the United States*, pp. 447-448.

323. "Politics . . . where ten years of honest toil . . ." Ridpath, *The Life and Work of James A. Garfield, Twentieth President of the United States*, p. 237.

324. "I think of you as away . . ." Ibid., p. 237

325. The Credit Mobilier scandal . . . Ibid., pp. 236-237.

326. "I never owned, received or agreed to receive . . ." McCabe, *Our Martyred President*, p. 351.

327. "General Garfield's answer has been received . . ." Ridpath, *The Life and Work of James A. Garfield, Twentieth President of the United States*, p. 260.

328. "If there be one thing upon this earth . . ." Thayer, *From Log Cabin to the White House: Life of James A. Garfield*, p. 388.

329. At this time, Garfield was the chairman . . . Ackerman, *Dark Horse.The Surprise Election and Political Murder of President James A. Garfield*, p. 145.

330. "It has been the plan of my life . . ." Thayer, *From Log Cabin to the White House: Life of James A. Garfield*, p. 379.

Chapter 17

331. "See two things in the United States . . ." Glazier, *Peculiarities of American Cities*, p. 157.

332. It was hard to believe . . . Ibid., p. 175.

333. Michigan Avenue, for example, was now fully paved . . . Ibid., p. 168.

334. "I did well . . ." Hayes and Hayes, *A Complete History of the Life and Trial of Charles Julius Guiteau, Assassin of President Garfield*, p. 27.

335. Despite her young age . . . Rosenberg, *The Trial of the Assassin Guiteau*, p. 27.

336. It was the last they saw of him . . . *Chicago Tribune*. July 3, 1881, p. 3.

337. "I cheated that old Jew!" Hayes and Hayes, *A Complete History of the Life and Trial of Charles Julius Guiteau, Assassin of President Garfield*, p. 74.

338. "I lived in continual anxiety . . ." Ibid., p. 73.

339. "I am your master! . . ." Rosenberg, *The Trial of the Assassin Guiteau*, p. 28.

340. "He was able to explain satisfactorily . . ." Hayes and Hayes, *A Complete History of the Life and Trial of Charles Julius Guiteau, Assassin of President Garfield*, p. 75.

341. "I remember one occurrence particularly . . ." Ibid., p. 82.

342. "There is not one man in five hundred . . ." Ibid.

343. "They also contained huge piles . . ." Colbert & Chamberlin, *Chicago & The Great Conflagration*, p. 175.

344. "It might be said, with considerable justice, . . ." Cromie, *The Great Chicago Fire*, p. 11.

345. In prior years the average amount of rain . . . Colbert & Chamberlin, *Chicago & The Great Conflagration*, p. 197.

346. Around midnight, the fire jumped across . . . Angle, *The Great Chicago Fire*, p. 13.

347. Over one hundred thousand people, . . . Colbert & Chamberlin, *Chicago & The Great Conflagration*, p. 9.

Chapter 18

348. The waterfront district contained . . . Santella, *Opium*, p. 66.

349. They had ten dollars between them . . . Ogilvie, *History of the Attempted Assassination of James A. Garfield*, p. 107.

350. "I don't know but that one of those mean . . ." Hayes and Hayes, *A Complete History of the Life and Trial of Charles Julius Guiteau, Assassin of President Garfield*, p. 135.

351. "I appreciate your kindness . . ." Ibid., p. 83.

352. "I will tell you what it is, . . ." Ibid.

353. "You have no sense . . ." Ibid., p. 84.

354. "That was his great objective . . ." Ibid., p. 86.

355. "He became infatuated with the idea . . ." Ibid., p. 94.

356. "We will have to put up with these things for a while . . ." Ibid., p. 95.

357. At that time he would occasionally . . . Ibid., p. 122.

358. In the summer of 1873 . . . Ibid., p. 119.

359. "Your will was never broken . . ." Ibid., p. 126.

360. Many times, while in such moods . . . Ibid., p. 127.

361. "When you make up your mind . . ." Ibid., p. 128.

362. "This conduct was repeated, time and time again . . ." Ibid., p. 129.

Chapter 19

363. "I do not object to Jefferson Davis . . ." Ridpath, *The Life and Work of James A. Garfield, Twentieth President of the United States*, p. 276.

364. "Toward those men who gallantly fought . . ." Ibid., p. 277.

365. President Grant personally thanked Garfield . . . Peskin, *Garfield*, p. 393.

366. When, for example, Congress failed to act . . . Garraty, *The American Nation to 1877. A History of the United States*, p. 443.

367. During his eight years in office . . . McFeely, *Grant*, pp. 404-406.

368. "The present good which we shall achieve . . ." Ridpath, *The Life and Work of James A. Garfield, Twentieth President of the United States*, p. 291.

369. "In my view, then, the foremost question . . ." Ibid.

370. "Since you have appointed me . . ." Ibid., p. 298.

371. He had no intention of trying . . . Garraty, *The American Nation to 1877. A History of the United States*, p. 185.

372. "Forgotten in the North . . ." Ibid., p. 447.

Chapter 20

373. On April 4, 1874, Justice Calvin E. Pratt of Kings County, . . . Hayes and Hayes, *A Complete History of the Life and Trial of Charles Julius Guiteau, Assassin of President Garfield*, pp. 104-105.

374. "Prior to the *Herald* publication I was doing well . . ." Ibid., p. 29.

375. Those odors were thought to cause ague . . . A Dictionary of Practical Medicine, A House Divided. Linda Wheeler, *The Washington Post*, March 4, 2013.

376. "I had no money and no relatives in the city, . . ." Ogilvie, *History of the Attempted Assassination of James A. Garfield*, p. 109.

377. "I was living with some friends . . ." Hayes and Hayes, *A Complete History of the Life and Trial of Charles Julius Guiteau, Assassin of President Garfield*, p. 107.

378. "It was a very severe, cold day . . ." Ibid., p. 108.

379. "He looked like a wild animal . . ." Ibid., p. 251.

380. "She and I are going to work together . . ." Ibid., p. 109.

381. "They are of no use to me . . ." Ibid., p. 111.

382. Most congregants belonged to . . . Glazier, *Peculiarities of American Cities*, p. 250.

383. The man Charles J. Guiteau . . . Rosenberg, *The Trial of the Assassin Guiteau*, p. 33.

384. "I weave the discourse out of my brain . . ." Ibid., p. 34.

Chapter 21

385. The convention was held in the immense hall . . . Glazier, *Peculiarities of American Cities*, p. 168.

386. "His flute-like tones . . ." Ridpath, *The Life and Work of James A. Garfield, Twentieth President of the United States*, p. 411.

387. Always ready for a good fight . . . Doenecke, *The Presidencies of James A. Garfield & Chester A. Arthur*, p. 12.

388. "His face lacked the lines of scorn . . ." Ridpath, *The Life and Work of James A. Garfield, Twentieth President of the United States*, p. 412.

389. "In speaking he had a deep . . ." Ibid.

390. "It remains to be seen how far the reckless assaults . . ." Brown & Williams, *The Diary of James A. Garfield*, p. 237.

391. A more beautiful day in June . . . Ridpath, *The Life and Work of James A. Garfield, Twentieth President of the United States*, p. 418.

392. "The Democratic party sees nothing of evil . . ." Balch, *The Life of James Abram Garfield, Late President of the United States*, pp. 380-381.

393. "Their food is simple, easily supplied . . ." Ibid., pp. 307-308.

394. "He wants all that we want . . ." Ibid., pp. 307-308.

395. "*Resolved*, As the sense of this Convention . . ." Ridpath, *The Life and Work of James A. Garfield, Twentieth President of the United States*, p. 423.

396. "Resolved, That the delegates who have voted . . ." Ibid.

397. "There never can be a convention . . ." Ibid., p. 425.

398. "When I want a thing . . ." Doenecke, *The Presidencies of James A. Garfield & Chester A. Arthur*, p. 14.

399. President Hayes had described Blaine as . . . Pletcher, *The Awkward Years*, p.5.

400. In the view of at least one historian . . . Garraty, *The American Nation to 1877. A History of the United States*, p. 191.

401. Lincoln himself had called Blaine . . . Ibid., p. 191.

402. "When asked whence comes our candidate . . ." Ridpath, *The Life and Work of James A. Garfield, Twentieth President of the United States*, p. 430.

403. "Gentlemen, we have only to listen above the din . . ." Ibid., p. 433.

404. "Mr. President . . . I have . . ." Ibid., pp. 433-434.

405. "How shall we do this great work? . . ." Ibid., p. 436.

406. "You ask for his monuments . . ." Ibid., p. 437.

407. "I do not present him [Sherman] as a better Republican . . ." Ibid.

Chapter 22

408. Like many of his fellow Republicans . . . Kelley and Lewis, *To Make Our World Anew: Volume I: A History of African Americans to 1880*, p. 250.

409. Later in life, Bruce would repay . . . Washington, *The Story of the Negro*, pp. 23-24.

410. The first ballot came on Monday . . . Ridpath, *The Life and Work of James A. Garfield, Twentieth President of the United States*, p. 439.

411. After twenty-eight ballots, . . . Ibid., p. 442.

412. "I think, Charlie . . ." Balch, *The Life of James Abram Garfield, Late President of the United States*, p. 470.

413. "No person having received a majority . . ." Ibid., p. 473.

414. "The people rose up and gave one tremendous cheer . . ." Lossing, *A Biography of James A. Garfield, Late President of the United States*, pp. 569-570.

415. Amidst the chaos, Vermont and Wisconsin . . . Ridpath, *The Life and Work of James A. Garfield, Twentieth President of the United States*, p. 442.

416. The changes in the vote by which the nomination . . . Ibid.

417. He looked "pale and death" . . . Ackerman, *Dark Horse.The Surprise Election and Political Murder of President James A. Garfield*, p. 114.

418. "Mr. Chairman . . . James A. Garfield . . ." McCabe, *Our Martyred President*, p. 472.

419. The chair, under the rules, . . . Ibid.

420. In 1871, Grant appointed him Collector . . . Doenecke, *The Presidencies of James A. Garfield & Chester A. Arthur*, p. 78.

421. A frail woman, she soon developed . . . Ibid.

422. Whatever the case, Arthur won . . . Ibid., p. 78.

423. On the day of the General's nomination . . . Balch, *The Life of James Abram Garfield, Late President of the United States*, p. 485.

Chapter 23

424. "Boston is a very stupid place . . ." Guiteau Testimony. *United States v. Charles Guiteau*, p. 583.

425. "A new line of thought runs through this book . . ." Ogilvie, *History of the Attempted Assassination of James A. Garfield*, p. 114.

426. "The Truth was simply a plagiarism . . ." Peskin, *Garfield*, p. 586.

427. All who died before A.D. to . . . Ogilvie, *History of the Attempted Assassination of James A. Garfield*, p. 116.

428. "He was possessed of the devil . . ." Hayes and Hayes, *A Complete History of the Life and Trial of Charles Julius Guiteau, Assassin of President Garfield*, p. 256.

429. "I am working for God, and it is God . . ." Ibid., p. 257.

430. Each carried a walking-beam engine . . . *New York Times*. June 13, 1880.

431. On a moonless night . . . *New York Times*. June 13, 1880.

432. By his own account, the night was . . . Ackerman, *Dark Horse. The Surprise Election and Political Murder of President James A. Garfield*, p. 136.

433. Unrestrained by belts, the buoyant pads . . . *New York Times*. June 13, 1880.

434. One gentleman walked to the rear of the ship . . . *New York Times.* June 13, 1880.

435. "We were in our state-room when the boat struck . . ." *New York Times.* June 13, 1880.

436. "I didn't jump till I saw the fire coming . . ." Ibid.

437. To keep up the courage of those who were struggling . . . Ibid.

438. Eighteen months later, in December 1881 . . . Ackerman, *Dark Horse.The Surprise Election and Political Murder of President James A. Garfield*, p. 137.

Chapter 24

439. Whatever merit "Garfield Against Hancock" may have had . . . Ogilvie, *History of the Attempted Assassination of James A. Garfield*, pp. 111-112.

440. As for Garfield, he wrote . . . Ibid., p. 113

441. "Ye men whose sons perished . . ." Ibid., p. 114.

442. The leading Republicans thought . . . Ibid., p. 127.

443. The *Saratogian* wrote about the affair . . . Ibid.

444. They were, in the words of one participant . . . Ibid., p. 125.

445. In a letter to John Guiteau . . . Rosenberg, *The Trial of the Assassin Guiteau*, p. 30.

446. Luther W. Guiteau was born . . . *The Boston Herald*. July 12, 1881.

447. "I met Guiteau in the Fifth Avenue Hotel . . ." Ogilvie, *History of the Attempted Assassination of James A. Garfield*, p. 128.

448. "This was my first introduction to them . . ." Hayes and Hayes, *A Complete History of the Life and Trial of Charles Julius Guiteau, Assassin of President Garfield*, p. 36.

449. "So, as a matter of fact . . ." Ibid.

450. Amid all the celebrating . . . Ibid.

Chapter 25

451. "Without any political experience . . ." Doenecke, *The Presidencies of James A. Garfield & Chester A. Arthur*, p. 25.

452. They were joined by New York Congressmen . . . Ackerman, *Dark Horse.The Surprise Election and Political Murder of President James A. Garfield*, p. 171.

453. Though never stated publicly . . . Ibid.

454. He remained deliberately ambiguous . . . Doenecke, *The Presidencies of James A. Garfield & Chester A. Arthur*, p. 27.

455. Nobody knows how the message . . . Peskin, *Garfield*, p. 491.

456. A few days later, he wrote to . . . Ackerman, *Dark Horse.The Surprise Election and Political Murder of President James A. Garfield*, p. 176.

457. As the race began, the field was crowded . . . Ridpath, *The Life and Work of James A. Garfield, Twentieth President of the United States*, p. 458.

458. The letter was written on House stationary . . . Ibid., p. 471.

459. At the very least, the Republicans . . . Doenecke, *The Presidencies of James A. Garfield & Chester A. Arthur*, p. 29.

460. "I will not break the rule . . ." Ridpath, *The Life and Work of James A. Garfield, Twentieth President of the United States*, p. 474.

461. In order to clear his name . . . Ibid., p. 474.

462. The prosecution failed to convict . . . Ibid., p. 476.

463. As far as the electoral vote . . . Peskin, *Garfield*, p. 510.

464. The General looks travel-tired . . . Ridpath, *The Life and Work of James A. Garfield, Twentieth President of the United States*, p. 485.

465. Garfield balked, telling the Stalwarts . . . Doenecke, *The Presidencies of James A. Garfield & Chester A. Arthur*, p. 30.

466. Its tasks ranged from collecting revenue . . . Ibid., p. 31

467. In April 1880, he had written . . . Ibid.

468. Hamilton Fish, who had served as . . . Pletcher, *The Awkward Years*, p.5.

Chapter 26

469. Garfield looked weary, and, according to at least one . . . Ridpath, *The Life and Work of James A. Garfield, Twentieth President of the United States*, p. 486.

470. "Looking in splendid condition . . ." Ibid., p. 487.

471. "Fellow citizens . . ." Ibid., p. 489.

472. The oath of office was administered by the Chief Justice . . . Lossing, *A Biography of James A. Garfield, Late President of the United States*, p. 604.

473. The ball was enhanced by . . . Ibid., p. 620.

474. On March 5, Garfield sent the Senate a list . . . Ibid., p. 622.

475. To apportion out these 100,000 offices . . . Balch, *The Life of James Abram Garfield, Late President of the United States*, p. 576.

476. In addition, he nominated Lewis F. Payne . . . Ridpath, *The Life and Work of James A. Garfield, Twentieth President of the United States*, p. 504.

477. First, that it was the President's . . . Ibid., p. 506.

478. President Garfield, said one able writer . . . Brown, *The Life and Public Services of James A. Garfield, Twentieth President of the United States,* p. 212.

Chapter 27

479. Throughout the city, contagious diseases were spreading . . . *New York Times.* February 20, 1881.

480. Back in November, he had sent his first letter . . . Hayes and Hayes, *A Complete History of the Life and Trial of Charles Julius Guiteau, Assassin of President Garfield*, p. 174.

481. Guiteau walked across the lawns . . . Ackerman, *Dark Horse. The Surprise Election and Political Murder of President James A. Garfield*, p. 266.

482. The first person he wrote to . . . Ibid., p. 267.

483. "I will talk with you about this . . ." Hayes and Hayes, *A Complete History of the Life and Trial of Charles Julius Guiteau, Assassin of President Garfield*, p. 175.

484. On the 25th, Guiteau sent another letter . . . Rosenberg, *The Trial of the Assassin Guiteau*, p. 37.

485. In later years, after sad experience . . . Peskin, *Garfield*, p. 549.

486. Guiteau was startled for a moment . . . Ackerman, *Dark Horse. The Surprise Election and Political Murder of President James A. Garfield*, p. 268.

487. Blaine saw no reason to act harshly . . . Ibid., p. 298.

488. The amenities of Dorsey's home . . . Pike, *Roadside New Mexico: A Guide to Historic Markers*, pp. 106-107.

489. On the importance of mail delivery . . . J. Martin Klotsche. The Mississippi Valley Historical Review. Vol. 22, No. 3. December, 1935, pp. 407-418.

490. When Dorsey was confronted . . ." Peskin, *Garfield*, p. 580.

Chapter 28

491. "I called to see you this a.m . . . ." Hayes and Hayes, *A Complete History of the Life and Trial of Charles Julius Guiteau, Assassin of President Garfield*, p. 204.

492. "I think I have a right to press . . ." Ibid.

493. "I have practiced law in New York . . ." Ibid., p. 205.

494. "I wish to say this about Robertson's nomination . . ." Ibid.

495. In the words of one Washingtonian . . . Rosenberg, *The Trial of the Assassin Guiteau*, p. 38.

496. During the Civil War, an entire regiment . . . *The New York Times.* August 20, 1881.

497. 'Do you know that it frightens . . ." *The New York Times.* March 3, 1891.

498. In the morning, she found her pillow . . . Ackerman, *Dark Horse. The Surprise Election and Political Murder of President James A. Garfield*, p. 329.

499. If Mrs. Garfield had returned to her room . . . *The New York Times.* July 24, 1881.

500. On May 7, he wrote . . . Hayes and Hayes, *A Complete History of the Life and Trial of Charles Julius Guiteau, Assassin of President Garfield*, p. 206.

501. On May 10 . . . Ibid.

502. Finally, on May 13, he wrote . . . Ibid., p. 207.

503. He stuck his finger in Guiteau's face . . . Ibid., p. 176.

504. "General Garfield—I have been trying to be . . ." Ibid.

505. Charles was coming to the end . . . Rosenberg, *The Trial of the Assassin Guiteau*, p. 38.

506. "By Roscoe Conkling's calculation . . ." Ackerman, *Dark Horse. The Surprise Election and Political Murder of President James A. Garfield*, p. 334.

507. On May 16, Vice-President Arthur . . . Ridpath, *The Life and Work of James A. Garfield, Twentieth President of the United States*, p. 512.

508. He hesitated for a moment . . . Ibid., p. 513.

509. As Doenecke noted . . . Doenecke, *The Presidencies of James A. Garfield & Chester A. Arthur*, p. 45.

Chapter 29

510. "He appeared to have a cat-like tread, . . ." Ogilvie, *History of the Attempted Assassination of James A. Garfield*, p. 63.

511. The position was a good one . . . Ibid., p. 106.

512. With Garfield removed . . . Ackerman, *Dark Horse. The Surprise Election and Political Murder of President James A. Garfield*, p. 346.

513. At first this was a mere impression . . . Hayes and Hayes, *A Complete History of the Life and Trial of Charles Julius Guiteau, Assassin of President Garfield*, p. 42.

514. Such was the case in March when, three days before . . . Radzinsky, *Alexander II. The Last Great Tsar*, pp. 405-407.

515. "I never had the slightest doubt . . ." *United States v. Charles Guiteau*. p. 593.

516. Days and weeks would pass before . . . Ridpath, *The Life and Work of James A. Garfield, Twentieth President of the United States*, p. 515.

517. "From here on . . ." Ackerman, *Dark Horse.The Surprise Election and Political Murder of President James A. Garfield*, p. 351.

518. "Two weeks after I conceived the idea . . ." Hayes and Hayes, *A Complete History of the Life and Trial of Charles Julius Guiteau, Assassin of President Garfield*, p. 43.

519. "I sent to Boston for a copy of my book . . ." Ibid.

520. He returned on the eighth, . . . Ibid., pp. 59-60.

521. "I looked at it as if it was going to bite me . . ." Ackerman, *Dark Horse.The Surprise Election and Political Murder of President James A. Garfield*, p. 355.

522. The purpose, as he later explained . . . *United States v. Charles Guiteau*. p. 637.

523. This time, he walked in and stood at the rear door . . . Ackerman, *Dark Horse.The Surprise Election and Political Murder of President James A. Garfield*, p. 356.

524. "I made up my mind that the next Sunday . . ." *New York Herald*. October 6, 1881.

525. "I conceived of the idea of removing the President . . ." Rosenberg, *The Trial of the Assassin Guiteau*, pp. 40-41.

526. "He [Garfield] got out of his carriage . . ." Hayes and Hayes, *A Complete History of the Life and Trial of Charles Julius Guiteau, Assassin of President Garfield*, p. 45.

527. "She looked so thin and she clung . . ." Ibid., p. 179.

528. By the end of the month . . . Ackerman, *Dark Horse.The Surprise Election and Political Murder of President James A. Garfield*, p. 366.

Chapter 30

529. Before he left, Guiteau peeked inside . . . Ackerman, *Dark Horse. The Surprise Election and Political Murder of President James A. Garfield*, p. 365.

530. "I noticed in the papers that . . ." Hayes and Hayes, *A Complete History of the Life and Trial of Charles Julius Guiteau, Assassin of President Garfield*, p. 46.

531. "I got up one morning at half-past five . . ." Ibid., p. 47.

532. "In the evening, after dinner . . ." Ibid.

533. "I hung around the park . . ." Ibid., p. 48.

534. "Within minutes, half a dozen of them . . ." Ackerman, *Dark Horse. The Surprise Election and Political Murder of President James A. Garfield*, p. 368.

535. "I do not known why it haunts me . . ." Bundy, *The Life of Gen. James A. Garfield*, pp.241-242.

536. "Now, I thought to myself . . ." Hayes and Hayes, *A Complete History of the Life and Trial of Charles Julius Guiteau, Assassin of President Garfield*, p. 49.

537. "I walked along on the opposite side . . ." *United States v. Charles Guiteau*, pp. 692-693.

538. "This scene made a striking . . ." Hayes and Hayes, *A Complete History of the Life and Trial of Charles Julius Guiteau, Assassin of President Garfield*, p. 50.

539. The President's tragic death was a sad necessity . . . Rosenberg, *The Trial of the Assassin Guiteau*, pp. 41-42.

540. To Gen. Sherman: I have just shot the President . . . *The New York Times*. July 3, 1881.

Chapter 31

541. "His nerve is remarkable . . ." McCabe, *Our Martyred President*, p. 546.

542. The night [July 6th] was very warm . . . Ibid., p. 557.

543. Suggestions for cooling the sick-room . . . Peskin, *Garfield*, p. 601.

544. Years later, he would describe the President . . . William E. Carter and Merri Sue Carter, *Simon Newcomb, America's First Great Astronomer*. Physics Today. Volume 62, Issue 2. February 2009, pp. 46-51.

545. It also consumed half a million . . . Peskin, *Garfield*, p. 602.

546. "With such a machine . . ." Kevles, *Naked To The Bone: Medical Imaging in the Twentieth Century*, p. 10.

547. The instrument consisted of two . . . Ridpath, *The Life and Work of James A. Garfield, Twentieth President of the United States*, p. 569.

548. The patient was bolstered up in bed . . . McCabe, *Our Martyred President*, p. 595.

549. Bell himself published his finding . . . Richard Menke, *Media in America, 1881: Garfield, Guiteau, Bell, Whitman*. Critical Inquiry 31. The University of Chicago, 2005.

550. The President was more than willing . . . Conwell, *The Life, Speeches, and Public Services of James A. Garfield, Twentieth President of the United States*, pp. 354-355.

551. To keep the car cool . . . Peskin, *Garfield*, p. 605.

552. To many he looked like a corpse . . . McCabe, *Our Martyred President*, p. 650.

553. "May God in his infinite goodness . . ." Morgan, *From Hayes to McKinley National Party Politics, 1887-1896*, p. 140.

554. During the day his pulse shot up . . . McCabe, *Our Martyred President*, p. 681.

555. Though the gravity of the President's condition . . . Ibid., p. 681.

556. "Oh, Swaim. I am in terrible pain here . . ." Conwell, *The Life, Speeches, and Public Services of James A. Garfield, Twentieth President of the United States*, p. 357.

557. Bliss ran into the sick-room . . . Thayer, *From Log Cabin to the White House: Life of James A. Garfield*, p. 421.

558. "Oh! Why am I made to suffer . . ." McCabe, *Our Martyred President*, p. 685.

559. Bliss placed a hand on the President's chest . . . *The New York Times*. September 20, 1881.

560. "Because it was on the nineteenth day . . ." Thayer, *From Log Cabin to the White House: Life of James A. Garfield*, p. 425.

Chapter 32

561. "I hope—my God, I do hope it is a mistake . . ." Howe, *Chester A. Arthur: A Quarter-Century of Machine Politics*, pp. 1-2.

562. "It becomes our painful duty . . ." *The New York Times*. September 20, 1881.

563. "I, Chester Alan Arthur, do solemnly swear . . ." Ackerman, *Dark Horse.The Surprise Election and Political Murder of President James A. Garfield*, pp. 428-429.

564. Arthur obtained the writ . . . The Historical Society of the Courts of the State of New York. The Lemmon Slave Case. John D. Gordan, III, Issue 4, 2006.

565. So zealous was he of his integrity . . . Brisbin, *The Early Life and Public Career of James A. Garfield*, p. 545.

566. "If I misappropriated a cent . . ." Ibid.

567. The allegation was laughable . . . *Austin American-Statesman*. August 19, 2009.

568. *The Washington Post*, engaging in the worst form . . . *The Washington Post*. July 9, 1881.

569. In an effort to sell newspapers . . . Ibid.

570. Reports have come in from our trusted sources . . . Ibid.

571. "My dear Mary, why have I been . . ." Personal letter from Vice President Chester A. Arthur to his sister, Mary McElroy. September 2, 1881.

572. This upset all the key people . . . Holland, *Hail To The Chiefs*, pp. 150-151.

Chapter 33

573. "During the summer of 1881, when the President's physicians . . ." Thayer, *From Log Cabin to the White House: Life of James A. Garfield*, p. 432.

574. Because it was on the nineteenth . . . Ibid., p. 433.

575. The bulletin was signed by . . . Brown, *The Life and Public Services of James A. Garfield, Twentieth President of the United States*, p. 259.

576. "The message was addressed to . . ." Ridpath, *The Life and Work of James A. Garfield, Twentieth President of the United States*, p. 651.

577. On Wednesday morning, September 21 . . . Thayer, *From Log Cabin to the White House: Life of James A. Garfield*, p. 434.

578. Outside, the coffin was placed . . . Ridpath, *The Life and Work of James A. Garfield, Twentieth President of the United States*, p. 655.

579. Nobody had ever seen anything like it . . . Ibid., p. 662.

580. A simple wreath . . . "The man and the Mausoleum. Dedication of the Garfield Memorial Structure in Cleveland, Ohio." Anonymous. May 30, 1890. The Cleveland Printing & Publishing Company, pp. 88-89.

581. Not surprisingly, Arthur's first public act . . . Thayer, *From Log Cabin to the White House: Life of James A. Garfield*, p. 433.

582. "It is proper that he should . . ." Brown, *The Life and Public Services of James A. Garfield, Twentieth President of the United States*, p. 280.

583. The docks along the water-front . . . *The New York Times*. September 21, 1881.

584. The list included . . . Brown, *The Life and Public Services of James A. Garfield, Twentieth President of the United States*, pp. 368-387.

585. Oliver Wendell Holmes wrote a sweet poem . . . Conwell, *The Life, Speeches, and Public Services of James A. Garfield, Twentieth President of the United States*, p. 384.

586. Alfred, Lord Tennyson, wrote . . . Ibid., p. 381.

587. "I have sometimes thought . . ." James A. Garfield, "Oration on Congressman Starkweather."

Chapter 34

588. In addition to the corps . . . Balch, *The Life of James Abram Garfield, Late President of the United States*, p. 711.

589. "It was found that the ball . . ." Ridpath, *The Life and Work of James A. Garfield, Twentieth President of the United States*, pp. 649-650.

590. The ruptured lining was . . . Balch, *The Life of James Abram Garfield, Late President of the United States*, p. 711.

591. "An abscess cavity, six inches . . ." Ibid., p. 712.

592. The embalmer had injected . . . Brown, *The Life and Public Services of James A. Garfield, Twentieth President of the United States*, p. 506.

593. The area over the sacrum . . . Ibid., p. 507.

594. Hemorrhoidal tumors, some the size . . ." Ibid.

595. No evidence of bullet damage . . . Ibid., p. 511.

596. The right kidney weighed . . . Ibid., pp. 511-512.

597. The heart weighed eleven ounces . . . Ibid., p. 516.

598. The head, [Garfield's] which is . . . Bundy, *The Life of Gen. James A. Garfield,* p. 237.

599. The theory was popularized . . . The New Columbia Encyclopedia. New York: Columbia University Press. 1875.

600. "If the man [Guiteau] only had . . ." Hayes and Hayes, *A Complete History of the Life and Trial of Charles Julius Guiteau, Assassin of President Garfield*, pp. 342-343.

Chapter 35

601. "Captain, I have tried to kill . . ." P.S. Ruckman, Jr. *Pardoned: America's Favorite Would-Be Murderer.* www.pardonpower.com, October 27, 2011.

602. After a short trial . . . Legal Information Institute. Cornell University Law School. "Ex Parte Mason," Supreme Court, U.S.

603. In their view, the sergeant had . . . *The New York Times.* March 11, 1882.

604. Efforts to secure the sergeant's release . . . *The New York Times.* March 16, 1882.

605. Mr. Lincoln was roundly criticized . . . *The New York Times.* April 1, 1863.

606. The plea had been used . . . West's Encyclopedia of American Law. Volume 6. St. Paul: West Group, 1998.

607. "He's no more insane than I am . . ." Rosenberg, *The Trial of the Assassin Guiteau*, p. 77.

608. "And so the Grand Jurors . . ." *The New York Times*. October 9, 1881.

609. "I plead not guilty to the indictment . . ." Hayes and Hayes, *A Complete History of the Life and Trial of Charles Julius Guiteau, Assassin of President Garfield*, p. 155.

610. "I undertake to say that the Lord . . ." Ibid.

611. In the court of public opinion . . . D. Jamez Terry. *The "Assassin Instrument" of God*. The Graduate Journal of Harvard Divinity School. Spring, 2011.

612. By denying the possibility . . . West's Encyclopedia of American Law. Volume 6. St. Paul: West Group, 1998.

613. It took all of three days . . . Hayes and Hayes, *A Complete History of the Life and Trial of Charles Julius Guiteau, Assassin of President Garfield*, p. 168.

614. As Guiteau looked on, appraising each juror . . . Ibid.

Chapter 36

615. "Counsel have been assigned to you . . ." Hayes and Hayes, *A Complete History of the Life and Trial of Charles Julius Guiteau, Assassin of President Garfield*, pp. 169-170.

616. Finally, after months of harassment . . . Mike McIntyre. "*Was Charles Guiteau Insane?*" Studies by Undergraduate Researchers at Guelph. Volume 2, Number 2, Spring 2009, pp. 3-7.

617. The list included the Minister of Venezuela, . . . Hayes and Hayes, *A Complete History of the Life and Trial of Charles Julius Guiteau, Assassin of President Garfield*, p. 190.

618. "I want first-class talent . . ." Ibid.

619. "I do not propose to be interrupted . . ." Ibid., p. 191.

620. Finally, after berating his own counsel . . . Ibid., p. 192.

621. Some referred to the trial . . . *New York Daily Tribune*. Summary of Events for 1881.

622. After a moment of nervous laughter . . . Hayes and Hayes, *A Complete History of the Life and Trial of Charles Julius Guiteau, Assassin of President Garfield*, p. 211.

623. The van gave chase . . . *The Evening Critic*. November 19, 1881.

624. "I wish you to say in your paper . . ." *New York Times*. November 20, 1881.

625. "It wasn't I that shot at him . . ." *New York Times*. November 21, 1881.

626. "Gentlemen . . . this is not the man . . ." *New York Times*. November 21, 1881.

627. "Jones has a light complexion . . ." *New York Times*. November 21, 1881.

628. The horse that Jones rode . . . *New York Times*. November 21, 1881.

Chapter 37

629. Autographed photographs could be purchased . . . Clark, *The Murder of James A. Garfield. The President's Last Days and the Trial and Execution of His Assassin.*, p. 140.

630. "I have to say that I am not . . ." Ibid., p. 70.

631. After studying the work of Louis Pasteur . . . "*Some Causes of Excessive Mortality After Surgical Operations.*" British Medical Journal. Volume 2, 1864, pp. 384-388.

632. Incredibly, most surgeons did not wear . . . Reverend Ed Hird. *Deep Cove Crier*, North Vancouver, B.C., January, 1998.

633. Agnew praised some of Lister's work, . . . Agnew, *The Principles and Practices of Surgery*, p. 331.

634. "Dr. Lister would later be described . . ." Ibid.

635. One paper wrote that . . . *New York Daily Tribune*. Summary of Events for 1881.

636. Surgeon-General Barnes . . . Hayes and Hayes, *A Complete History of the Life and Trial of Charles Julius Guiteau, Assassin of President Garfield*, p. 218.

637. "I was not aware that I was expected . . ." Ibid., p. 220

638. On the other hand . . . Ibid., p. 222.

639. Mrs. Guiteau never recovered . . . Ibid., p. 249.

640. Without making eye contact . . . Ibid., p. 251.

641. "Inspiration, as I understand it . . ." Ibid., p. 265.

642. Thirty to seventy passengers died . . . Millard, *Destiny of the Republic: A Tale of Madness, Medicine and the Murder of a President*, pp. 1-4.

643. The defendant was convinced . . . Hayes and Hayes, *A Complete History of the Life and Trial of Charles Julius Guiteau, Assassin of President Garfield*, p. 271.

Chapter 38

644. "In our opinion, Mr. Porter . . ." John K. Porter collection, 1851-1882, New York State Library, NYSED.Gov.

645. In 1861, he successfully defended . . . *New York Times*. September 9, 1861.

646. His honor would later describe . . . Tilton v. Beecher, John K. Porter collection 1851-1882, New York State Library, p. 225.

647. One doctor died from the effects . . . Wellman, *The Art of Cross-Examination*, p. 357.

648. "I said, or intended to say . . ." Hayes and Hayes, *A Complete History of the Life and Trial of Charles Julius Guiteau, Assassin of President Garfield*, p. 274.

649. "I say the Deity furnished the money . . ." Wellman, *The Art of Cross-Examination*, pp. 359-360.

650. "The Deity confirmed my act . . ." Ibid., p. 361.

651. They decided it had traveled . . ." Clark, *The Murder of James A. Garfield. The President's Last Days and the Trial and Execution of His Assassin*, p. 78.

652. "The immediate cause of death . . ." McCabe, *Our Martyred President. The Life and Public Services of Gen. James A. Garfield*, p. 691.

653. "No, sir, I do not like the word murder . . ." Wellman, *The Art of Cross-Examination*, pp. 361-362.

654. "Did you suppose that the Supreme Ruler . . ." Ibid., p. 366.

655. "I decline to discuss this matter . . ." Ibid., pp. 367-368.

656. "Is there any higher divine authority . . ." Ibid., pp. 371-372.

657. "I don't know whether it would or not . . ." Ibid., pp. 375-376.

658. "The cross-examination is closed . . ." Hayes and Hayes, *A Complete History of the Life and Trial of Charles Julius Guiteau, Assassin of President Garfield*, pp. 307-308.

Chapter 39

659. In a sense, the trouble out West . . . Lubet, *Murder in Tombstone. The Forgotten Trial of Wyatt Earp*, p. 44.

660. Few presidents have been as concerned . . . Doenecke, *The Presidencies of James A. Garfield & Chester A. Arthur*, p. 78.

661. Twenty-four wagonloads of furniture . . . Ibid.

662. Since Arthur was a bachelor . . . Reeves, *Gentleman Boss: The Life of Chester A. Arthur*, pp. 252-253.

663. In Garfield's Inauguration Speech . . . Ridpath, *The Life and Work of James A. Garfield, Twentieth President of the United States*, p. 495.

664. In Utah, in 1882, Mormons outnumbered . . . Doenecke, *The Presidencies of James A. Garfield & Chester A. Arthur*, p. 84.

665. "He also proposed that all Mormon . . ." Chester A. Arthur. First Annual Message to the Senate and House of Representatives of the United States. December 6, 1881.

666. "In its decision, the court held . . ." *George Reynolds v. United States*. Supreme Court of the United States. May 5, 1879.

667. The act would make plural marriage . . . The Edmunds Act. Tribune Printing and Publishing Company. Salt Lake City, Utah. 1883.

668. "Arthur would veto the bill . . ." Doenecke, *The Presidencies of James A. Garfield & Chester A. Arthur*, p. 83.

669. Furthermore, he warned that . . . Ibid.

670. "The race of red men would be . . ." Peskin, *Garfield*, p. 298.

671. He went on to suggest . . . Ibid.

672. He was determined to introduce . . . Chester A. Arthur. First Annual Message to the Senate and House of Representatives of the United States. December 6, 1881.

673. "Their hunting days are over . . ." Ibid.

674. With the press and the public . . . Doenecke, *The Presidencies of James A. Garfield & Chester A. Arthur*, p. 183.

Chapter 40

675. According to Charles E. Rosenberg . . . Rosenberg, *The Trial of the Assassin Guiteau*, p. 144.

676. That such effect is exerted . . . Ibid.

677. After his dismissal, both orderlies . . . *New York Times*. December 5, 1877.

678. Considering these facts, did Dr. Kiernan . . . Hayes and Hayes, *A Complete History of the Life and Trial of Charles Julius Guiteau, Assassin of President Garfield*, pp. 313-314.

679. "Assuming these propositions to be true . . ." Ibid., p. 314.

680. The term "moral insanity" was coined . . . Macpherson, *Mental Affections; An Introduction to the Study of Insanity*, p. 300.

681. Kiernan's testimony was supported by . . . Hayes and Hayes, *A Complete History of the Life and Trial of Charles Julius Guiteau, Assassin of President Garfield*, pp. 316-319.

682. The prosecution began its rebuttal . . . Ibid., p. 323.

683. In an incredible display of hubris . . . Ibid.

684. Smiling, Guiteau told the court . . . Ibid., p. 326.

685. Under oath, the eminent physician . . . Ibid., p. 340.

686. While on the stand, he testified . . . Rosenberg, *The Trial of the Assassin Guiteau*, p. 157.

687. The admission provoked the following exchange: . . . Hayes and Hayes, *A Complete History of the Life and Trial of Charles Julius Guiteau, Assassin of President Garfield*, p. 341.

688. There is not a scintilla of doubt . . . Rosenberg, *The Trial of the Assassin Guiteau*, p. 155.

689. Spitzka remained calm, despite the calculated attempt . . . Ibid., p. 166.

690. The trial lasted seventy-two days . . . Hamilton, *Recollections of an Alienist*, p. 356.

691. Hamilton was followed by a steady stream . . . Rosenberg, *The Trial of the Assassin Guiteau*, p. 173.

692. Gray testified that Guiteau . . . Gosling, *Before Freud. Neurasthenia and The American Medical Community*, p. 21.

693. The mere recital of his credentials . . . Rosenberg, *The Trial of the Assassin Guiteau*, p. 189.

694. Twenty-four medical specialists . . . "*The Man who Murdered Garfield*." Stewart Mitchell. Massachusetts Historical Society. (October, 1941-May, 1944.), p. 469.

695. Insane or not, Americans were of one mind . . . "*Was Charles Guiteau Insane?*" Mike McIntyre. Studies by Undergraduate Researchers at Guelph. Volume 2, Number 2. Spring 2009, pp. 3-7.

696. "All this time possibly the reader . . ." Balch, *The Life of James Abram Garfield, Late President of the United States*, p. 664.

Chapter 41

697. During his five-day oration . . . Rosenberg, *The Trial of the Assassin Guiteau*, p. 210.

698. "Scoville was a type of the abusive . . ." Hamilton, *Recollections of an Alienist*, p. 357.

699. "Gray is a big gun . . ." Hayes and Hayes, *A Complete History of the Life and Trial of Charles Julius Guiteau, Assassin of President Garfield*, p. 461.

700. "I am going to sit down . . ." Ibid., p. 464.

701. "Put my body in the ground . . ." Ibid., p. 465.

702. A man without a conscience or a soul . . . Ibid., p. 467.

703. "The prisoner tells you, with his characteristic . . ." Guiteau trial: Closing Speech to the Jury of John K. Porter of New York. January 23, 1882, pp. 42-46.

704. Once again, Judge Porter answered his own question . . . Ibid.

705. "It is the direct question . . ." Ibid., pp. 53-54.

706. In closing, he asked the jury . . . Ibid., p. 123.

707. Guiteau was brought back . . . Hayes and Hayes, *A Complete History of the Life and Trial of Charles Julius Guiteau, Assassin of President Garfield*, p. 517.

708. One by one, the members were called . . . Ibid., p 518.

709. The judge told him to be quiet . . . Ibid., p. 520.

710. "You have been doing well . . ." Ibid., p. 523.

711. "You convicted me with your jackass theories . . ." Ibid., p. 524.

712. Mercifully, the District Attorney . . . Ibid., p. 525.

713. He paused again, then added . . . Ibid., p. 527.

714. "And may God have mercy on your soul! . . ." Ibid.

715. "I will have a flight to glory . . ." Ibid., p. 528.

Chapter 42

716. Supposedly, Ridgeway wanted to exhibit . . . *New York Times.* February 1, 1882.

717. Toward the slayer of her husband . . . *New York Times.* February 18, 1882.

718. "Whenever I think of any of those people . . ." Clark, *The Murder of James A. Garfield. The President's Last Days and the Trial and Execution of His Assassin*, p. 142.

719. A motion for a new hearing . . . John D. Lawson. *The Trial of Charles J. Guiteau for the Murder of President Garfield.* American State Trials. Volume 14, 1923, p. 155.

720. "Another night watch will be the last . . ." *New York Times.* June 28, 1882.

721. He ordered the exact same meal . . . *New York Times.* June 29, 1882.

722. The bouquet was immediately removed . . . *New York Times.* October 4, 1882.

723. George Corkhill, the District Attorney . . . Ibid.

724. "I, John S. Crocker, Warden of the jail . . ." *New York Times.* August 3, 1882.

725. "I don't think I can go through . . ." Clark, *The Murder of James A. Garfield. The President's Last Days and the Trial and Execution of His Assassin.* p. 142.

726. Not surprisingly, the event had drawn . . . *New York Times.* June 29, 1882.

727. "The American press has a large bill . . ." *Boston Evening Transcript.* June 30, 1882.

728. In a final display of characteristic hubris . . . Ackerman, *Dark Horse. The Surprise Election and Political Murder of President James A. Garfield*, p. 445.

729. After an autopsy that discovered . . . *New York Times.* July 1, 1882.

730. The catalog description boasted . . . *New York Times.* August 19, 1882.

731. In the words of the *New York Times* . . . Ibid.

BIBLIOGRAPHY

Ackerman, Kenneth D. *Dark Horse. The Surprise Election and Political Murder of President James A. Garfield.* New York: Carroll & Graf Publishers, 2003.

Agnew, D. Hayes *The Principles and Practices of Surgery.* Philadelphia: J.B. Lippincott, 1878

Angle, Paul M. *The Great Chicago Fire.* Chicago: The Chicago Historical Society, 1946.

Balch, William Ralston. *The Life of James Abram Garfield, Late President of the United States.* Philadelphia: Hubbard Bros., 1881.

Bliss, Dr. Willard. "*The Story of President Garfield's Illness.*" Century Magazine (Vol. 23, Issue 2), December 1881.

Bonadio, Felice A. *North of Reconstruction: Ohio Politics, 1865-1870.* New York: New York University Press, 1970.

Brisbin, James S. *The Early Life and Public Career of James A. Garfield.* Philadelphia: Hubbard Bros., 1880.

Brown, E.E. *The Life and Public Services of James A. Garfield, Twentieth President of the United States.* Boston: D.L. Guernsey, Cornhill, 1881.

Brown, Harry James, Frederick D. Williams. *The Diary of James A. Garfield. Volume II 1872-1874*, East Lansing: Michigan State University Press, 1967.

Bundy, J.M. *The Life of Gen. James A. Garfield.* New York: A.S. Barnes & Co., 1880.

Caldwell, Robert Granville. *James A. Garfield: Party Chieftain.* New York: Dood, Mead & Company, 1931.

Cist, Henry Martyn. *The Army of the Cumberland.* New York: Charles Scribner's Sons, 1909.

Clark, James C. *The Murder of James A. Garfield. The President's Last Days and the Trial and Execution of His Assassin.* Jefferson: McFarland & Company, Inc. 1993.

Colbert, Elias, Everett Chamberlin. *Chicago &The Great Conflagration.* New York: The Viking Press, 1971.

Conwell, Russell H. *The Life, Speeches, and Public Services of James A. Garfield, Twentieth President of the United States.* Portland: George Stinson & Company, 1881.

Cromie, Robert. *The Great Chicago Fire*. New York: McGraw-Hill Book Company, Inc., 1958.

Doenecke, Justus D. *The Presidencies of James A. Garfield & Chester A. Arthur*. Lawrence: The Regents Press of Kansas, 1981.

Fogarty, Robert S. *Desire and Duty at Oneida: Tirzah Miller's Intimate Memoir*. Bloomington: Indiana University Press. 2000.

Gammon, Frederic T. *The Canal Boy Who Became President*. London: S.W. Partridge & Co., 1881.

Garfield, James A. *The Diary of James A. Garfield. Edited by Harry J. Brown and Frederick D. Brown*. East Lansing: Michigan State University Press, 1981.

Garraty, John A. *The American Nation to 1877. A History of the United States*. New York: American Heritage Publishing Co., 1966.

Glazier, Captain Willard. *Peculiarities of American Cities*. Philadelphia: Hubbard Brothers, 1886.

Gosling, F.G. *Before Freud. Neurasthenia and The American Medical Community, 1870-1910*. Champaign, Illinois: University of Illinois Press, 1987.

Hamilton, Allen McLane. *Recollections of an Alienist*. New York: George H. Doran Company, 1916.

Hayes, H.G. and Hayes, C.J. *A Complete History of the Life and Trial of Charles Julius Guiteau, Assassin of President Garfield.* Philadelphia: Hubbard Bros., 1882

Heidler, David S., Jeanne T. Heidler. *Encyclopedia of the American Civil War.* New York: W.W. Norton & Company, Inc., 2000.

Hesseltine, William B. *Ulysses S. Grant: Politician.* New York: Frederick Ungar Publishing Co., 1957.

Hindsdale, Mary L., ed. *Garfield—Hinsdale Letters: Correspondence Between James Abram Garfield and Burke Aaron Hinsdale.* Ann Arbor: University of Michigan Press, 1949.

Holland, Barbara. *Hail To The Chiefs.* New York: Ballantine Books, 1989.

Howe, George F. *Chester A. Arthur: A Quarter-Century of Machine Politics.* New York: Eaton Press 1935.

Josephson, Matthew. *The Robber Barons: The Great American Capitalists 1861-1901.* New York: Harcourt, Brace and Company, 1934.

Kelley, Robin D.G., Earl Lewis. *To Make Our World Anew: Volume I: A History of African Americans to 1880.* Oxford: Oxford University Press, 2000.

Kevles, BettyAnn Holtzmann. *Naked To The Bone: Medical Imaging in the Twentieth Century.* Rutgers: Rutgers University Press, 1997.

Kingsbury, Robert. *The Assassination of James A. Garfield*. New York: The Rosen Publishing Group, Inc. 2002.

Long, Everette Beach. *The Civil War. Day By Day*. Garden City, New York: Doubleday, 1971.

Lossing, Benson John. *A Biography of James A. Garfield, Late President of the United States*. New York: Henry S. Goodspeed & Co., 1882.

Lubet, Steven. *Murder in Tombstone. The Forgotten Trial of Wyatt Earp*. Harrisonburg: R.R. Donnelley, 2004.

Macpherson, John. *Mental Affections; An Introduction to the Study of Insanity*. London: MacMillan and Co., Limited, 1899.

McCabe, James D. *Our Martyred President. The Life and Public Services of Gen. James A. Garfield*. Philadelphia: National Publishing Company, 1880.

McCullough, David. *John Adams*. New York: Simon & Schuster, 2001.

McFeely, William S. *Grant*. New York: W.W. Norton & Company. 1981.

Millard, Candice. *Destiny of the Republic: A Tale of Madness, Medicine and the Murder of a President*. New York: Anchor Books, 2011.

Morgan, H. Wayne. *From Hayes to McKinley National Party Politics, 1887-1896*. Syracuse: Syracuse University Press, 1969.

Muzzey, David S. *James G. Blaine: A Political Idol of Other Days*. New York: Dodd, Mead & Company, 1934.

Ogilvie, J.S. *History of the Attempted Assassination of James A. Garfield*. Cincinnati: Cincinnati Publishing Co., 1881.

Parker, Robert Auerton. *A Yankee Saint: John Humphrey Noyes and the Oneida Community*. New York: G.P. Putnam's Sons, 1935.

Peskin, Allan. *Garfield*. Kent, Ohio: The Kent State University Press, 1978.

Pike, David. *Roadside New Mexico: A Guide to Historic Markers*. Albuquerque: University of New Mexico Press, 2004.

Pletcher, David M. *The Awkward Years. American Foreign Relations Under Garfield and Arthur*. Columbia: University of Missouri Press, 1962.

Radzinsky, Edvard. *Alexander II. The Last Great Tsar*. New York: Simon & Schuster, Inc., 2005.

Reeves, Thomas C. *Gentleman Boss: The Life of Chester A. Arthur*. New York: Alfred A. Knopf, 1975.

Ridpath, John Clark. *The Life and Work of James A. Garfield, Twentieth President of the United States*. Cincinnati: Jones Brothers and Company, 1881.

Rosenberg, Charles E. *The Trial of the Assassin Guiteau*. Chicago: The University of Chicago Press, 1968.

Santella, Thomas M. *Opium*. New York: Chelsea House, 2007.

Shaw, John, ed. *Crete and James: Personal Letters of Lucretia and James Garfield*. East Lansing, Michigan: Michigan State University Press, 1994.

Sides, Hampton. *Blood and Thunder*. New York: Doubleday, 2006.

Stanwood, Edward. *James Gillespie Blaine*. New York: Houghton Mifflin Company, 1905.

Stout, H.R. *Our Family Physician*. Boston: George M. Smith & Co., 1885.

Taylor, John M. *Garfield of Ohio. The Available Man*. New York: W.W. Norton and Company, 1970.

Thayer, William M. *From Log Cabin to the White House*. Boston: James H. Earle, Publisher, 1881.

The United States vs. Charles G. Guiteau. In the Supreme Court of the District of Columbia, Criminal Case No. 14056. June Term, 1881.

Washington, Booker T. *The Story of the Negro. (The Rise of the Race From Slavery.)* New York: Doubleday & Company, 1969.

Wellman, Francis L. *The Art of Cross-Examination*. New York: Gordon Press, 1978.

Manuscript Collections:

Chester Alan Arthur Papers, Library of Congress

Joseph Stanley-Brown Papers, Library of Congress

Roscoe Conkling Papers, Library of Congress

James A. Garfield Papers, Library of Congress

Charles Guiteau Papers, Georgetown University

John Sherman Papers, Library of Congress

Newspapers:

Albany Times

Boston Globe

Boston Post

Brooklyn Eagle

Chicago Inter Ocean

Chicago Times

Chicago Tribune

Cleveland Herald

New York Herald

New York Times

New York Tribune

Washington Evening Star

Washington Post

Made in the USA
Middletown, DE
21 February 2017